Theorizing Feminist Ethics of Care in Early Childhood Practice

Feminist Thought in Childhood Research

Series editors: Jayne Osgood and Veronica Pacini-Ketchabaw

Drawing on feminist scholarship, this boundary-pushing series explores the use of creative, experimental, new materialist and post-humanist research methodologies that address various aspects of childhood. *Feminist Thought in Childhood Research* foregrounds examples of research practices within feminist childhood studies that engage with post-humanism, science studies, affect theory, animal studies, new materialisms and other post-foundational perspectives that seek to decentre human experience. Books in the series offer lived examples of feminist research praxis and politics in childhood studies. The series includes authored and edited collections – from early career and established scholars – addressing past, present and future childhood research issues from a global context.

Also available in the series

Feminist Research for 21st-Century Childhoods: Common Worlds Methods,
edited by B. Denise Hodgins
Feminists Researching Gendered Childhoods: Generative Entanglements,
edited by Jayne Osgood and Kerry H. Robinson

Theorizing Feminist Ethics of Care in Early Childhood Practice

Possibilities and Dangers

Edited by

Rachel Langford

BLOOMSBURY ACADEMIC
LONDON • NEW YORK • OXFORD • NEW DELHI • SYDNEY

BLOOMSBURY ACADEMIC
Bloomsbury Publishing Plc
50 Bedford Square, London, WC1B 3DP, UK
1385 Broadway, New York, NY 10018, USA

BLOOMSBURY, BLOOMSBURY ACADEMIC and the Diana logo
are trademarks of Bloomsbury Publishing Plc

First published in Great Britain 2019
This paperback edition published in 2021

Series design by Anna Berzovan
Cover image © Qweek / iStock

ISBN: HB: 978-1-3500-6747-9
        PB: 978-1-3502-0136-1
        ePDF: 978-1-3500-6748-6
        eBook: 978-1-3500-6749-3

Series: Feminist Thought in Childhood Research

Typeset by Integra Software Services Pvt. Ltd.

To find out more about our authors and books visit www.bloomsbury.com
and sign up for our newsletters.

Contents

List of Figures

Contributors

Sonja Arndt is Senior Lecturer in early childhood education in the Early Years Research Centre. She is a Director of the Centre for Global Studies at the University of Waikato, New Zealand. Her teaching covers a wide range of topics across the early childhood education and teacher education programs, with a particular interest in using post-structural, philosophical, and feminist perspectives to question taken-for-granted truths and assumptions.

Marian Barnes is Professor Emeritus of social policy at the University of Brighton, UK. She is the author of *Caring and Social Justice* (2006) and *Care in Everyday Life: An Ethic of Care in Practice* (2012) as well as the lead editor of *Ethics of Care: Critical Advances in International Perspective* (2015). She has written numerous articles on her research that seeks to conceptually and empirically draw connections between care, social cohesion, and social justice.

B. Denise Hodgins is the Executive Director of the Early Childhood Pedagogy Network in British Columbia, Canada, and Adjunct Assistant Professor at the University of Victoria. Her work as a researcher, pedagogist, and educator is rooted in feminist materialism and explores the implications that postfoundational theories and methodologies have for twenty-first-century childhood studies.

Maria Karmiris is a PhD student at Ontario Institute for Studies in Education of the University of Toronto, Canada, in the Department of Social Justice Education. Some of her research interests include disability studies, elementary curriculum studies, post-structural feminist research methodologies, and decolonial studies. She is also an elementary school teacher with the Toronto District School Board (TDSB). Since beginning her career in 2002, she has taught students from Kindergarten to Grade 6 in both the "regular" classroom and in segregated special needs settings.

Rachel Langford is Associate Professor in the School of Early Childhood Studies at Ryerson University, Toronto, Canada. From 2006 to 2016 she served as the director of the School. She is a co-editor of *Caring for Children: Social*

Movements and Public Policy in Canada (UBC Press, 2017). Other publications focus on the inclusion of children with disabilities in early childhood settings, early childhood pedagogy, and ECE workforce issues. Her current research project, *Caring about Care: An Examination of Care in Canadian Childcare*, is funded by the Social Sciences and Humanities Research Council of Canada.

Amy Mullin is Professor of Philosophy at the University of Toronto, Canada. She is the author of "Reconceiving Pregnancy and Childcare" and numerous articles about children, caregiving, and ethical responsibility.

Colette Rabin (Associate Professor—Elementary Education) teaches in the joint credential/master's program at San Jose State University, United States. She teaches educational foundations, research, classroom management, and student teaching courses. Prior to teaching graduate school, she taught grades kindergarten through middle school for twelve years. Her research interests are in care ethics, aesthetics, sustainability, and social justice. Colette has explored the nature of relationships in schools from multiple perspectives and how to create and sustain them from the perspective of an ethic of care as a conceptual schema.

Griet Roets is a tenure track Professor of Social Work in the Department of Social Work and Social Pedagogy, Ghent University, Belgium. Her research is mainly inspired by feminist theory and attempts to challenge binary and categorical thinking in social work and social welfare issues. Her research interests include concepts of citizenship and welfare rights; intersections of gender, poverty, disability, and age; and interpretative and biographical research methodologies.

Rachel Rosen is Lecturer in Childhood at University College London, UK. Her current research is focused on the care *of* children, *by* children, on migration journeys, as well as how these caring practices are taken into account (or not) in children's efforts to settle and claim asylum in the UK and the perceived commonalities and conflicts between children's interests and women's interests and, more broadly, intersections and antagonisms between feminisms and the politics of childhood. She is a co-editor of two books: *Feminism and the Politics of Childhood: Friends or Foes?*, with Katherine Twamly (UCL Press), and *Reimagining Childhood Studies*, with Spyros Spyrou and Daniel Cook (Bloomsbury Press).

Geoff Taggart is Lecturer at the University of Reading, UK. He teaches and researches on the subject of care, reflective practice, and professionalism in the preparation of people for "caring professions." He is also an ordained interfaith minister with an interest in contemplative pedagogy.

Marek Tesar is Associate Professor in Childhood Studies and Early Childhood Education at the University of Auckland, New Zealand, with a focus on the philosophy and sociology of childhood, and the history of education/childhood. His research is concerned with the construction of childhoods, notions of place/space of childhoods, and newly qualified teachers.

Michel Vandenbroeck is Professor in Family Pedagogy and Head of the Department of Social Work and Social Pedagogy at Ghent University, Belgium. His research focuses on early childhood care and education, parent support, and family policies, with a special interest for processes of inclusion and exclusion in contexts of diversity.

Katrien Van Laere works in VBJK, Centre for Innovation in the Early Years, affiliated with the Department of Social Work and Social Pedagogy, Ghent University, Belgium. Recently she finished a doctoral research project on conceptualizations of care and education. Her research interests include feminist ethics of care, social justice, and accessibility of ECEC services.

Kelsey Wapenaar is an early childhood educator at the University of Victoria Child Care Services. With a background in early education and arts, her interest in a common worlds framework, multi-species relationships, and sustainability influences her approach to teaching. She is intrigued by the entanglements that are entwined within assemblages of gardens and how the arts can be a vehicle to make sense of these relationships.

Jacqueline White is an undergraduate student in the School of Social Work at Ryerson University. She is currently involved in the Caring about Care Project. Her interests include feminist ethics of care, social policy, and disability.

Sherri-Lynn Yazbeck is an early childhood educator at the University of Victoria Child Care Services. Drawing on her background in psychology, philosophy, and early childhood education and inspired by "everyday moments" with children, she is interested in the entangled multi-species relationships and encounters that take place in the classroom, playground, nearby forests, and gardens. She is intrigued by how human and more-than-human assemblages create place and pedagogy in early education and interested in what it might mean to practice care and sustainability through relationships.

Series Editors' Introduction

The series *Feminist Thought in Childhood Research* considers experimental and creative modes of researching and practicing in childhood studies. Recognizing the complex neoliberal landscape and worrisome spaces of coloniality in the twenty-first century, the *Feminist Thought in Childhood Research* books provide a forum for cross-disciplinary, interdisciplinary, and transdisciplinary conversations in childhood studies that engage feminist decolonial, anticolonial, more-than-human, new materialisms, post-humanist, and other post-foundational perspectives that seek to reconfigure human experience. The series offers lively examples of feminist research praxis and politics that invite childhood studies scholars, students, and educators to engage in collectively to imagine childhood otherwise.

Until now, childhood studies has been decidedly a human matter focused on the needs of individual children (Taylor, 2013). In the Anthropocene (Colebrooke, 2012, 2013), however, other approaches to childhood that address the profound, human-induced ecological challenges facing our own and other species are emerging. As Taylor (2013) reminds us, if we are going to grapple with the socio-ecological challenges we face today, childhood studies need to pay attention to the *more*-than-human, to the *non*-human others that inhabit our worlds and the *in*human. Toward this end, *Feminist Thought in Childhood Research* series challenges the humanist, linear, and moral narratives (Colebrook, 2013; Haraway, 2013) of much of childhood studies by engaging with feminisms. As a feminist series, the books explore the inheritances of how to live in the Anthropocene and think about it in ways that are in tension with the Anthropocene itself.

The third book in the series, *Theorizing Feminist Ethics of Care in Early Childhood Practice: Possibilities and Dangers*, makes a significant contribution to the series through a rich engagement with care. Discussions on care, the authors show, require complex theoretical and methodological considerations. Thus, they deliver a rich treatment of care: as love, as labour, as gendered, as political, as located within the milieu. Several feminist frameworks are deployed in the volume—from phenomenological and poststructural to posthumanist and new materialist understandings of care. It is the treatment of care as an ethical response in early childhood education that connects the chapters in the volume. Through carefully crafted studies, the authors think with an ethics of care to offer creative ways to enact education beyond the current neoliberal story.

Aligned with this series, the compendium also provokes readers to think outside of human-centered perspectives on care. In the introduction, Rachel Langford reminds us that "feminist care ethics is one such feminism that seeks to unseat the dominance of a moral narrative that privileges human independence and separateness and denies human interdependence and relationality."

Acknowledgments

I gratefully acknowledge the support of the Social Sciences and Humanities Research Council of Canada for funding the "Caring about Care" research project. The project seeks to theorize and frame a robust and coherent integration of care and care work into Canadian childcare advocacy, policy, and practice. This edited volume emerged out of the many rich and lively conversations about how to care about caring in early childhood that I have had with my research project colleagues: Patrizia Albanese, Kate Bezanson, and Susan Prentice. Special thanks go to research assistants for the project: Madison Banks, Alana Powell, Brooke Richardson, and Jacqueline White who continually push my thinking about care. A commitment to feminist analysis in early childhood studies by the Series Editors, Jayne Osgood and Veronica Pacini-Ketchabaw, motivated this volume. The contributions of Maria Giovanna Brauzzi at Bloomsbury Academic in the development of the volume and Susan Girvan and Janette Lush in the editing of my sections are greatly appreciated. This edited volume is dedicated to educators around the world who care for young children. One day, I hope, our world is turned around and your care is central to politics, policy, and practice in early childhood education.

Introduction

Rachel Langford

The idea for this edited volume emerged from a failure to resist thinking about *care* in early childhood education and care (ECEC). In the 1980s, when I worked in both early childhood and elementary school settings, I bristled when others described my care of young children as natural, an assumption no doubt based on my gender. Later, taking a graduate studies course on the philosophy of care in education, I was suspicious of readings by Nel Noddings (1988) and drawn to Claudia Card's article on caring and evil (1990). I found some middle ground in Robin Dillon's (1992) concept of *care respect*, which Amy Mullin takes up in this volume's chapter on nurturing hope to support children's autonomy. Later in my working life I focused on professionalism while teaching postsecondary early childhood education (ECE) students, but something about *care* continued to hover at the back of my thinking.

In 2013, I began to think about teaching a course on children and care as a way to investigate my conflicts with care in ECEC. This course, now delivered for several years to university students across many disciplines, explores the possibilities and controversies in ethics of care literature in relation to the lives of children and families at the personal, political, and global levels.

At the same time, my research shifted from a focus on professionalization as a Canadian childcare advocacy strategy to theorizing and framing a robust and coherent integration of care, ethics of care, and care work into Canadian childcare advocacy, policy, and practice. (This is not to suggest that professionalization and care are incompatible.) It could be said that I have now embraced care ethics as a focus of my teaching and research. As Carol Gilligan (2011: 177), often associated with the origins of care ethics, has urged, rather than resisting care, I have "joined the resistance" to patriarchy and other forms of oppression that seek to deny the caring capacities that constitute the humanity of all citizens of a democracy. Gilligan writes:

Once the ethic of care is released from its subsidiary position within a justice framework, it can guide us by framing the struggle in a way that clarifies what is at stake and by illuminating a path of resistance grounded not in ideology but in our humanity. If along the path we lose our way, we can remind ourselves to listen for voice, to pay attention to how things are gendered, and to remember that within ourselves we have the ability to spot a false story. (2011: 43)

This edited volume draws on the spirit of this resistance to meet two aims. The first is to lift the "aura of invisibility" of "the very common and everyday nature" of care relations in ECEC (Bowden 1997: 5–6). As Gilligan states, this aim is pressing in a time in which false stories distort what really matters in ECEC. To this end, chapter authors offer contemporary and in-depth theorizations of feminist ethics of care in early childhood practice, illuminating its possibilities for personal, professional, and social transformation.

The second aim is to assert that everything about care in ECEC is inescapably political and dangerous. Chapter authors address these dangers by highlighting political and policy priorities and decisions that constrain early childhood practices and reproduce social inequalities in care relations and care work. In addressing these dangers, chapter authors point to openings for social change. Overall, this unique volume seeks to contribute to ethics of care scholarship that is "burgeoning across many disciplines" (Engster and Hamington 2015: 4).

A growing field of study in ECEC

In this introduction, selected ideas from an emerging body of literature on care and ethics of care in early childhood practice are explored to serve as a foundation for this volume. Three overlapping motivations for this literature can be traced:

1. to address the split systems of market-based childcare and public education in many countries;
2. to assert *care* as central to early childhood practice; and
3. to examine care work as a site of gendered exploitation and emotional labor.

What links these motivations is an overarching concern with questioning and contesting the dominance of neoliberal and technocratic discourses in ECEC that exclude narratives of care. Moss et al. (2016) connect and frame these discourses as a story with a plot in which early intervention leads happily to quality, improved child outcomes, and "national success in a competitive global economy." They describe the style and tone of this story thus:

> Instrumental, calculative, economistic, technical, avid for certainty, control and closure—with a distinctive vocabulary, having frequent resource to words such as "evidence-based," "programmes," "quality," "investment," "outcomes," "development," "effects," "returns" and "human capital." Last but not least, the story is entirely lacking in self-criticism or awareness of possible alternative narratives. (3)

One such alternative narrative seeks to imagine a different kind of system of early childhood services for children and families.

The split systems of childcare and education

Currently, an entrenched split between the early childhood systems of care and education reflects a private and public divide in which care is relegated to a highly gendered workforce and counted only in the private domain (Delaune 2017; Gibbons 2007; Langford et al. 2016; Moss 2006; Tronto 2013; Van Laere and Vandenbroeck 2016; Warin 2014). One approach to dismantling this care–education divide has been to rethink the discourses that shape and direct ways of looking at the childcare system. Moss (1992: 63) stated almost twenty-five years ago that what is needed is a "new terminology to express the concept of a system of services that is coherent and comprehensive." Later, in an article titled "Farewell to Childcare," Moss (2006), perhaps optimistically, documents a nascent turn from childcare discourses to pedagogical discourses in two waves, first in Nordic countries, then in countries such as New Zealand and England. Moss's argument (2006: 82) is that "childcare is [an] increasingly inadequate and outdated" concept, particularly with its linkages to wider discourses of maternalism and childcare as a substitute for home with caregivers who act as substitute mothers. Moss (2006: 73) maintains that an alternative concept of pedagogy promotes the integration of care and education services in early childhood whereby "reflective and researching educators" provide experiences for children that are qualitatively different than those in the home. Other terms have emerged to emphasize this integration: *compassionate pedagogy* (Taggart 2014) and *relational pedagogy* (Papatheodorou 2009). The care–education dualism in some European countries has also been reimagined as *educare* (Van Laere and Vandenbroeck 2016; Warin 2014). In this edited volume, Katrien Van Laere, Griet Roets, and Michel Vandenbroeck explore, through an analysis of a child's use of a pacifier all day long in an early childhood setting, in what ways the professional, reflective language of educare has some value in enabling early childhood staff who think of themselves as teachers "to utilise their embodied potential to care."

Another approach to dismantling, at least discursively, the split systems of care and education has been to transform the concept of *care* in ECEC into an *ethics of care* that represents an overarching moral framework for understanding how people can engage with each other in various spaces in civil society, including education (Dahlberg and Moss 2005: 90). This approach is evident in this volume in chapters by Geoff Taggart, Colette Rabin, and Rachel Langford and Jacqueline White, with the significant tensions between care as ethic and care as labor explored in a chapter by Rachel Rosen. Throughout this book, authors persist with and amplify the language of the ethics of care: care as unknowing (Sonja Arndt and Marek Tesar), care as hope (Amy Mullin), care as presence and absence (Maria Karmiris), and care as ethical interactions (Langford and White). In their chapter, Denise Hodgins, Sherri-Lynn Yazbeck, and Kelsey Wapenaar reflect on care(ing) as curriculum, drawing on Maria Puig de la Bellacas's rereading of feminist ethics of care as both human and nonhuman relationality and interdependence. This persistence with the concept of the ethics of care throughout the book reflects an underlying belief that in the "ruins" of care and education there are many possibilities for meanings of care ethics in early childhood to emerge creatively (Gibbons 2007: 123).

The assertion of care in ECEC

A second motivation for literature on care in early childhood is the belief that the ECEC field needs to reexamine central assumptions about social relationships in early childhood services. Two overlapping streams of literature can be identified that focus on:

1. the assertion of maternalism, care, love, and intimacy (Ailwood 2017; Aslanian 2015; Campbell-Barr et al. 2015; Davis and Degotardi 2015; Luff 2013; Luff and Kanyal 2015; Page 2011, 2018; Page and Elfer 2013; White and Gradovski 2018); and

2. tensions between care and professionalism (Brooker 2010; Campbell-Barr et al. 2015; Harwood et al. 2013; Osgood 2006; Rabin and Smith 2013; Rouse and Hadley 2018; Shin 2015; Taggart 2015).

Some writers concerned with asserting maternalism, care, love, and intimacy make use of Sara Ruddick's (1989) book, *Maternal Thinking*, which argues that mothering yields a distinctive moral outlook that could be relevant beyond mothering. In the context of ECEC, maternalism is typically understood as natural care and love that enhances the dyadic attachment between a practitioner and child, particularly a very young child. For example, Luff and Kanyal (2015) apply Ruddick's three characteristics of maternal thinking (protecting the child, promoting the holistic growth of the child, and training the child toward social acceptance) to their research on practitioners' understandings, interpretation, and enactment of their observations of children. These researchers propose the term *care-full pedagogy* to capture the maternal thinking practitioners appear to employ in their relationships with children. Other writers invoke the importance of love in these relationships. In editing a special issue of the *International Journal of Early Years Education*, Page (2018: 128) states that "the legitimisation of love in Early Childhood Education and Care is undergoing a (re)birth and some reinforcement." Page's evidence is that parents value professional pedagogues' love of and intimacy with their children more than their professional training or expertise; in addition, professional pedagogues know from practice the value of love and intimacy. In her own article for the special issue, Page draws on various attachment theories of care theorist Nel Noddings to set out a phenomenology of professional love constructed as an intellectual capacity. In this volume, a discourse of love is found in chapters by Geoff Taggart as well as Sonja Arndt and Marek Tesar, who write "love can be seen as the root of conceptualising education as a moral undertaking."

Nevertheless, criticisms of discourses of maternalism, care, and love in ECEC are evident since the 1990s (e.g., Cannella 1997). Ailwood (2017: 305) remarks more than two decades later that "the word *care* sits within the language of the early years associated with providing a safe place for children to be supervised and have their needs attended to, an association that raises problematic nostalgia about home and family life where care, mothering, and maternalism are idealized." Furthermore, while Ruddick (1989) proposes a politics of peace that extends from the preservation of life in maternal relations, she was also cautious about generalizing maternal thinking to other kinds of thinking about care in different activities. She states: "It is disrespectful to each kind of thinking and to the rationality of care as a whole to combine the varieties of thinking without attempting to describe them individually and mark their connections and differences" (47). A further concern is the conflation of care and love:

White and Gradovski (2018: 201), for example, suggest this conflation "sets a risky precedent [because] it ignores the loving relationships that exist beyond caregiving acts—as an integral part of the pedagogical experience." Conceptual differences between care and love are more evident when love is considered in relation to a *feminist ethics of care* that pays attention to the social locations of and power relations between those giving and receiving care in specific times, places, and institutions. As Tronto (2013: 159) stresses, the family, unlike the early childhood institution, is a particular institution in which "there are clearly understood lines of power and obligation" and care has a clear purpose "as an expression of love."

In tracing historical and current discourses of love, care, and maternalism, Aslanian (2015) concludes that practices of care and love in early childhood settings are currently perceived as threats to workforce professionalism. The push toward professionalizing the ECEC sector represents responses by the workforce to well-documented conditions of their work. As the focus on upgrading the professional status of the sector through acquired and technical competencies has increased, some researchers have documented the disappearance of care discourses from professional documents (Campbell-Barr et al. 2015; Davis and Degotardi 2015; Löfdahl and Folke-Fichtelius 2015; Rouse and Hadley 2018). Osgood (2006) argues that early childhood educators themselves are preoccupied with these externally imposed discourses of professionalism, leaving little opportunity for them to consider counter-discourses of care. Still, these researchers suggest that, at the level of everyday practice, the care of young children prevails although talk about it is underground and in tentative assertions of professional identity. For example, in their study of early childhood educator (ECE) perspectives on professionalism in three countries, Harwood et al. (2013: 15) found that an "ethic of care orientation emerged as an integral aspect of the conceptualizations of 'being a professional.'" Building on earlier work (Rabin and Smith 2013; Taggart 2014, 2015), Colette Rabin and Geoff Taggart describe in this volume sites in higher education where care ethics is integrated into professional preparation programs. It could be said, then, that for many working directly with children and for some in higher education early childhood education programs, "care is serious professional work" (Ailwood 2017: 307).

ECEC work as a site of exploitation

A final area of literature selected for this introduction is concerned with ECEC as a site of gendered, classed, and increasingly racialized care work deeply marked by exploitation (Andrew 2015; Cooper 2017; Page and Elfer 2013; Rockel 2009; Taggart 2011; Vincent and Braun 2013; Warin and Gannerud 2014). Although Vincent and Braun (2013: 754) note that "the role, scope and application of care, caring and emotion is not often openly discussed," three overlapping concepts that point to workforce exploitation at the *emotional* level of caring are evident in some literature—emotionality, emotional labor, and emotional capital. As an example of literature on emotionality, Page and Elfer (2013) describe the logistical and emotional complexity of facilitating consistent, accountable, and reflective attachment interactions with young children all day and every day. Cooper (2017) conceptualizes emotionality as emotional labor, a term coined by Alie Hochschild (1979) to describe how care workers are required to demonstrate a set of positive emotions (and conversely to suppress negative emotions), established by management as "feeling rules," to induce a desired emotional state in clients. Emotional labor thus requires care workers to act and perform as though they feel emotions that, in reality, they do not have. These enacted emotional scripts often reflect middle-class values (Colley 2006; Vincent and Braun 2013). Vincent and Braun, who studied working-class women's experiences in an ECEC training program, distinguish between emotional labor that is "alienating and oppressive" from that which is "agentic and skillful." Similarly, Andrew (2015: 357) uses the term "emotional capital," which he defines as a dispositional understanding "which results from engaging reflexively about how empathy, insight and resilience are experienced by early childhood educators" and which potentially mediate the effects of workforce issues, such as burnout and low morale.

Emotions are central to the valuing and practice of a feminist ethics of care. Objective rationalistic calculations are rejected and subjective emotions, such as sympathy, empathy, sensitivity, and responsiveness, are accepted and appreciated for guiding acts of care (Held 2006). These emotions, or care feelings, cultivated through thought and experience, are expected to be sincere, arising from genuine concern for those receiving care. For this reason, Held (2006: 37) states that care cannot simply be reduced to emotional work or labor; rather she conceptualizes an ethics of care as values and practices that involve authentic emotions that foster the flourishing and well-being of both caregivers and care receivers. However, feminist care ethics recognizes that when care responsibilities are unequal and care practices are burdensome, care feelings can become distorted, inauthentic, and transformed into emotional labor (Goldstein 1998). A feminist ethics of care also asks why the pleasures and burdens of caring for children fall disproportionately on women and aims to produce radical change in who assumes caring responsibilities and under what conditions (Mahon and Robinson 2011). And as Rachel Rosen explores in her chapter, care work analyzed in early childhood literature without feminist theories of social reproduction and political economy of care do little to challenge "the unequal terrain in which … [care] relations are lived."

Ethics of care as a feminist project

Together chapters in this edited volume explore how feminist theory on care is constantly shifting to reconfigure the human experience. Ethics of care's "feminist background" (Held 2006: 23) began in the 1980s with the premise that the private caring experience of women (and children) in the family are "as important, relevant and philosophically interesting as the experience of men." This experience of care was soon situated within the public and political realm. Tronto (1993, 2013), for example, explores how taken-for-granted gendered, racially, and class-biased assumptions about care responsibilities can be questioned through feminist theory for its limited scope of questions addressed by democratic politics. More recently, Raghuram (2016: 511) argues that feminist theories of care have the capacity to take account of the diversity of care practices globally, and how different notions of care are often and increasingly enacted across space and in dialogue with each other. In this volume, feminist ethics of care is layered with Kristeva's (1998) feminist theories of the subject in process, Braidotti's (2013) posthuman theory, Puig de la Bellacasa's (2017) theories of feminist materialism, and Black feminist theories of Spelman (1997) and Scheurich and Young (1997), as well as feminist critiques of mind–body dualism. In drawing on a range of feminist thinkers, some chapter authors explore the complex relationship between an ethics of care and an ethics of justice–rights within a highly ideological neoliberal political landscape (Engster and Hamington 2015). As Robinson (2006: 178) states, care ethics is not an ideology but rather "a set of values, practices and responsibilities which exist in societies, but which lack the attention and recognition they deserve."

Collectively volume authors contribute to the perspectives of the series, *Feminist Thought in Childhood Research*. The goal of this volume is consistent with the series' intention to challenge dominant neoliberal "humanist, linear and moral narratives" by engaging with a range of feminist theories. Feminist care ethics is one such feminism that seeks to unseat the dominance of a moral narrative that privileges human independence and separateness and denies human interdependence and relationality. Moreover, feminist care theorists are less interested in a unified, linear, and precise definition of care ethics and more interested in political, contextual, and emotional nuances in caring experiences (Hamington 2018: 309). There is room, therefore, in feminist care ethics to push thinking about the human experience to include decolonial, posthumanist, new materialisms, and other postfoundational perspectives that are the focus of the series *Feminist Thought in Childhood Research*. As Hamington (2018: 316), a leading care scholar, writes, the human caring experience is being decentered by concerns with "the care of non-human entities and objects as a means to develop non-exploitive caring relationships for humans and non-humans alike." Thus, feminist care ethics in conversations with other feminist theories offers possibilities for envisioning and affirming interconnections between human and more-than-human caring worlds in the twenty-first century.

Organization of volume

The chapters in this volume form an assemblage of ideas, arguments, agreements, and disagreements that does not easily conform to a straightforward organization. Terminology (e.g., educator vs. teacher vs. childcare worker) is inconsistent, reflecting the interdisciplinary orientation of the volume and the countries where the authors are located: early childhood studies (e.g., Katrien van Laere, Griet Roets, and Michel Vandenbroeck, Belgium), educational studies (Colette Rabin, United States), sociology (Marian Barnes, England), philosophy (Amy Mullin, Canada), and critical disability studies (Maria Karmiris, Canada). Chapters also reflect a broad understanding of early childhood as encompassing children from birth to eight-years-old; therefore, the sites of practice discussed are diverse. Some authors locate these practices in larger contexts of institutions, policies, politics, and discourses, moving analyses between the personal, institutional, political, and global levels. Despite these complexities, the volume has been divided into three parts: "Beginning the Conversation: Possibilities and Dangers," "Preparing Educators to Practice a Feminist Ethics of Care," and "Practicing a Feminist Ethics of Care." Readers can, of course, creatively undertake the chapters in any order—all contribute to theorizing feminist ethics of care in early childhood practice.

The first four chapters examine major developments in ethics of care scholarship over the last three decades and then begins a conversation about the possibilities and dangers of feminist ethics of care, particularly in the middle of intersecting social differences and power imbalances between those who give and receive care.

In Chapter 1, Marian Barnes provides an overview of the development of the ethics of care as a moral framework as well as its key themes, with attention to sociopolitical contexts for care practices. She describes her own introduction to the ethics of care and her "unashamedly pro-care approach" to critically analyzing care policies and politics in relation to the care needs of citizens, and the responsibilities of a democracy for enabling both care and justice.

In Chapter 2, authors Sonja Arndt and Marek Tesar revisit research data collected in culturally diverse early childhood settings and call for rethinking practices shaped by normative constructions of childhood. Central to Arndt and Taser's analyses is the rethinking of concepts, such as children's "dependencies and needs" and "secret and hiding places" that expose what and who are in center, and in the margins of early childhood practice. Kristeva's philosophical lens is used in a retheorization of children's narratives, opening up the possibilities of an ethics of unknowing.

In Chapter 3, Rachel Langford and Jacqueline White explore a conceptual move beyond care as particular activities to an ethical practice of being and doing in interactions and sustained relations in the context of an early childhood institution. A feminist analysis illuminates how educators and children cannot be separated from their social locations and power relationships as they recognize, give, and receive care, particularly when the purposes of this care are articulated.

In Chapter 4, Rachel Rosen argues that while the ethics of care offers the possibility of framing interdependence and social relations in early childhood practice, it is limited in exposing the labor of care practices. In particular, she maintains that early childhood literature avoids discussing the mundane and "dirty" in care work revealed through the application of social reproduction and political economy theories. Rosen proposes putting the "materialist feminist" into an ethics of care to broaden the discussion on care as labor.

Chapters 5 and 6 authors challenge the foundations of conventional ethics education in higher education programs for early childhood education students in two countries: England and the United States. The authors embrace a holistic pedagogy and a "slow ethics" in which a more relational, situated response to ethical dilemmas is required. Geoff Taggart's chapter (5) proposes that to philosophically reframe early childhood practice as ethical, psychological research in attachment and moral development needs to be considered. To understand the work of early childhood teachers and maintain a political ethic of care, Taggart argues that the growing psychology of compassion as well as a contemplative approach can contribute to understanding care philosophically and psychologically. In Chapter 6, Colette Rabin explores several common misconceptions of care held by higher education teacher candidates. Suggestions for translating care ethics into early childhood pedagogies, such as the use of narrative methods, are proposed so that teacher candidates can learn the "contours of a care ethic." Rubin suggests that the complexity of caring becomes apparent as teacher candidates engage in dramatic rehearsal of these stories and reflect on their interpretations and choices for action in a given context.

The last group of chapters offer offers more specific explorations into the practice of a feminist ethics of care through a range of theoretical orientations. Drawing on the picture book, *Each Kindness*, in Chapter 7, Maria Karmiris considers the simultaneous absence and presence of impressions teachers and children leave upon each other and the effects of these impressions on care relations amid power imbalances. Applying the work of feminist ethics of care, disability, and social justice education scholars, Karmiris explores how care requires both the stability and instability of a caring "self" deeply mired in social injustices. An interdisciplinary–intersectional approach is proposed to reconfigure feminist care ethics so that teachers and children may turn toward one another rather than turn away.

In their chapter (8), Katrine van Laere, Griet Roots, and Michel Vandenbroeck draw on feminist theory that problematizes the mind–body dualism evident in early childhood settings where education and care responsibilities are allocated to different groups of educators. They analyze data from professionals' and parents' discussions of the situation of Ravza, a two-and-a-half-year-old Turkish girl who holds her pacifier and schoolbag all day. They recommend professionals "embrace" the value of interdependence and differences in dependencies, underpinned by notions of community solidarity that foster practices of embodied care in early childhood settings.

In Chapter 9, Amy Mullin explores children's capacity to act in accordance with what they care about and to demonstrate relational autonomy. Mullin argues, however, that to develop these capacities children must be able to hope and sustain that hope in the face of obstacles. Mullin distinguishes hope, a neglected but key condition for autonomy, from optimism which is not grounded in plans for actions. Nurturing and sustaining hope calls on early childhood practices of attentiveness and responsiveness to children's differing capacities and goals.

In the final chapter, Denise Hodgins, Sherri-Lynn Yazbeck, and Kelsey Wapenaar analyze data from action research inquiries within a large multiprogram childcare center. They consider how conceptualizations of ethico-political and more-than-human relations help educators question Euro-Western developmental and anthropocentric knowledge. Puig de la Bellacasa's feminist materialist triptych of care as work–ethics–affect is used to imagine pedagogies as caring for and with children who are living with colonial and environmental legacies.

Together the chapters in this volume offer many insights, raise many questions, and will, it is hoped, stimulate the next wave of thinking about the possibilities and dangers of theorizing feminist ethics of care in early childhood practice.

References

Ailwood, J. (2017), "Exploring the Care in Early Childhood Education and Care," *Global Studies of Childhood*, 7 (4): 305–310.

Andrew, Y. (2015), "What We Feel and What We Do: Emotional Capital in Early Childhood Work," *Early Years*, 35 (4): 351–365.

Aslanian, T. (2015), "Getting behind Discourses of Love, Care and Maternalism in Early Childhood Education," *Contemporary Issues in Early Childhood*, 16 (2): 153–165.

Bowden, P. (1997), *Caring: Gender-Sensitive Ethics*, London: Routledge.

Braidotti, R. (2013), *The Posthuman*, Cambridge: Polity Press.

Brooker, L. (2010), "Constructing the Triangle of Care: Power and Professionalism in Practitioner/Parent Relationships," *British Journal of Educational Studies*, 58 (2): 181–196.

Campbell-Barr, V., J. Georgeson, and A. N. Varga (2015), "Developing Professional Early Childhood Educators in England and Hungary: Where Has All the Love Gone?," *European Education*, 47: 311–330.

Cannella, G. S. (1997), *Deconstructing Early Childhood Education*, New York: Peter Lang.

Card, C. (1990), "Caring and Evil," *Hypatia*, 5 (1): 101–119.

Colley, H. (2006), "Learning to Labour with Feeling: Class, Gender and Emotion in Childcare Education and Training," *Contemporary Issues in Early Childhood*, 7 (1): 15–29.

Cooper, M. (2017), "Reframing Assessment: Reconceptualizing Relationships and Acknowledging Emotional Labour," *Contemporary Issues in Early Childhood*, 18 (4): 375–386.

Dahlberg, G. and P. Moss (2005), *Ethics and Politics in Early Childhood Education*, London: Routledge.

Davis, B. and S. Degotardi (2015), "Who Cares? Infant Educators' Responses to Professional Discourses of Care," *Early Child Development and Care*, 185 (11–12): 1733–1747.

Delaune, A. (2017), "'Investing' in Early Childhood Education and *Care* in Aotearoa New Zealand: Noddings' Ethics of Care and the Politics of *Care* within the Social Investment Approach to Governance," *Global Studies of Childhood*, 7 (4): 335–345.

Dillon, R. (1992), "Respect and Care: Towards Moral Integration," *Canadian Journal of Philosophy*, 22 (1): 105–132.

Engster, D. and M. Hamington (2015), *Care Ethics and Political Theory*, Oxford: Oxford University Press.

Gibbons, A. (2007), "Playing the Ruins: The Philosophy of Care in Early Childhood Education," *Contemporary Issues in Early Childhood*, 8 (2): 123–132.

Gilligan, C. (2011), *Joining the Resistance*, Cambridge: Polity Press.

Goldstein, L. (1998), "More Than Gentle Smiles and Warm Hugs: Applying the Ethic of Care to Early Childhood Education," *Journal of Research in Childhood Education*, 12 (2): 244–261.

Hamington, M. (2018), "The Care Ethics Moment: International Innovations," *International Journal of Care and Caring*, 2 (3): 309–318.

Harwood, D., A. Klopper, A. Osanyin, and M. L. Vanderlee (2013), "'It's More Than Care': Early Childhood Educators' Concepts of Professionalism," *Early Years*, 33 (1): 4–17.

Held, V. (2006), *The Ethics of Care: Personal, Political, and Global*, New York: Oxford University Press.

Hochschild, A. (1979), "Emotion Work, Feeling Rules and Social Structures," *American Journal of Sociology*, 85 (3): 551–575.

Kristeva, J. (1998), "The Subject in Process," in P. French and R. L. Lack (eds), *The Tel Quel Reader*, 133–178, London: Routledge.

Langford, R., A. Di Santo, A. Valeo, K. Underwood, and A. Lenis (2016), "The Innovation of Ontario's Full Day Kindergarten Teams: Have They Reproduced the Split Systems of Care and Education?" *Gender and Education*, doi:10.1080/09540 253.2016.1258456.

Löfdahl, A. and M. Folke-Fichtelius (2015), "Preschool's New Suit: Care in Terms of Learning and Knowledge," *Early Years*, 35 (3): 260–272.

Luff, P. (2013), "Reclaiming Care in Early Childhood Education and Care," in C. Rogers and S. Weller (eds), *Critical Approaches to Care: Understanding Caring Relations, Identities and Cultures*, 18–29, New York: Routledge.

Luff, P. and M. Kanyal (2015), "Maternal Thinking and Beyond: Towards a Care-Full Pedagogy for Early Childhood," *Early Child Development and Care*, 185 (11–12): 1748–1761.

Mahon, R. and F. Robinson (2011), *Feminist Ethics and Social Policy: Towards a New Global Political Economy of Care*, Vancouver: UBC Press.

Moss, P. (1992), "Do Early Childhood Services Need a Coherent and Comprehensive Approach?" *Educare in Europe: A Report of the European Childcare Conference*, 51–63, Paris, France: UNESCO.

Moss, P. (2006), *Farewell to Childcare?*, National Institute Economic Review, No. 195.

Moss, P., G. Dahlberg, L. M. Olsson, and M. Vandenbroeck (2016), *Why Contest Early Childhood?* https://www.book2look.com/book/CGQqJCANOX?utm_source=Routledge&utm_medium=cms&utm_campaign=160701429

Noddings, N. (1988), "An Ethic of Caring and Its Implications for Instructional Arrangements," *American Journal of Education*, 96 (2): 215–230.

Osgood, J. (2006), "Deconstructing Professionalism in Early Childhood Education: Resisting the Regulatory Gaze," *Contemporary Issues in Early Childhood*, 7 (1): 5–14.

Page, J. (2011), "Do Mothers Want Professional Carers to Love Their Babies?" *Journal of Early Childhood Research*, 9 (3): 310–323.

Page, J. (2018), "Characterising the Principles of Professional Love in Early Childhood Education and Care," *International Journal of Early Years Education*, 26 (2): 125–141.

Page, J. and P. Elfer (2013), "The Emotional Complexity of Attachment Interactions in Nursery," *European Early Childhood Education Research Journal*, 21 (4): 553–567.

Papatheodorou, T. (2009), "Exploring Relational Pedagogy," in T. Papatheodorou and J. Moyles (eds), *Learning Together in the Early Years: Exploring Relational Pedagogy*, 3–17, London: Routledge.

Puig de la Bellacasa, M. (2017), *Matters of Care in Technoscience: Speculative Ethics in More Than Human Worlds*, Minneapolis: University of Minnesota Press.

Rabin, C. and G. Smith (2013), "Teaching Care Ethics: Conceptual Understandings and Stories for Learning," *Journal of Moral Education*, 42 (2): 164–176.

Raghuram, P. (2016), "Locating Care Ethics beyond the Global North," *ACME: International Journal for Critical Geographies*, 15 (3): 511–533.

Robinson, F. (2006), "Ethical Globalization? States, Corporations, and the Ethics of Care," in M. Hamington and D. C. Miller (eds), *Socializing Care: Feminist Ethics and Public Issues*, 163–182, Lanham, MD: Rowman and Littlefield.

Rockel, J. (2009), "A Pedagogy of Care: Moving beyond the Margins of Managing Work and Minding Babies," *Australasian Journal of Early Childhood*, 34 (3): 1–8.

Rouse, E. and F. Hadley (2018), "Where Did Love and Care Get Lost? Educators and Parents' Perceptions of Early Childhood Practice," *International Journal of Early Years Education*, 26 (2): 159–172.

Ruddick, S. (1989), *Maternal Thinking: Toward a Politics of Peace*, Boston, MA: Beacon Press.

Scheurich, J. J. and M. D. Young (1997), "Colouring Epistemologies: Are Our Research Epistemologies Racially Biased?" *Educational Researcher*, 26 (4): 4–16.

Shin, M. (2015), "Enacting Caring Pedagogy in the Infant Classroom," *Early Child Development and Care*, 185 (3): 496–508.

Spelman, E. V. (1997), *Fruits of Sorrow: Framing Our Attention to Suffering*, Boston, MA: Beacon Press.

Taggart, G. (2011), "Don't We Care?: The Ethics and Emotional Labour of Early Years Professionalism," *Early Years*, 31 (1): 85–95.

Taggart, G. (2014), "Compassionate Pedagogy: The Ethics of Care in Early Childhood Professionalism," *European Early Childhood Education Research Journal*, http://dx.doi.org/10:1080/1350293X.2014.970847.

Taggart, G. (2015), "Sustaining Care: Cultivating Mindful Practice in Early Years Professional Development," *Early Years*, 35 (4): 381–393.

Tronto, J. (1993), *Moral Boundaries: A Political Argument for an Ethics of Care*, New York: Routledge.

Tronto, J. (2013), *Caring Democracy: Markets, Equality and Justice*, New York: New York University Press.

Van Laere, K. and M. Vandenbroeck (2016), "The (In)Convenience of Care in Preschool Education: Examining Staff Views on Educare," *Early Years*, doi: 10.1080/09575146.2016.1252727.

Vincent, C. and A. Braun (2013), "Being 'Fun' at Work: Emotional Labour, Class, Gender and Childcare," *British Educational Research Journal*, 39 (4): 751–768.

Warin, J. (2014), "The Status of Care: Linking Gender and 'Educare,'" *Journal of Gender Studies*, 23 (1): 93–106.

Warin, J. and E. Gannerud (2014), "Gender, Teaching and Care: A Comparative Global Conversation," *Gender and Education*, 26 (3): 193–199.

White, J. E. and M. Gradovski (2018), 'Untangling (Some) Philosophical Knots Concerning Love and Care in Early Childhood Education," *International Journal of Early Years Education*, 26 (2): 201–211.

1

Contesting and Transforming Care:
An Introduction to a Critical Ethics of Care

Marian Barnes

The premise of this book is that care is both an opportunity and a danger in relation to work with young children.

Care for young children is not the only context in which care evokes ambivalent or negative responses. In many instances, care has been seen as something to be avoided, resisted, or challenged. Many disabled people have rejected care in favor of more neutral terms such as support or help, for example. So why is care a problem? The word care is ubiquitous in everyday language. It is used it when evaluating people or attitudes: "that was careless," "he doesn't care," or "she's a caring person." It is used positively but more frivolously to persuade consumers that cosmetics will improve hair or skin by caring for them. It can apply to burdens or worries: "the cares of the world." It is used not only to describe close or intimate relationships between friends and family members, but also to describe a diverse range of services and work roles: health care, social care, care workers of all kinds. Perhaps one of the word's problems is its diversity of meanings. We need to go beyond that to understand why many people resist being cared for, and why caring for others can feel and be an unwelcome burden. Such resistance reflects not only a desire to avoid being seen as needy, but also the demands of caregiving and gendered assumptions about who should care. We need to take seriously and understand these resistances, but we also need to advocate for care. To those who want to abandon or avoid care, we need to ask about the consequences of an absence of care both for individuals and for society.

The last three decades have seen major developments in care scholarship. This has coincided with political assaults on the funding of care services and the emergence of a hegemonic discourse celebrating autonomous individualism and viewing dependency as a moral failing. Scholars working with a care ethics perspective across disciplines have offered transformative insights into the political as well as personal significance of care. In addition to renewing debate about the potential of care to challenge oppression and achieve justice, this work has also enabled care thinking to expand beyond fields traditionally associated with care (Barnes 2012). The relevance of care thinking to topics such as international relations, urban design, and domestic violence reflects the breadth of the definition of care offered by Tronto and Fisher and the opportunities this offers for alternative imaginings of social relations:

> On the most general level, we suggest that caring be viewed as a species activity that includes everything that we do to maintain, continue, and repair our "world" so that we can live in it as well as possible. That world includes our bodies, our selves, and our environment, all of which we seek to interweave in a complex, life-sustaining web. (quoted in Tronto 1993: 103)

The power of this definition is also a challenge because of the diversity of contexts and ideas deployed when scholars and practitioners across disciplines talk of care. But these are challenges worth taking on.

In providing an introductory chapter to this book from a perspective outside the field of early childhood education and care (ECEC), I want to consider how feminist care ethics offers a critical framework and resource for those concerned with how we nurture and support young children, as well as other fields of social practices and social relations. I do so by emphasizing the significance of care ethics not only to the practice of childcare workers or relationships between workers, parents, and children, but also in critical policy analysis: in thinking about participative policymaking, the institutional context within which care work takes place, and in relation to the generation of solidarity and social justice. The growth of interest in care ethics has generated considerable literature on this topic. What follows is a selective discussion of developments in care ethics, but one that is structured to draw on literatures that may be less familiar to ECEC scholars and offers perspectives relevant to the challenge of both reconceptualizing care and developing policy and practice.

Care is political

The political dimensions of care have been examined from a political economy perspective and from feminist analyses of who cares and what this means for women's lives. But feminist care ethics offers other critical and potentially transformative approaches to the politics of care (Williams 2001). Here I explore ways in which feminist care ethics has contributed to critical policy analysis, to thinking about how we do politics, and to broader thinking about the type of democracy capable of enabling both care and justice. The examples I consider come from different areas of policy, including child and family policy. A key part of my argument is the significance of care thinking across diverse domains of policy and everyday lives, and the value of thinking laterally about the significance of care.

Care and justice

My own introduction to the ethics of care was Selma Sevenhuijsen's (1998) book *Citizenship and the Ethics of Care: Feminist Considerations on Justice, Morality and Politics*. I was attracted to her work because of my previous work on citizenship and social justice in the context of collective action by users of welfare services. Aspects of positions taken by some disabled activists troubled me because of a rejection of care associated with claims for civil rights. While I agreed that discrimination against disabled people, people with mental health problems, and others falls firmly within the sphere of social justice, I felt uncomfortable with the association of rejection of care with appeals to rights and citizenship. Discovering care ethics enabled me to resolve these concerns while still recognizing both the reality of the oppressive nature of "bad care" and the necessity of realizing rights in practice. Sevenhuijsen's book contains five essays that start with an everyday scene in a residential home for older people, a context most would recognize as a location for care and pans out from this scene to interrogate the uneasy relationship between feminism and ethics and the separation of care and politics in most mainstream and feminist scholarship, before zooming in to interrogate two areas of Dutch social policy: child custody and public health care. She summarizes her objectives in these essays as a "plea to integrate care into conceptions of democratic citizenship and social justice, and to look for suitable moral epistemologies and forms of public debate which make this possible" (33). She thus squarely locates care, justice, democracy and epistemology within a shared field.

Subsequently, Sevenhuijsen carried out critical policy analysis in other contexts, including an analysis of the influential "Third Way" discourse of the late 1990s and early 2000s (Sevenhuijsen 2000); Dutch policies regarding combining work, care, and generation-sensitive polices (Sevenhuijsen 2003); and social welfare policy in South Africa (Sevenhuijsen et al. 2003). She also, importantly, set out the analytical process and framework she had developed through these policy analyses. The goal of policy analysis is to:

> trace the normative framework(s) in policy reports in order to evaluate and renew these from the perspective of an ethic of care. The background motivation to this approach is the wish to further develop care into a political concept and to position care as a social and moral practice in notions of citizenship. (Sevenhuijsen 2004: 1)

The purpose is thus not only critical, evaluative analysis but also renewal through applying insights from political care ethics. This should not be seen as replacing an ethic of justice but rather as providing a moral vocabulary that alerts us to questions about social relations different from those raised by a more abstract and disembodied justice ethic.

The origins of care ethics emerge from Carol Gilligan's (1982) work in which she distinguishes a different moral voice from that expressed through an ethic of justice. In another early work, Noddings (1984) supports the notion that care and justice are distinct ethical positions and also argues that they are irreconcilable. However, the emphasis in more recent care ethics scholarship has been on understanding how both care thinking and justice thinking are necessary to achieve social justice.

One important contributor to this work is Eva Kittay. Kittay's development of care ethics arises not only from her professional work as a moral philosopher, but also from her insights as the mother of a daughter with severe cognitive disabilities (Kittay 1999). This experience confronts her with the disjuncture between concepts of autonomous individualism and the reality of her daughter's dependence. She understands the human condition as involving "inevitable dependencies" and argues for theories of justice based on this understanding rather than, as in Rawls and other liberal theorists, relegating the challenges offered by such inequalities to a footnote. She writes: "The domains of caring and equality, an ideal of justice, need to be brought into a dialectical relation if we are to genuinely meet both the concerns of dependency and the demands of equality" (Kittay 1999: 19).

More recently, Kittay articulates a theory of justice that starts from the concept of humans as inevitably interdependent. Creating a just society requires creating fair terms of social life given our inevitable dependence and interdependence. Thus, collective action is not a matter of choice but of necessity (Kittay 2015). While degrees of dependence vary across time, everyone is vulnerable to being or becoming dependent. A just society must meet the needs of both those who are dependent and those she calls "dependency workers": that is, both those who receive and those who give care. To view relations between them as solely a private concern fails the justice test: "Just social arrangements require attention to our dependency needs and the relationships that sustain ourselves in our dependency" (Kittay 2015: 11). From this understanding flows questions about the institutions required to support such arrangements, and political priorities and resourcing decisions necessary to support them.

Others have adopted different approaches to the care–justice relationship. Virginia Held (2006) considers the distinctiveness of care and justice as moral ideals and the dilemma of choosing which framework to apply to different personal and political issues. She concludes that care provides the underpinning moral framework within which issues of justice are embedded. She writes:

> When, for instance, necessities are provided without the relational human caring children need, children do not develop well, if at all. When in society individuals treat each other with only the respect that justice requires but no further consideration, the social fabric of trust and concern can be missing or disappearing. (p. 71)

Care, values, and public policy

From a social science perspective, Virginia Held's statement reflects the importance of working with both ethical and empirical insights when considering the significance of care. Sayer (2011) argues that humans are evaluative beings and thus a critical social science should not try to avoid questions of value and evaluation. He comes to conclusions similar to those reached by Walker (2007) from her position as a moral philosopher. She argues that morality is woven into the texture of everyday life, and, thus, moral understandings are expressed through social ones and social identities include moral understandings. While neither Sayer nor Walker identify themselves specifically as care ethicists, both point to feminist care ethics as offering one of the clearest examples of the necessity and value of bringing ethics and epistemology together. With Tronto, each recognizes that seeking to sustain boundaries between ethics and politics reinforces the exclusion of the concerns of those with least power from the political concerns of society.

The transformative objective Sevenhuijsen proposes for policy analysis is thus one of the distinctive characteristics of care ethics. It is evident in the definition of care offered by Fisher and Tronto that not only emphasizes the active, purposive nature of care, but also its role in repairing our world to enable both well-being and justice. While the concept of repair might be considered backward looking, not only Tronto's work but also that of others who have adopted, applied, and developed this way of thinking demonstrate its progressive intention and potential (Barnes et al. 2015). Moral concepts and arguments are often concealed in apparently empirical policy statements, and these also contain contradictions and inconsistencies in their normative frameworks. These can cause dilemmas but also opportunities for those working in public services.

Sevenhuijsen's TRACE analysis considers how policy texts are produced and how the policy problems to be addressed are defined. It then identifies the leading values at work within the document and whether these values are made explicit. Related to this are the suppositions about human nature contained within the text, for example assumptions about rational self-interest or interdependence. Analysis focuses on the way in which care is defined, whether the role of gender in caring arrangements is acknowledged, and how the role of the state vis-á-vis responsibilities of individuals and private institutions is defined. But it then goes on to offer a renewed articulation of the policy under consideration from within the ethics of care. In applying the framework of care ethics to the analysis of personalization policy[1] in social care in the UK, I suggest that one of the limitations of TRACE could be to base policy analysis solely on documentary analysis rather than an understanding of what practitioners do when they implement policy in their day-to-day practices (Barnes 2011). Linking the two—policy analysis and analysis of practice—from an ethics of care perspective holds the possibility of understanding the tensions often experienced by practitioners when their everyday experience does not match assumptions within official discourse and of locating spaces in which alliances for change might be forged.

An example of such tensions in the context of eldercare is offered by Liveng (2015). She focuses on the consequences of different philosophical conceptualizations of human beings—in this case, neoliberal constructions of older people as autonomous consumers. Not only did this construction not tally with the lives of older people who attended Danish activity centers, but a failure to recognize care workers' experiences of the lives and circumstances of older service users meant that care workers felt an infringement that challenged their capacity to give good care. Liveng concludes: "The ideology embedded in the described transformations potentially affects all citizens. Without an alternative

---

[1] Implemented through the allocation of an individual budget that enables users to choose and purchase services.

understanding of the human condition, the basic purpose of a welfare state disappears" (138).

In work with both older people and social care practitioners, colleagues and I demonstrate how creating spaces to deliberate *with care about care* enable re-imaginings of practices that are more attentive to the lived experiences of older people using social care services (Ward and Barnes 2016). This offers one example of how applying care ethics can open the possibility of transformation.

Others who have undertaken policy analysis from an ethic of care have not applied TRACE in its entirety, but the objective of not only critiquing but also offering alternatives is often shared. Thus Hankivsky (2004) has offered a care-based alternative to how victims of institutional abuse might be compensated; Lloyd (2012) considers what care ethics suggests about health policy in the context of a global, aging population; and Robinson (1999) addresses an area of policy rarely considered from a care perspective, that of international relations, to propose an alternative way of approaching responsibilities for relieving poverty across national borders.

Fiona Williams (2004a) suggests parameters of what family policy informed by a care ethic rather than a work ethic might look like. Her work demonstrates another strength of care ethics: its capacity to connect analysis of everyday life and the lay ethics that inform the difficult decisions people make about the right or best thing to do in terms of care for children and other family members, with the implications of such understandings for social policies. This is a connection that I have also made in my work on family caregivers (Barnes 2006) and in broader consideration of a care ethics approach to caring relations in diverse contexts (Barnes 2012).

In relation to child and family policy, Williams draws on a significant body of empirical research undertaken in the Care Values and Future of Welfare (CAVA) program that considers issues such as how mothers decide whether to return to paid work or to stay at home with a child and decisions made about childcare post-divorce, to offer critical analysis of UK policies such as "Every Child Matters" (ECM). Her conclusion that ECM both opens up and closes down opportunities for transforming the lives of children and their parents relates this to the absence of an explicit vision and values underpinning the policy. Advocating the importance of trust and respect to enable professionals to understand the diversity of children's experiences in the context of different cultures and the networks in which they are embedded, she writes:

> The care ethic demands that *interdependence* be seen as the basis of human interaction in which the values of solidarity, reciprocity, commitment, and love

are recognized and respected; in these terms, autonomy and independence for
children and adults are about the capacity for self-determination rather than the
expectation of individual adult self-sufficiency. (Williams 2004b: 423)

Williams's reference to "interdependence" in this quote reflects a relational
understanding of what it means to be human that is fundamental to care ethics.
The implications for policies and practices of starting from an understanding
of humans as relational beings are profound. If the human condition is one of
interdependence, then policy objectives, whether in relation to older people or
children (Langford et al. 2017) that are predicated on achieving independence
must be rethought. We need, as Williams suggests, to reconsider what we mean
by independence, but we also need to promote rather than denigrate the values
associated with interdependence if we are to build supportive social relations.

One of the most ambitious attempts to apply care ethics to social policy analysis
was undertaken by Engster (2007, 2015). Engster set himself the challenge of
renewing justice theory with care theory and then proposing what this would
mean for a welfare state based on an integrated concept of care and justice. In
his second book, he proposes detailed social policies relating to children, old
people, disabled people, people living in poverty, and health care. The result
is a somewhat didactic set of proposals that, from my perspective, fails to
acknowledge another key insight of care ethics. That is the necessity for dialogue
about needs and experiences within specific contexts to determine the right or
best thing to do to care in that context. This also applies to policymaking. Care
ethics requires us to consider how we do politics, who is involved in making
policy, and the nature of the dialogue through which this takes place.

Care, justice, and knowledge: Participatory policymaking

Here we need to introduce a new concept to those of care and justice: knowledge.
Sevenhuijsen names the "knowing and thinking subject" summoned by care
ethics (1998: 89). Concepts of care that associate it solely or primarily with
emotions such as compassion fail to acknowledge the epistemological basis
of care. These concepts contribute to a view of care as something that comes
naturally to some people.

At the level of policy, we hope that those who make policy both care about
and know about the issues they are addressing. We expect policymakers to
recognize that decisions about specific policies embody different values and
that those values are contested and should be a matter of public debate. We also
expect policymakers to access expert knowledge in the process of policymaking

and to recognize that such expertise is held by those who have direct experience of the issue at hand: living in poverty, being a parent of a disabled child, living with mental illness, for example, as well as by those professionally educated to know about such issues from a practitioner perspective. Recognition of such experiential knowledge is itself a political issue and one that has been the basis for much of the challenge offered to welfare professionals by service users (Barnes and Cotterell 2012). A political ethic of care requires us to enable both caregivers and care receivers to take part in making policy as well as determine how their own needs should be met.

Julie White (2000) elaborates one example of the consequences of this participatory approach. Basing her suggestions on a study of two different school–community collaboration programs and applying Tronto's political ethic of care, she develops a different critique of paternalism from liberal ideologies that can be used to justify nonintervention in situations where needs do exist. She argues for a participatory politics of needs interpretation to create effective policies and trusting relationships between communities and public officials. Sevenhuijsen (2003) links an analysis of specific policies from an ethic of care with a broader argument about the need to relocate both care and politics to create more responsive government with policymakers who actively listen to their citizens:

> In the public sphere people will exchange narratives of what counts in their lives and become acquainted with the stories of others. In this way, they will arrive at systems of shared meanings that will make sustainable forms of co-existence possible. (Sevenhuijsen 2003: 180)

This argument for deliberative and participatory practices at the level of both policy and service delivery is one familiar to me from my work on user involvement and collective action among disabled people, mental health service users, old people, and others (Barnes 2005; Barnes and Bowl 2001). This has led me to argue not only the necessity for those often regarded as recipients of care to be present in forums in which policies are made, but also that the way in which conversations take place and contributions can be supported requires "deliberating with care" (Barnes 2008). Such processes require not only "emotional morality," that is, recognizing that emotions are central to the experiences that need to be communicated and that talking about them with others cannot be done dispassionately, but also that the phases and principles of care that Tronto outlines and subsequently develops (Tronto 1993, 2013) can be applied to such processes and help develop the ethical sensibilities necessary to making good decisions about care.

Attentiveness in the context of participative policymaking requires a preparedness to listen to the particularity of the circumstances, experiences, and ideas of others, even when these are expressed in ways that do not conform to official modes of deliberation. Those inviting participation must take responsibility not only for the competent organization of spaces in which conversations can take place, but also for being aware of how participants are responding—whether they are becoming upset or withdrawn, for example. Organizers also need to accept that listening presages responsibility for acting on what is heard. If these conditions are present, then such processes contain the possibility of building solidarity based on an experience that public officials and others do genuinely care and that there is a collective acceptance of responsibility to ensure that needs are met.

Colleagues and I applied this approach to participatory research into well-being in old age, working with old people, and to a subsequent knowledge exchange involving social care practitioners and old people in applying research findings to the development of learning resources (Ward and Barnes 2016). Not only did we consider what old people and practitioners said *about* care during their deliberations about how practitioners can enhance well-being, but we were also attentive to the significance of care in developing relationships among the group in order to facilitate debate. Recognition that care is relevant in all our lives is important in building the connections between old people and practitioners that can contribute to solidarity. This recognition is based in personal experiences of relating to older relatives as well as professional responsibilities to ensure quality services.

Similar shared experiences can be anticipated in conversations between childcare workers and parents in the context of participatory processes concerning childcare policy and services. Langford et al. (2017) argue that not only children but also workers in ECEC settings have been excluded from policy deliberations and that this contributes to an understanding of care that is both too narrow and too simplistic to enable good judgments of the complexity of effective childcare. Deliberation among those differently positioned in relation to care can not only enable good care within day-to-day practice, but also contribute to broader political debate about the significance of care in achieving collective good.

Thus, in reviewing the contribution of care ethics to an understanding of care as political, we have moved from critical policy analysis, the relationship between care and justice and assumptions made about the nature of humans, through a renewed understanding of participatory practices in policymaking, needs analysis, and service delivery to what Tronto (2013) has called a "caring democracy." Tronto argues that care deficits—the failure of advanced countries to find sufficient workers to care for old people, children, and others—and democratic deficits—the incapacity of government to reflect the values of citizens—are two sides of the same coin. Fundamental to her argument is the necessity for democratic life to involve citizens in ongoing practices in which people who recognize themselves as both givers and receivers of care engage in making judgments about responsibility. One implication is that the type of spaces my colleagues and I created for old people and social care practitioners to talk together about care, well-being, and how this might be supported would become much more widely available. Such spaces would encompass a diverse range of citizens in conversation about factors impacting how we can live well together and explore responsibilities for action to achieve positive change. Calder (2015) discusses examples of the type of spaces that can be created with the aim of encouraging deliberation about care among academics, social care practitioners, caregivers, and care receivers. Unlike Engster (2015), Tronto does not propose specific policies arising from the type of engagement she envisages: "That task, after all, is the work of caring, democratic citizens" (2013: 170). Her emphasis is on the necessity to identify the "get out passes" that have enabled powerful people to avoid any responsibility for care and to create the political processes through which such "privileged irresponsibility" can be interrogated and challenged. This is significant in thinking about what care ethics can offer ECEC. Care ethics offer a distinctive way of thinking about how policy relating to ECEC is made, who is involved in that process, and what that requires in terms of participatory practices. It suggests ways of thinking about the purpose or objectives of services for young children—in terms of what sort of people such services seek to help to create, and the kind of values that are promoted and prioritized within those services. I now want to connect the political analysis and hope of transformation that care ethics points to with the way in which care ethics helps us think about and develop caring relationships.

Caring relationships

A strength of care ethics is its capacity to address everyday lives, politics, and policymaking as well as offering a perspective on specific care practices. I also argue that linking these domains is important in developing a critical perspective that reflects how people seek to do the right things in different contexts. In this section I focus more directly on caring relationships.

A view of caring relationships as comprising only one-to-one relationships between a person identified as caregiver and another as care receiver is neither empirically nor morally adequate (Barnes 2015). Not only is care a process that can facilitate political engagement; caring involves diverse relationships, not all of which are face-to-face, and which frequently involve different people who occupy different positions at different times.

The archetypal care relationship is often considered to be that between a parent (usually a mother) and their very young child. This is a source of one of the problems associated with care. It emphasizes complete dependence, a private relationship in which the caregiver is much more powerful than the care receiver. Such an image makes it hard to think of care receivers as people who can also give care or even as people who can contribute to the care process. It feeds the expectation and assumption that people will grow out of this situation and thus leave behind the need for care.

The rejection of care on the part of many disabled people has some of its origins in the experience of infantilization that can come with being a care receiver. But care ethics helps all of us recognize that not only will we all need care, but also that people are both caregivers and care receivers during their lives, sometimes at the same time (Barnes 2006). By naming *responsiveness* as the fourth phase of care, Tronto (1993) also identified the contribution of the care receiver to the process of care.[2] While acknowledging that caring relationships involve relationships of unequal power, it needs to be acknowledged that receiving care is not the same as passivity and that intersectional identities can encompass identities as both caregivers and care receivers (Ward 2015a).

Nicki Ward (2015b) explores the ethical significance of unsettling the caregiver–care receiver dichotomy in relation to people with learning disabilities. They are a social group often defined in relation to their need for care, but many also care for parents and others growing older. Ward argues that exploring their experiences as caregivers "enables us to see how they express the attributes of caring moral citizenship in their everyday lives, through mutual and reciprocal relationships of care" (168–169). Demonstrating their moral agency as caregivers can contribute to both personal and publicly recognized worth. In an earlier article, Ward (2011) also illustrates how shared identities as caregivers can unsettle distinctions regarding the social positions of people with learning

---

[2] Tronto (1993) identified four phases of care linked to four principles: caring about—attentiveness; caring for—responsibility; care giving—competence; and care receiving—responsiveness. In her later work (2013), she added a fifth phase: caring with, linked to solidarity.

disabilities and non-learning-disabled people. She does this by recounting a recognized equivalence between herself as someone caring for her mother and the experience of a neighbor being cared for by her daughter.

Other examples and contexts in which people often thought of as care receivers are also caregivers illustrate another point: that care can be given and received collectively as well as in one-to-one relationships (Barnes 2015). Ruth Emond (2003) studied children and young people in residential care to explore ways in which relationships between the young people could be understood as caring relationships that were important sources of support in situations in which they had been removed from families. An important factor in the care given and received among the young people is shared experience of the difficulties many are experiencing and the capacity to draw on shared experiential knowledge in being attentive to distress. I discuss this example and others in Chapter 5 of *Care in Everyday Life* (Barnes 2012). These include observations of similar ways in which people with mental health problems active in self-advocacy groups recognize and understand the variable capacity of their co-advocates to take on responsibilities and use this to build networks that enable support to be offered when necessary. Shared experiential knowledge facilitates reciprocity in relationships that often encompass personal support as well as political activism. Care can and does emerge through relationships established among those who use services, whether that be people with learning difficulties, with mental health problems, or among children and young people in early childhood settings or residential facilities. This not only unsettles assumptions about distinctions between caregivers and receivers, but also enlarges understanding of what care consists of and how responsibilities of those paid to care need to be exercised.

I discussed above Kittay's arguments that caregivers need to be cared for to ensure justice for dependence workers as well as dependents. In the context of unpaid care this is well recognized. Not only do we all need care, the capacity to care is impacted by care received, and a caring democracy cannot be achieved through the exploitation of those who accept responsibility to care for family or friends. Kittay discusses this by reference both to the role of the *doula*—who helps a mother so she can care for her newborn child—and to the concept of "nested dependencies": "these nested dependencies link those who need help to those who help, and link the helpers to a set of supports. The equality concept inherent in the idea that we are all some mother's child utilizes such a notion of nested dependencies" (1999: 132).

I discuss a similar point using the concept of care networks (Barnes 2015). Care networks can involve complex relationships. Kittay (1999) discusses her own relationship with Peggy, the woman who came to stay to help her look after her disabled daughter Sesha. Kittay recognizes both relief and discomfort in her relationship with Peggy and acknowledges her privilege in being able to afford to pay another woman to share care of her daughter. While the intensity of this relationship derives from Peggy's live-in position and the depth and complexity of Sesha's needs, paid childcare generally illustrates the importance of understanding both the significance and complexity of care networks.

In the context of early childhood care and education, Garrity and Canavan (2017) use the concept of care communities to highlight their significance. Their focus is on the relationships that develop between early years practitioners and the mothers of the children they care for. The relationships the authors considered from the perspective of the ethics of care were thus between paid and unpaid caregivers:

> This exploration of mother–caregiver relationships highlights how mothers are rendered vulnerable and potentially powerless in their need for care for their child. Acting on trust, mothers surrender the care of their child to practitioners, who in turn justify these trusting actions through reinforcing behaviours. The dynamic aspect of these relationships supports the longer-term development of caring, mutually beneficial relationships with the child at the centre. (15)

But beyond support for the care of the child, Garrity and Canavan argue that these relationships contribute to enabling mothers to feel part of wider communities of care with others who understand the difficult decisions they have to make about handing over care of their children to people who are at first strangers.

It is not only unpaid caregivers who need to experience care. There has been comparatively little work done on the needs of care workers to be cared for, but there is some within the care ethics tradition. Teodora Manea (2015) studied the experiences of Romanian doctors who migrated to the UK and identified their care needs as they sought to find a place in an unfamiliar culture while separated from their care networks. Peta Bowden (1997: 104) identified the "needs and well-being of nursing practitioners [as] an important dimension of the ethical import of their relations with patients." She, like Tronto (2010), recognized that face-to-face caring relations between paid caregivers and those they care for must be understood within the institutional and organizational context that both frames and provides the opportunities and constraints within which caring relationships can be established. A positive valuing of care is more likely to generate a context in which practitioners are able to both discuss the ethical dilemmas they face in their everyday practice and acknowledge their own vulnerabilities and need for support.

I suggested above that collective forms of service provision hold potential as spaces in which people can learn to care for each other. If the idea of shared responsibilities for caregivers is added to ensure that they are not overburdened or exploited, this brings us back to Tronto's arguments for a fifth phase of care: *caring with*, which embodies the value of solidarity. Early childhood care and education has an important role to play here in the creation of caring citizens as well as productive citizens.

If we are arguing for care as a basis on which solidarity can be built, who is included within the sphere of social relations of solidarity? This question relates to questions about who we have responsibility to care for. Engster (2007) argues there is a hierarchy of such responsibilities, with self-care the primary caring responsibility and general duties to care for all others in need coming last. Robinson's (1999) work on care in the context of international relations argues that interdependencies are not only interpersonal but also link nation states in a web of responsibility relationships. Scuzzarello et al. (2009) discuss care ethics in the context of multiculturalism and increased movement of peoples across the globe. I argue that stranger relationships should be considered among relationships of care, both in terms of an awareness of the impact of national policies on those who leave families behind to care for strangers and also those who care for those who are different (Barnes 2012). Elena Pulcini (2009) addresses issues of time in arguing that we all need to care for the future, while issues of intergenerational relations raise the question of how to think about responsibilities for people in different generations and the implications of this not only for personal relationships, but also for public policy. Others working in the tradition of care ethics suggest how thinking about care can be informed by different cultures, philosophies, and ways of conceptualizing care and caring relations (Boulton and Brannelly 2015).

These contributions may seem a long way from the challenges and pressures experienced by practitioners working with young children and their families. Their significance can be understood in two ways: first in terms of reinforcing the ethical significance of care and thus the need to challenge those who would argue that care is limited to bodily and emotional tending; and second, to locate the practice of childcare within a broader understanding of what kind of people we hope children will be both as children and as they become adults. This should influence both the way practitioners approach children as moral agents capable of giving as well as receiving care and the relationships that children are supported to develop among themselves and in relation to others who are different from them and/or who they may never meet.

Feminist care ethics helps us understand what is necessary to create caring relationships that can enable personal as well as political transformations. In the context of social practices of various types and of interactions between people who share varying degrees of intimacy, care involves both talking and doing. Elisabeth Conradi (2015) writes of this in terms of communicative contact, practice, and interactivity:

> To develop the liberating aspects of care it is important to see the inclusiveness of persons within a common action and notice collective and interrelational processes of change …. What is central here are the relations people develop while participating in a concrete caring practice. Individuals are not subjects isolated from one another and independent of the dynamics of the process in which they are involved. Rather, the dynamics of the process *changes all the participants,* including outsiders and institutions. (118–119)

By doing care through interrelational activity, both the caregiver and care receiver are changed and such changes link to the broader transformations that feminist care ethics seeks to achieve. Care is purposive and necessary to respond to the experiences of those who are marginalized and disrespected to both meet immediate needs and create the conditions in which injustices can be addressed. Brannelly (2015) writes about this in relation to people with mental health difficulties, and Evans and Atim (2015) make similar arguments regarding children caring for relatives with HIV/AIDS in sub-Saharan Africa. Above, I cited Nicki Ward about the way that being recognized as a caregiver contributes to the moral worth experienced by people with learning disabilities. Again, in the context of HIV/AIDS, Anke Niehof (2015: 148) argues that "women's responsibilities for arranging care and finding support confer authority and express women's decision-making power," and, hence, that this matriarchy of care can have broader influence on social structures. Closer to home, my interviews with caregivers demonstrate important ways in which women make connections between personal caring relations and collective action to achieve change (Barnes 2006). In all these examples, the link between care and social justice is made through the way in which caring relations reveal the connections between respect, recognition, and the acceptance of collective responsibility to support people who may be marginalized or oppressed. We have come full circle, back to the political nature and implications of care.

Conclusion

In this chapter, I have adopted an unashamedly pro-care approach to argue that it is essential for care to occupy a strong but critical place within early childhood care and education. In doing so, I have emphasized the political nature of feminist care ethics rather than focusing on care practices. Arguably ECEC occupies a key point at which we need to transform both the concept and the experience of care to minimize the risk that care is associated only with the tending of those who are not capable of self-care. To do this, those who work at care in these settings need to feel cared for in their work and be able to work within networks of care that involve policymakers, parents, and the children themselves and also embody care as a value that supports solidarity and social justice.

References

Barnes, M. (2005), "Same Old Process? Older People, Participation and Deliberation," *Ageing and Society*, 25 (2): 245–259.

Barnes, M. (2006), *Caring and Social Justice*, Basingstoke: Palgrave.

Barnes M. (2008), "Passionate Participation: Emotional Experiences and Expressions in Deliberative Forums," *Critical Social Policy*, 28 (4): 461–481.

Barnes, M. (2011), "Abandoning Care? A Critical Perspective on Personalisation from an Ethic of Care," *Ethics and Social Welfare*, 5 (2): 153–167.

Barnes, M. (2012), *Care in Everyday Life: An Ethic of Care in Practice*, Bristol: Policy Press.

Barnes, M. (2015), "Beyond the Dyad: Exploring the Multidimensionality of Care," in M. Barnes, T. Brannelly, L. Ward, and N. Ward (eds), *Ethics of Care: Critical Advances in International Perspective*, 31–44, Bristol: Policy Press.

Barnes, M. and R. Bowl (2001), *Taking over the Asylum: Empowerment and Mental Health*, Basingstoke: Palgrave.

Barnes, M. and P. Cotterell (eds) (2012), *Critical Perspectives on User Involvement*, Bristol: Policy Press.

Barnes, M., T. Brannelly, L. Ward, and N. Ward (eds) (2015), *Ethics of Care: Critical Advances in International Perspective*, Bristol: Policy Press.

Boulton, A. and T. Brannelly (2015), "Care Ethics and Indigenous Values: Political, Tribal and Personal," in M. Barnes, T. Brannelly, L. Ward, and N. Ward (eds), *Ethics of Care: Critical Advances in International Perspective*, 69–82, Bristol: Policy Press.

Bowden, P. (1997), *Caring: Gender Sensitive Ethics*, London: Routledge.

Brannelly, T. (2015), "Mental Health Service Use and the Ethics of Care: In Pursuit of Justice," in M. Barnes, T. Brannelly, L. Ward, and N. Ward (eds), *Ethics of Care: Critical Advances in International Perspective*, 219–232, Bristol: Policy Press.

Calder, G. (2015), "Caring about Deliberation, Deliberating about Care," *Ethics and Social Welfare*, 9 (2): 130–146.

Conradi, E. (2015), "Redoing Care: Societal Transformation through Critical Practice," *Ethics and Social Welfare*, 9 (2): 113–129.

Emond, R. (2003), "Putting the Care into Residential Care: The Role of Young People," *Journal of Social Work*, 3 (3): 321–337.

Engster, D. (2007), *The Heart of Justice: Care Ethics and Political Theory*, Oxford: Oxford University Press.

Engster, D. (2015), *Justice, Care and the Welfare State*, Oxford and New York: Oxford University Press.

Evans, R. and A. Atim (2015), "HIV Care and Interdependence in Tanzania and Uganda," in M. Barnes, T. Brannelly, L. Ward, and N. Ward (eds), *Ethics of Care: Critical Advances in International Perspective*, 151–164, Bristol: Policy Press.

Garrity, S. and J. Canavan (2017), "Trust, Responsiveness and Communities of Care: An Ethnographic Study of the Significance and Development of Parent–Caregiver Relationships in Irish Early Years Settings," *European Early Childhood Education Research Journal*, https://doi.org/10.1080/1350293X.2017.1356546.

Gilligan, C. (1982), *In a Different Voice: Psychological Theory and Women's Development*, Cambridge, MA: Harvard University Press.

Hankivsky, O. (2004), *Social Policy and the Ethic of Care*, Vancouver: UBC Press.

Held, V. (2006), *The Ethics of Care: Personal, Political and Global*, Oxford: Oxford University Press.

Kittay, E. F. (1999), *Love's Labor. Essays on Women, Equality and Dependency*, London and New York: Routledge.

Kittay, E. F. (2015), "A Theory of Justice as Fair Terms in Social Life Given Our Inevitable Dependency and Our Inextricable Interdependency," in D. Engster and M. Hamington (eds), *Care Ethics and Political Theory*, Oxford Scholarship Online, 51–71. doi: 10.1093/acprof:oso/9780198716341.001.0001.

Langford, R., B. Richardson, P. Albanese, K. Bezanson, S. Prentice, and J. White (2017), "Caring about Care: Reasserting Care as Integral to Early Childhood Education and Care Practice, Politics and Policies in Canada," *Global Studies of Childhood*, 1–12. doi: 10.1177/2043610617747978.

Liveng, A. (2015), "Paradoxical Constructions in Danish Elderly Care," in M. Barnes, T. Brannelly, L. Ward, and N. Ward (eds), *Ethics of Care: Critical Advances in International Perspective*, 125–138, Bristol: Policy Press.

Lloyd, L. (2012), *Health and Care in Ageing Societies. A New International Approach*, Bristol: Policy Press.

Manea, T. (2015), "Care for Carers: Care in the Context of Medical Migration," in M. Barnes, T. Brannelly, L. Ward, and N. Ward (eds), *Ethics of Care: Critical Advances in International Perspective*, 207–218, Bristol: Policy Press.

Niehof, A. (2015), "Contours of Matriarchy in Care for People Living with AIDS," in M. Barnes, T. Brannelly, L. Ward, and N. Ward (eds), *Ethics of Care: Critical Advances in International Perspective*, 139–150, Bristol: Policy Press.

Noddings, N. (1984), *Caring: A Feminine Approach to Ethics and Moral Education*, Berkeley: University of California Press.

Pulcini, E. (2009), *Care of the World. Fear, Responsibility and Justice in the Global Age*, Dordrecht: Springer.

Robinson, F. (1999), *Globalizing Care: Ethics, Feminist Theory and International Relations*, Boulder: Westview Press.

Sayer, A. (2011), *Why Things Matter to People: Social Science, Values and Ethical Life*, Cambridge: Cambridge University Press.

Scuzzarello, S., C. Kinnvall, and K. R. Monroe (eds) (2009), *On Behalf of Others: The Psychology of Care in a Global World*, Oxford: Oxford University Press.

Sevenhuijsen, S. (1998), *Citizenship and the Ethics of Care: Feminist Considerations of Justice, Morality and Politics*, London and New York: Routledge.

Sevenhuijsen, S. (2000), "Caring in the Third Way: The Relation between Obligation, Responsibility and Care in Third Way Discourse," *Critical Social Policy*, 20 (1): 5–37.

Sevenhuijsen, S. (2003), "The Place of Care: The Relevance of the Feminist Ethic of Care for Social Policy," *Feminist Theory*, 4 (2): 179–197.

Sevenhuijsen, S. (2004), "TRACE: A Method for Normative Policy Analysis from the Ethic of Care," in S. Sevenhuijsen. and A. Švab (eds), *The Heart of the Matter: The Contribution of the Ethic of Care to Social Policy in Some New EU Member States*, 8–9, Ljubljana: Peace Institute.

Sevenhuijsen, S., V. Bozalek, A. Gouws, and M. Minnaar-McDonald (2003), "South African Social Welfare Policy: An Analysis Using the Ethic of Care," *Critical Social Policy*, 23 (3): 299–321.

Tronto, J. (1993), *Moral Boundaries: A Political Argument for an Ethic of Care*, London and New York: Routledge.

Tronto, J. (2010), "Creating Caring Institutions: Politics, Plurality and Purpose," *Ethics and Social Welfare*, 4 (2): 158–171.

Tronto, J. (2013), *Caring Democracy: Markets, Equality and Justice*, New York and London: New York University Press.

Walker, M. U. (2007), *Moral Understandings. A Feminist Study in Ethics*, Oxford: Oxford University Press.

Ward, L. and M. Barnes (2016), "Transforming Practice with Older People through an Ethic of Care," *British Journal of Social Work*, 46 (4): 906–922.

Ward, N. (2011), "Care Ethics and Carers with Learning Disabilities: A Challenge to Dependence and Paternalism," *Ethics and Social Welfare*, 5 (2): 168–180.

Ward, N. (2015a), "Care Ethics, Intersectionality and Poststructuralism," in M. Barnes, T. Brannelly, L. Ward, and N. Ward (eds), *Ethics of Care: Critical Advances in International Perspective*, 57–68, Bristol, Policy Press.

Ward, N. (2015b), "Reciprocity and Mutuality: People with Learning Disabilities as Carers," in M. Barnes, T. Brannelly, L. Ward, and N. Ward (eds), *Ethics of Care: Critical Advances in International Perspective*, 165–178, Bristol: Policy Press.

White, J. A. (2000), *Democracy, Justice and the Welfare State. Reconstructing Public Care*, Philadelphia: Pennsylvania State University Press.

Williams, F. (2001), "In and beyond New Labour: Towards a New Political Ethics of Care," *Critical Social Policy*, 21 (4): 467–493.

Williams, F. (2004a), *Rethinking Families*, London: Calouste Gulbenkian Foundation.

Williams, F. (2004b), "What Matters Is Who Works: Why Every Child Matters to New Labour. Commentary on the DfES Green Paper Every Child Matters," *Critical Social Policy*, 24 (3): 406–427.

2

An Ethics of Care in Culturally Diverse Early Childhood Settings: Toward an Ethics of Unknowing

Sonja Arndt and Marek Tesar

Education is about producing better people, better in "all aspects of a complete life: moral, physical, social, vocational, aesthetic, intellectual, spiritual, and civic."

Noddings 2015: 1

What do we want for our children? Who do we think the child is—what is our image of the child? What is the role of the preschool or school in society? What do we mean by terms such as "education," "knowledge," "care"? ... our evaluation of pedagogical work can never be divorced from ethics and politics.

Dahlberg and Moss 2005: 89

In this chapter, we engage in reconceptualizing the notion of an ethics of care in the sometimes messy, blurred places and spaces of early childhood settings. Such a reconceptualization complicates pedagogies through a re-theorization of what a feminist ethics of care might be, look like, and feel like for children and teachers, considering the added complexities that arise in the often culturally diverse communities of early childhood settings. The chapter is, on the one hand, a response to, and, on the other, a new way of viewing recent work that emphasizes the need for more nuanced articulations of the implications of a feminist ethics of care (Taggart 2016).

It also responds to the recent calls by the foundational thinkers and activists in the reconceptualist movement (Bloch et al. 2018) when they enquire into the progress that has been made over the decades of reconceptualist work since the early 1990s. As they ask, "Are we/how are we making life better when young human beings are living with war, abuse, hunger, disaster, and death" (8)?

And in what ways "do oppression, injustice, and violence imposed on younger human beings" (8) become affected by privileges and wider social justice issues in societies? These calls cannot be taken lightly, as they expose the severity and comprehensive nature of the task of ongoing imaginings and enactments of a critical, feminist ethics of care. In this chapter, we propose an argument for a new ethics of early childhood pedagogy that takes these calls seriously: an ethics of unknowing.

Seeking to elevate children as already complete, complex, and closely entwined in their lives and contexts, this re-theorization of an ethics of care seeks to de-elevate certainty and the constant need to know that commonly drives early childhood pedagogies. As we write, Aotearoa New Zealand's need "to do better" (Harris 2018) for children is recognized in a new report by the group responsible for monitoring implementations of the United Nations Convention on the Rights of the Child (UNCRC). Both timely and disturbing, this report unravels the moral endeavor that is implied by Noddings's opening statement and in the reconceptualist calls from Bloch and colleagues. The report makes clear from the beginning the impossibility of separating concerns with care from concerns with rights. It inserts care–rights concerns into such fundamental questions as those raised by Dahlberg and Moss in the opening of this chapter. Rethinking an ethics of care involves rethinking underlying orientations toward teaching, learning, and education, but, most importantly, toward children. It means unsettling the contextual limitations of our orientations that direct, constrain, and control the "production" of better people through education, for example, in the neoliberal, outcomes-and-profit-oriented framings of teaching and assessment (Arndt and Tesar 2015).

Reconceptualizing an ethics of care within early childhood education compels us to consider education as a moral and political, as well as a social, act that is both uncontrollable and unknowable. Julia Kristeva's feminist post-structural philosophical lens helps us challenge the ethics of plannable, profitable, and comfortable educational practices. In this chapter we draw particularly on Kristeva's work on subject formation, the idea of being the foreigner, and on the notion of exile. Kristeva's philosophical approach is useful to outline possibilities for an ethics of care that follows an orientation of openness to the Other and to our own humility, that is, to the idea that we do not, and maybe cannot, know or control all within the teaching environment. It raises the idea of an ethics of the unknown.

Our reflections on two recent research projects, one in Aotearoa New Zealand, and one in Kenyan early childhood settings, serve as brief examples to illustrate our thinking. In our analysis of these reflections, we demonstrate a conceptual broadening and deepening of an ethics of care to strengthen our argument for the potential of an ethics of unknowing.

Reinserting Dahlberg and Moss's questions, the concerns that are central to this chapter focus on what and whose needs are considered, how they are determined, who is being served, and who is left at the margins in early childhood settings. We place a particular emphasis on the notion of the Other—the concept of the stranger—to include both diverse human Othernesses and the ethics of other-than-human relationships. In other words, we emphasize the relational dependencies as well as the responsibilities invoked in the wider conceptions of care ethics (Collins 2015).

The responsive and reciprocal relational nature of early childhood education is affirmed in the Aotearoa New Zealand early childhood curriculum framework *Te Whāriki* (Ministry of Education 2017), situating the idea of an ethics of care as an ethics of an encounter. As such, it is not an encounter as a one-off interaction or engagement but rather a commitment to the long-term maintenance, nourishing, and hard work of sustaining the relationship. As an ethics of an encounter, then, rethinking an ethics of care in early childhood settings is implicated and exacerbated by local and worldly concerns, such as the violence and injustices raised by Bloch and colleagues above. This ethics of care is dependent, then, on being attentive and having certain understandings of and sensitivities to children's and teachers' day-to-day realities. "Acting ethically is based on interaction with and attentiveness to others," Dahlberg and Moss (2005) note, "not derived from an ethical code" (89). That is, ethical care arises in and because of the encounter in each localized situation. Our argument for an ethics of unknowing through "interaction with and attentiveness to others" arises from the unknowability of the intricacies of these situations in early childhood settings.

ECE settings as *loci* for ethical practice

Early childhood education settings are posited as the *loci* for ethical practices (Dahlberg and Moss 2005). In many countries, this means that ethics and care practices are becoming increasingly complex in terms of diverse cultural pluralities, histories, and orientations. From where we write, Aotearoa New Zealand early childhood settings offer an example of the relational ethics arising from such pluralities. Auckland is the largest city in the country and is one of the most ethnically diverse cities in the world (Global Migration Trends

Factsheet 2018). This implicates an ethics of care as multilayered encounters with the heterogeneity of the diverse backgrounds, histories, cultures, and lifestyles of children and teachers who live, work, play, and grow up here.

Such a plurality of diverse cultures was evident in the settings where the images referred to later in this chapter were taken: in a central Auckland suburb. These images were gathered as a part of a project that was aimed at learning about children's understandings and meaning-making in culturally diverse early childhood spaces and places. Reporting on the findings, Tesar (2017) argues, on the one hand, for recognition of the potential complexities arising when families and teachers interpret children's learning, behaviors, and needs from diverse perspectives, life goals, and aspirations. He also argues for the acceptance of a "childhood underground"—of children's resistance to adult urges to control and know and order children's activities, movements, and learning through an increased recognition of children's rights and agentic direction of their own learning and encounters.

Positing early childhood settings as *loci* for such a complex ethics of care affects orientations. It provokes questioning, of what, for example, is the purpose of early childhood education? How do we see the nature and purpose of childhoods? What does it mean to be a "good" person who may or may not be able to direct their own life? Osgood (2010) points out that the discourses and counter-discourses of professionalism itself, when related to early childhood education, depend on such diverse orientations. Multiple and often intimate conceptions arise out of very localized and historicized constructions of the professional teacher and the type of relationships and responsibilities teachers ought to have with children and society, among other things. On this basis, professional and ethical responsibilities and encounters are always moral engagements with relational, emotional, cultural, political, and highly localized ways of being and knowing. Framing our argument within *a need to unknow* and to humbly accept this state of unknowing as an ethical imperative is critical to elevating marginalized, subjugated, or oppressed knowledges and ways of being.

This need to unknow became strongly evident in another study conducted in Kenyan early childhood settings that we have previously examined together with colleagues involved in the project in Kwale, Kenya (Arndt et al. 2016). Kwale County is located in coastal southern Kenya and represents a range of sub-counties that feature coastal plains, semi-arid, and plateau regions. This study was conducted as an aid project and elevated the ways in which the development discourses perpetuate, among other orientations, particular images and experiences of power, deficiency, and lack. Further blurring interpretations of an ethics of care and relational encounters, some of the complexities that arose in that context involved negotiating the boundaries of care alongside notions of charity, hopefulness, and agency in children and childhoods, that are embedded within a postcolonial political web of aid and localized development. Following Osgood's argument above, both in the Auckland context and in the Kwale context, the close connections between relational and local stories, mythologies, histories, and day-to-day, mundane realities underlie the meanings and responsibilities evoked by an ethics of care—sometimes knowingly and sometimes unknowingly.

Our revisiting of these prior studies compels us to rethink an ethical relational lens of "producing better people," as Noddings asks. The prior studies importantly do not give us answers to the complicated question of what "better" means in any one instance. Instead, our reflections raise further questions about the ways that reinterpreting an ethics of care might help reconfigure our approaches as researchers and as educators, to everyday conceptions and practices of an ethics of care in early childhood settings.

Reconceptualizing a feminist ethics of care

Dahlberg and Moss (2005) suggest that teaching and learning begin from a foundation grounded in ethics. They draw on Levinas's thinking of an ethics of an encounter, where to be in relation with an Other places upon individuals the responsibility to respond. As we reinterpret the images and reflections from our earlier research project, we feel within us the ethics of a re-encounter with that context, with those children, and with our relationships surrounding these encounters.

In Levinas's notion of the ethics of an encounter, there is a sense of a constant danger that ethics becomes a concern to which we pay attention once and then assume that it is "done," "sorted," ticked off, once and for all. Rather, the ethics of an encounter with an Other, with the stranger—with the children and contexts in our research—is "renewed at every moment, in every conversation with every other" (Guenther 2009). An understanding of ethics in this encounter-focused way thus eludes certainty and never ends. It opens up a conceptual and relational space of uncertainty, of a responsibility that is placed on all encounters as an ongoing obligation.

That early childhood education is a moral endeavor that affects the everyday, mundane practices in early childhood settings, locates it within such encounters as relational obligations. Indeed, Dahlberg and Moss's (2005) questions in the opening quote illustrate an openness to interrogating conceptions of the everyday to understand how ethics and politics are constant elements in early childhood practices. Considering a feminist ethics of care inserts gender issues into understandings of ethics and, also, in its wider constructions, a feminist ethics of care implies a concern with all elements of marginalization, subjugation, power relations, and exclusionary behaviors that move beyond male domination and gender issues of traditional patriarchal orientations and structures, to concerns with other forms of difference and othernesses (Stanford Encyclopedia of Philosophy 2009). Notions of the Other, the stranger, and that which is strange or different are at the forefront of this recognition of difference, coinciding with the ethics of an encounter, of every encounter, questioning the obligations that the encounter might entail and the responsibility to respond in appropriate ways, ethically, culturally, and politically. This orientation blurs multiple boundaries, inviting further encounters, and, to borrow further from Noddings (2015), it "is delightfully vague":

> There need be no intention to fill it out with highly specific, number-sustainable, details. It invites dialogue, moral and social analysis, imaginative exploration, tender concern for the young, intelligent consideration for the health of the Earth on which we live ... it guides everything we do. (234)

The usefulness of rethinking an ethics of unknowing as "delightfully vague" allows us to strengthen our own unknowing.

Adding the Kristevan influence

Thinking through Kristeva's work informs our re-encounter with the early childhood instances in our earlier research, drawing on her theories of the subject in process, the idea of the foreigner within, and her notion of exile. Specifically, a Kristevan lens underlies the unknowability, reciprocal implicatedness, and humility that we see as closely interwoven with a feminist ethics of care.

Subjects always in process

As a post-structural feminist philosopher, Kristeva theorizes Otherness through her philosophy of the subject and subjectivity formation. Claiming that all subjects are always in process—i.e., in ongoing construction—Kristeva (2008) insists that all of our identities are "infinitely in construction, de-constructible, open and evolving" (2). She asserts that some aspects of this process are conscious and knowable, while other aspects of the process are unconscious and remain unknowable. Kristeva's (1998) theory of the subject in process is at the root of the openness to the unknown in this ethics that we propose. It helps us see ourselves as always in construction and reciprocally in relation and implicated with those around us. For this reason, it is at the root of our argument for humble and tentative encounters with the ethics of care in pedagogical engagements. Even as we become more aware of what was previously unknown to us about ourselves, Kristeva (1991) claims there will always be elements of ourselves that we do not know.

Affirming this unknowability, Stone (2004) argues that Kristeva's idea on the subject in process can be seen as a mystery that "works" through four elements. These elements include the notion of the semiotic, love, abjection, and revolt. The semiotic operates mostly in the subject's unconscious, and is what makes meaning for the subject, that is, for us as researchers, or for teachers, or children (Kristeva 1998). The semiotic works alongside its context and realities, counters homogeneity by highlighting the "the heterogeneity of meaning" (Prud'homme and Légaré 2006: 4) and energizes the subject through meaning-making. In other words, the semiotic works with and makes meaning of the complex interrelationships in which the subject is implicated and by which it is formed and governed.

The other elements at work in subjects in process include the notion of love. Love is the very foundation of relationships and of ethical encounters with and through the Other (Stone 2004). Love can be seen as the root of conceptualizing education as a moral undertaking. The notion of love works alongside a further Kristevan concept: abjection. Abjection serves the literal and figurative purpose of expulsion. That is, it is that element that helps us as individuals to recognize the inarticulable—our "gut" feelings—through which we might become aware of and refrain from engaging in what feels wrong, repulsive, off-putting, and uninviting. Abjection might be the sense that causes a teacher to remove herself from a situation that could cause offence, pain, or harm. Abjection has the potential to alert a teacher to a sense of ethical obligation, in response to particular situations, encounters, or pressures. Abjection works within all of us as subjects in process, helping us sense ethical responsibilities, for example, and respond in ways that take heed of ethical dangers and tensions.

The final element at work in Kristeva's subject in process, according to Stone (2004), is the element of revolt. Revolt implies a constant state of questioning. It seeks the deep and critical thought that moves teachers' thinking beyond surface-level practices to engage with the cultural and relational day-to-day realities that complicate an ethics of encounters in early childhood settings. Revolt in a Kristevan (2014) sense should not necessarily be seen as a revolution or an overthrowing of any particular regime—although those too may be necessary! Instead, it could also be a form of mini-revolt. That is, an inner questioning and transformation that causes us as early childhood teacher educators or teachers to think and behave in more nuanced ways, in our pedagogical, ethical encounters. Kristeva laments the lack of revolt in contemporary society, pointing to a dominant preference for what is comfortable, known, and predictable. This concern mirrors our argument for critical reconceptualizations of the intricacies and unfathomabilities of the ethics of early childhood pedagogies and care.

These elements, Stone (2004) contends in her analysis of Kristeva's theory, form us as subjects in process that are never completely products of only our own experiences. Instead, she says, we are always "split subjects" and as such "we must call ourselves (continually) into question" (Stone 2004: 124). As subjects in process, then, we are always, at least a little bit unknown, even to ourselves.

The foreigner within

Unknown to ourselves, as strangers to ourselves, we are all, to various extents, foreigners. Through a Kristevan (2008) lens, this places us in an "unsettling fragility" and "vigorous subtlety" (2) of unknowing. Kristeva's (1991) notion of the foreigner illustrates the "incoherences and abysses ... the strangenesses" (2) that these unknowabilities, even of ourselves, evoke. Extending the idea that we are all foreigners, where we balance on a cusp of the known and the strange, the comfort of familiarity and the fear of the unknown, our communication always interconnects not only to ourselves as the speaker or the listener, but also to all of what has informed, shaped, and affected us in our past and present. Confronting our own foreignness is crucial to the humility for which we argue in the ethics of encounters within early childhood settings. Kristeva's (1991) claim, that "strangely, the foreigner lives within us: [s]he is the hidden face of our identity" (1), implies for us that the foreignness inside each of us is the hidden face of our identities. This unknowability of ourselves shapes who we are and what we communicate in verbal or nonverbal ways and is formed, shaped, and permeated by what has affected us in the past and present, directly or indirectly.

Reconfiguring an ethics of unknowing

Kristeva's influence through the idea that we are all subjects in process and foreigners to ourselves alerts us to a concern. The precarity and unpredictability of these notions raise what might be seen as the dangerous aspects of ethics in care and encounters. That is, they provoke more tentative responses, for example, in claiming what is good, right, or proper, in relation to Dahlberg and Moss's opening questions. They add a certain humility, in our practice as researchers and educators and in our formulation of an ethics of care for early childhood settings. They compel us to take notice of the unknowability in relational encounters. From a Kristevan (1998) perspective, the unfolding transformation of all of us as subjects in process always occurs as a result of and alongside the wider context. This means that we are constantly affected by the physical environment (our structural context), that is, the local and wider social and political policy structures and by the relationships with the people, places, and things around us. Each child's and each teacher's histories and potential futures thus influence the process of their constant transformation. This, then, also affirms that what is considered ethical in a particular culture, space, or physical or conceptual situation may be considered to be highly offensive or dangerous in another. Kristeva's feminist thinking compels us to make space for and insert nuanced complexities, marginalizations, violence, or dominations that call forth and alert us to the risks in making ethical assertions and decisions.

 This caution applies, for example, to the nuances and specificities of difference arising when children and teachers in early childhood settings come from different cultural or indigenous backgrounds. In the Aotearoa New Zealand context, this tentative, humble positioning creates an opening for elevating the realities of children and teachers from the indigenous Māori culture as well as for children from the many diverse cultures represented in Aotearoa New Zealand society. It blurs the care and rights discourses (to which Taggart (2016) points) in a confluence of rights–vulnerability–care. Such an ethics of care calls for a conception of agency in which the subject is not only "simultaneously critical and vulnerable" (173), but also strong, as highlighted in Tesar's (2017) childhood underground, and unknowable. The Kwale research in Kenya highlighted what Noddings (2013) sees as a reciprocity of care and commitment by illustrating ways in which the "cared for," that is the children themselves, embodied their own care responsibilities in their daily encounters by being "keenly aware of the commitments, contributions and efforts made by those caring for them" (Arndt et al. 2016: 298). The children demonstrated this by sharing stories on how they take on roles that are necessary in the daily life of their families and communities: to gather food, to look after the shop, and to go to school. Each of these roles is deeply embedded in local practices, stories, and beliefs (Mbugua 2013). In that research, the children's engrossment as a close and interdependent engagement with the local landscape, people, and things in deeply relational acts and attitudes of caring alerts particularly to our outsider role as researchers. Notwithstanding the close and reciprocal care and agentic engagements by Kwale children and communities in their local practices and lives, the confluence of care and rights through diverse lenses inserts an element of danger—and the humility referred to above—that pushes us to argue for thinking through another Kristevan concepts: the necessity of exile.

Exile

Utilizing a Kristevan lens in this rethinking of a feminist ethics of care offers what might be seen as a safeguard against "the danger of ethics" alerted to above through Kristeva's notion of the ethics of exile and philosophical thought. According to Kristeva (1977/1986), exile is a form of dissidence. By its very nature, exile involves uprooting ourselves from what is familiar, comfortable, known, and understood to venture into the strange and unknown. Exile requires standing back and undertaking, as Kristeva states, a "specific and detailed analysis which will take us beyond romantic melodrama and beyond complacency" (298). In other words, exile from the depths of a situation allows us to, as Kristeva continues, "patiently and meticulously" (299) dismantle our own assumptions. This makes possible a deeper examination of a situation by becoming removed from the immediacy of, for example, assumptions about particular collegial misunderstandings or from the constraints and limitations of monocultural or otherwise narrow policy structures or expectations of aid and development work. Exile, according to Kristeva, allows a more ruthless and irreverent engagement in the workings of the discourses of a situation, to analyze responses in more ethical, tentative, and, as we argue, unknowing ways. In the following section we outline further how an ethics of unknowing could be seen in relation to our reflections on an ethics of care.

An exilic ethics of unknowing

Examining unknowability

An ethics of care as involving a fundamental orientation toward unknowing calls for rethinking the importance placed on predictability and certainty. In Kristevan terms, this could be the space for revolt as a form of dissidence that questions the expectations of certainty and of teachers being in control. Such a shift, or mini-revolt, might arise by conceiving the early childhood settings and actors within it as unknowable subjects that are constantly in process and foreigners within. When the self and the Other are seen as strangers, there is already a problem if we are aiming for certainty or predictability. That is, when we take a step back, exiling ourselves from definitive expectations, in order to see ourselves and others as always being foreign, even to ourselves, then ideas on what are respectful, sensitive, and ethical practices will necessarily be based on an element of unknowing.

Let us use the image below to illustrate a shift to an ethics of unknowing. This image was taken during the Auckland-based research referred to earlier. (see Figure 2.1) It emerged in the course of examining children's engagements within a multicultural early childhood setting. To interpret this image through an ethics of care means to take seriously Tesar's (2017) call for the impact of children's "private and public life" and their "power and resistance" (25). As we recognize how little we can determine or assert on the basis of this photograph, we are

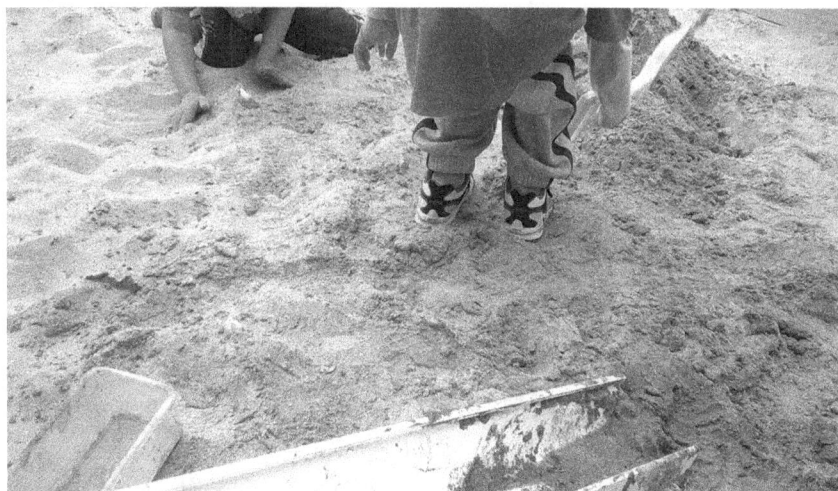

Figure 2.1 Image used with permission ECREA 2015 project, University of Auckland.

compelled to move ourselves farther away. That is, we are compelled to exile ourselves from the situation and downplay our importance in it.

Reciprocal implicatedness

From our exilic, stepped-back position, we recognize this photograph as representing a particular, reciprocal implicatedness of care and an encounter. If early childhood settings are imbued in many complicated ways with the knowledges and ways of being that have surrounded every person and thing within it, then, according to our theorization above, this implicates this educational setting as morally and ethically bound. At the same time, it necessitates an acceptance that *we cannot know* those past influences, and, nor, then, can we know the subjects or the intricacies of the encounters. In this image, this means that we cannot know the children or their motives or relationships to this sand activity, their relational intentions, and expectations (with each other, or with/for/because of somebody or something else in their private or public life), and what conceptual understandings are in place.

To connect this reflection to the Kwale example raises similar concerns. We do not know in which ways any private or public communal governance, expectations, or cultural commitments drive or inspire the children's seemingly mundane, day-to-day play. The idea of reciprocal implicatedness draws us back into the idea of the ethics of an encounter, as Dahlberg and Moss (2005) infer from Levinas, where we are obliged toward those by whom we are surrounded. This idea is not unfamiliar to teachers, but certain constraints might limit the depth to which they consider such an obligation. It implies also that we are obliged to acknowledge those intricate, often raw, perhaps sensitive, deeply embedded elements of the histories and realities of each member of the early childhood setting. It is this obligation that draws us, and perhaps teachers, into discomfort and uncertainty, as we too are reciprocally implicated through our own pasts and realities in known or unknown ways.

Examining humility and danger

We are reminded in our reflections on our research that the discomfort and uncertainty of unsettling, prior conceptions can lead to a regression into the safety and security of what is already known. In this instance, we draw on Kristeva's notion of revolt as mini, inner revolts, where we begin from what we already know in our ongoing questioning and transformation. Rethinking an ethics of care in early childhood education, then, is an attempt to elevate an engagement with the dangers of transgressing ethical boundaries of which we may previously be unaware, on the basis of what we can know, observe, or find out.

If we take as another example the set of images below, also from the project in Auckland, an examination of an ethics of care becomes an ethics of an encounter with what we know and what we do not know of this situation (see Figure 2.2). It could be that the teachers in this setting know something about the relationship between these two children. It could also be that they know something of their family histories, beliefs, cultural practices, or expectations. To draw any conclusions from the images, however, through a Kristevan lens and ethical exilic positioning, urges

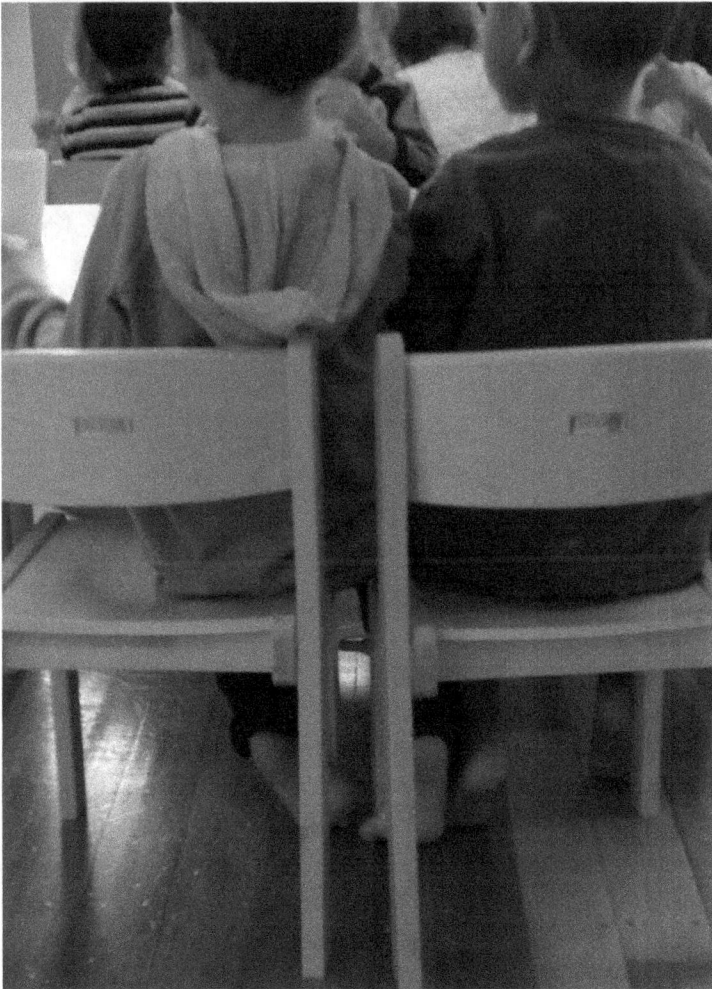

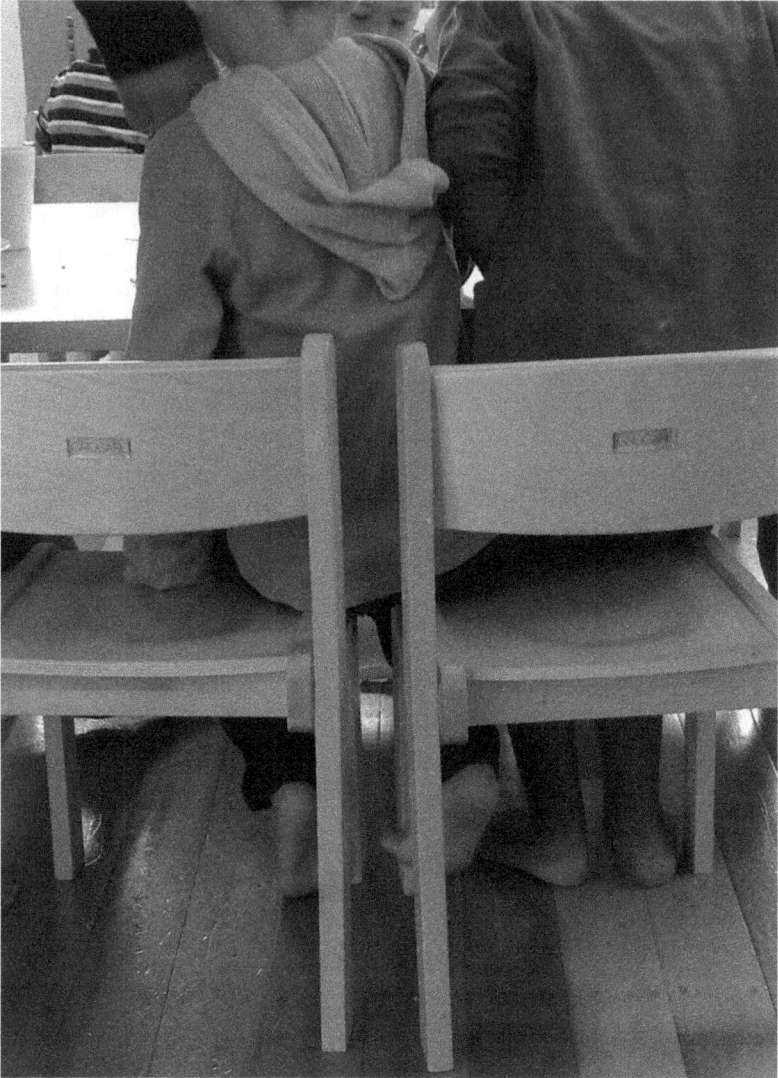

a deeper analysis and questioning of our own often subdued, overlooked, or surface-level assumptions. Even then, bearing in mind that we are unable to really know ourselves and even less likely to know these children and the things and influences on them on that particular day in that situation, renders an ethics of the unknown as the only careful way to proceed. To avoid the risk or danger of engaging in practices that offend, harm, or hinder the care–rights–agency of individuals within the setting, this requires an acknowledgment that there is much that we cannot know, and even that is sacred or otherwise valued in ways that it is *inappropriate* for us to know.

Figure 2.2 Images used with permission ECREA 2015 project, University of Auckland.

It is possible, through the Kristevan lens where the subject's formation is always imbued by everything that is happening within its surroundings, that these images of two children moving ever closer on their chairs at a food table, draw us into an ethical "danger zone." Such a situation might arise where we—adults, teachers, or researchers—make rapid, convenient decisions and respond without much thought. Seen through the concept of abjection, as an inner sense in subject formation, this could mean running the risk of disregarding our "sense" or "gut" feelings about a situation, let alone about that which we cannot know. In turn, this then puts us at risk of making assumptions about possible meanings of the children's behavior, of their worldviews, of their relationship to the space and things by which they are surrounded, or of any other aspect of their being and ways of knowing about food spaces, bodily contact, or each other. We can only speculate, for example, on what might be inspiring them to move together on the chair, and, of course, they may both be thinking and being in quite diverse ways.

Adopting Kristeva's notion of exile as a necessary prerequisite for sufficiently critical and deep thought in pedagogical–ethical situations or encounters means that such thought is more likely to occur if we remove ourselves from a situation. This may be a physical or metaphorical removal, allowing an examination of intentions and orientations in that situation. That is, we may take a step back from the children in the above images, from their play, from the various influences by teachers, from what happened in the morning before the children arrived at the center, and from the multilayered early childhood setting. A position of exile, Kristeva (1977/1986) argues, allows a more ruthless and irreverent examination of nuances and complexities, and elevates the uncertainty and unknowability of each situation.

Our reconceptualization of an ethics of care thus elevates not only the importance of accepting the unknowability of early childhood pedagogies and practices and of the adequacy of interpretations and responses to a situation. It also highlights, from a methodological perspective, the value and importance of exile and revolt as enabling tools and methodological practices in research and teaching. Placing a Kristevan lens on the unknowability, implicatedness, and humility of our earlier research illustrates how these concepts might shift, deepen, and unsettle pedagogical care practices. Furthering our argument in this chapter, these analyses are in themselves non-definitive, always shifting, open, and uncertain, and not intended to present answers or solutions. They lead us to a final construct that further adds to this uncertainty.

A posthuman ethics of care

Our final rethinking of an ethics of care and of an encounter must acknowledge research that has emerged in recent years that situates an ethics of care as significantly problematic: as a human-centric practice. In this final explication of an ethics of care we argue that the ethics of an encounter and of the unknown has implications beyond the human realm. Rethinking an ethics of encounters as more-than-human highlights the fact that the rights and care discourses to which Taggart (2016), for example, refers, and Noddings's (2013, 2015) work, are situated within a human-centric frame. We argue that there is a need for bridging the human and nonhuman theoretical space. From a posthuman (Braidotti 2013) perspective, we argue, then, that an ethics of care that decenters the human is both a deeply personal and a political matter that is social *as well as* material. By elevating humility and uncertainty, our theorizing of an ethics of care emerges from this need to de-elevate the adult, as well as the human, the rule-maker, as the privileged, powerful subject, as ever present in any ethics of care encounters.

Although an ethics of care is central to onto-epistemological thinking that embraces and celebrates the human subject and its multiple relations, it is also problematic. Braidotti's (2013) insistence on the posthuman as affirming "life beyond the self" (13) elevates the inner unknown, and such concepts as diversity and multiple ways of being and belonging: "Living matter itself," she asserts, "affects the very fiber and structure of social subjects" (Braidotti 2010: 201). Inserting a posthuman framing into an ethics of care affirms it as an always contingent, relational construct that is produced by and implicates both human and nonhuman. It inserts into the relational ethics of early childhood encounters not only possible interdependencies between and among humans, but also with and between the materialities and forces as affirmed by theorizations of the ontological and agentic engagements in new materialisms (Coole and Frost 2010). Reaffirming our argument for an ethics of unknowing explicates the wider realm of the energies and forces, exerted in relation to and beyond the human, through concepts such as the vibrancy and agency of matter (Bennett 2010; Tesar and Arndt 2016) and the new imaginaries arising in theorizing the co-, inter-, and intra-actions of matter (Barad 2015) and wider species relationships (Haraway 2007).

We see a human-centric focus in an ethics of care as problematic. This is especially so when the ethics of care remains centered on adult human subjects. In other words, we see humanistic ethics of care constructs as running the risk of limiting opportunities, particularly for children and oppressed or marginalized subjects. To de-center the human subject therefore primarily means for us to de-center the adult subject. Our explication of an ethics of care as something that is more than social draws on Kristeva's work to bridge the human with the post and more-than-human. By inserting the unknowability and constant formation of the subject, our theorization moves us to this wider ontological positioning of becoming. In the sense of Deleuze and Guattari's (1987) positioning, it (re) territorializes and (de)territorializes an ethics of care in early childhood settings through shifts and movements of assemblages of discrete pieces or elements. We have further theorized these "bridges" and more-than-social theorizations of early childhood education, the vibrancy of matter, and quality elsewhere (Arndt and Tesar 2016; Tesar and Arndt 2016) as a lens to more fully recognize the implicatedness, particularly of children, as deeply rooted in and arising from localized and global histories and ecologies.

Bringing these perspectives together, the ethics that we argue for involves strong elements of humility, acceptance, and trust. It bridges the paradigms of care and rights and provokes a shift beyond purely human, and even adult-centric constructs, to accommodate confluences of diverse epistemologies on gender, culture, race, abilities, other forms of Otherness, and more-than-social realities, things, and beings. It takes as its foundation a view of children as agentic, competent, and confident, as well as constantly and uncertainly becoming, in relation to and interdependent with other people, places, things, and forces. An ethics of unknowing involves a stepping back by the adults in early childhood settings and a restraint of the adults' frequent eagerness to capture and control children's development and learning.

Our argument in this chapter responds to the urgency of reconceptualizing feminist ethics of care and rethinking dominant orientations toward early childhood education as "merely" care, and well-suited to women (and not men). Most importantly, it inserts into the existing reconceptualist work a further— and hopeful—imagining: of an ethics of unknowing, humility, trust, and faith. It aims to do better for children and is never "divorced from ethics and politics" as Dahlberg and Moss urge in their opening quote, as it traverses the terrain of the human and the more-than-human world.

Conclusion

This chapter represents our exilic re-theorizing of an ethics of care. From our privileged, adult, human positioning, we have elevated Kristeva's philosophical constructions of unknowing the self to reconceptualize early childhood pedagogies beyond contemporary feminist conceptions of an ethics of care. We have inserted a Kristevan lens as a complicating articulation of the intricacies and specificities that underlie ethical encounters and the responsibilities of and by teachers' pedagogical thought and practice. Kristeva's philosophical and theoretical work on the "subject in process," the notion of the foreigner within, and the imperatives of exile have led our examination to bridge traditional care and rights discourses by inserting elements of unknowability, reciprocal implicatedness, and humility, even danger, into a nuanced and uncertain ethics of unknowing.

We are not certain that these conceptions will lead to the "production of better people," as Noddings seeks in her opening quote. Nor are we convinced that they can answer what we want for children, who we think the child is, or what society's image is of the child, as Dahlberg and Moss ask in their opening quote. Indeed, what we suspect is that if there were an answer to any of these questions, it would be fleeting, pass us by, and become superseded in the process of the known and unknown ongoing construction in which we are entangled as subjects in process. Furthermore, it would be incomplete on account of the human- and beyond-the-human-centric educational problem. We also suspect and, in fact, hope that the process of exile, in which we confront the "hidden face of our identity" and of our own foreignness will continue to help us to recognize the foreigner within ourselves. As Kristeva (1991) claims, it is only then that we will be spared "detesting" the foreign Other—which we understand as both the human and nonhuman Other (object, animal, plant, natural or man-made occurrence, and so on). While teachers may not necessarily "detest" those who are Other, Kristeva's assertion confronts the danger of unthinking approaches to the ethics of encounters in early childhood settings. Thinking through Kristeva both elevates and de-reifies our inner knowing and bridges the gap to move toward a wider, worldly ethics of an encounter with that which we sense but do not necessarily know, as an ethics of unknowing.

References

Arndt, S. and M. Tesar (2015), "Early Childhood Assessment in Aotearoa New Zealand: Critical Perspectives and Fresh Openings," *Journal of Pedagogy*, 6 (2): 71–86, doi: 10.1515/jped-2015-0014.

Arndt, S. and M. Tesar (2016), "The More-than-Social Movement: Post-Human Condition of Quality in Early Years," *Contemporary Issues in Early Childhood*, 17 (1): 16–25. doi: 10.1177/1463949115627896.

Arndt, S., M. Tesar, B. Pupala, O. Kascak, and T. Mbugua (2016), "Re-negotiating an Ethics of Care in Kenyan Childhoods," *Human Affairs*, 26: 288–303, doi: 10.1515/humaff-2016-0025.

Barad, K. (2015), "Transmaterialities: Trans*/matter/realities and Queer Political Imaginings," *GLQ: A Journal of Lesbian and Gay Studies*, 21 (2–3): 387–422, doi: 10.1215/10642684-2843239.

Bennett, J. (2010), *Vibrant Matter: A Political Ecology of Things*, Durham, NC: Duke University Press.

Bloch, M., B. Blue Swadener, and G. S. Cannella (2018), "Introduction: Reconceptualist Histories and Possibilities," in M. Bloch, B. Blue Swadener, and G. S. Cannella (eds), *Reconceptualizing Early Childhood Education and Care—A Reader: Critical Questions, New Imaginaries and Social Activism*, 2nd edn, 1–17, New York: Peter Lang.

Braidotti, R. (2010), "The Politics of 'Life Itself' and New Ways of Dying," in D. Coole and S. Frost (eds), *New Materialisms: Ontology, Agency, and Politics*, 201–220, Durham, NC: Duke University Press.

Braidotti, R. (2013), *The Posthuman*, Cambridge: Polity Press.

Collins, S. (2015), *The Core of Care Ethics*, Basingstoke: Palgrave Macmillan.

Coole, D. and S. Frost (2010), "Introducing New Materialisms," in D. Coole and S. Frost (eds), *New Materialisms: Ontology, Agency and Politics*, 1–43, Durham, NC: Duke University Press.

Dahlberg, G. and P. Moss (2005), *Ethics and Politics in Early Childhood Education*, London: RoutledgeFalmer.

Deleuze, G. and F. Guattari (1987), *A Thousand Plateaus: Capitalism and Schizophrenia*, Minneapolis: University of Minnesota Press.

Global Migration Trends Factsheet (2018), "International Migration: Stock, Characteristics, Geography," Retrieved from: http://gmdac.iom.int/global-migration-trends-factsheet.

Guenther, L. (2009), "Review of *The Ethics of Emmanuel Levinas* by Diane Perpich," *Notre Dame Philosophical Reviews*, 23 February.

Haraway, D. (2007), *When Species Meet*, Minneapolis: University of Minnesota Press.

Harris, S. (April 11, 2018), "Children's Convention Monitoring Group Releases Report to Better Child Wellbeing," Retrieved from: http://www.nzherald.co.nz/index.cfm?objectid=12029666&ref=twitter.

Kristeva, J. (1977/1986), "A New Type of Intellectual: The Dissident," in T. Moi (ed.), *The Kristeva Reader*, 292–300, Oxford: Blackwell Publishers.

Kristeva, J. (1991), *Strangers to Ourselves*, New York: Columbia University Press.

Kristeva, J. (1998), "The Subject in Process," in P. French and R. F. Lack (eds), *The Tel Quel Reader*, 133–178, London: Routledge.

Kristeva, J. (2008), "Does European Culture Exist?" Paper presented at the Dagmar and Vaclav Havel Foundation VIZE 97 Prize, Prague Crossroads, http://www.vize.cz/download/laureat-Julia-Kristeva-en-speech.pdf.

Kristeva, J. (2014), *New forms of revolt*. Keynote presented at The Kristeva Circle, March 27–30, Nashville, TN.

Mbugua, T. (2013), "From Montessori to Culturally Relevant Schools under the Trees," in S. C. Wortham (ed.), *Common Characteristics and Unique Qualities in Preschool Programs. Global Perspectives in Early Childhood Education*, 23–25, Dordrecht: Springer.

Ministry of Education (2017), *Te whāriki he whāriki mātauranga mō ngā mokopuna o Aotearoa early childhood curriculum*, Wellington, New Zealand: New Zealand Government.

Noddings, N. (2013), *Caring: A Feminine Approach to Ethics and Moral Education*, Berkeley: University of California Press.

Noddings, N. (2015), "A Richer, Broader View of Education," *Society*, 52 (3): 232–236.

Osgood, J. (2010), "Reconstructing Professionalism in ECEC: The Case for the 'Critically Reflective Emotional Professional,'" *Early Years*, 30 (2): 119–133.

Prud'homme, J. and L. Légaré (2006), "The Subject in Process," *Signo [online], Rimouski (Quebec)*.

Stanford Encyclopedia of Philosophy (2009), "Feminist Ethics," Retrieved from: https://plato.stanford.edu/entries/feminism-ethics/#FemAppEth.

Stone, L. (2004), "Julia Kristeva's 'Mystery' of the Subject in Process," in J. D. Marshall (ed.), *Poststructuralism, Philosophy, Pedagogy*, 119–139, Dordrecht: Kluwer Academic Publishers.

Taggart, G. (2016), "Compassionate Pedagogy: The Ethics of Care in Early Childhood Professionalism," *European Early Childhood Education Research Journal*, 24 (4): 173–185.

Tesar, M. (2017), "Childhood Undergrounds: Power, Resistance, Secrets, Objects and Subversion in Early Childhood Education," *Early Childhood Folio*, 21 (1): 22–26, doi: 10.18296/ecf.0033.

Tesar, M. and S. Arndt (2016), "Vibrancy of Childhood Things: Power, Philosophy, and Political Ecology," *Cultural Studies<-> Critical Methodologies*, 1–8, doi: 10.1177/1532708616636144.

3

Conceptualizing Care as Being and Doing in Ethical Interactions and Sustained Care Relationships in the Early Childhood Institution

Rachel Langford and Jacqueline White

There are few detailed accounts of what care is and how it happens specifically in the early childhood institution (Dahlberg and Moss 2005; Pacini-Ketchabaw et al. 2015 are exceptions). Following phenomenological descriptions of care (i.e., Hamington 2015; Noddings 2010; Pettersen 2012), this chapter seeks to provide such an account through an exploration of care as being and doing in ethical interactions between educators and children. This exploration addresses several questions about our choice to use the term *interactions* in relation to care and to regard these interactions to be ethical. We begin the chapter with an explanation of our choices.

A substantial portion of the chapter then explores processes of care as ethical interactions identified by Noddings (2010) in three stages: recognizing the need for care, giving care, and receiving care. Integral to this account is a critical examination of children's needs and their participation in care as a series of ethical interactions. In addition, a feminist analysis illuminates how educators and children cannot be separated from their social locations and power relationships as they recognize, give, and receive care. In a final discussion, we address Tronto's (2010, 2013: 161) challenge to consider the purposes of our account of care for the early childhood institution and to answer a final question for the chapter: What do we want to achieve by describing a particular kind of care?

Explanation of terms and choices

We use the term *early childhood institution* to distinguish, as Tronto (2010: 159) does, the purposes of family life from the purposes of an institutional and sociopolitical context where "certain elements of care that go unspoken and that we take for granted in the family setting" must be made explicit. However, we reject the term *institutional care*, which is typically used as an attack on early childhood education. And while recognizing the current stratification of those working with young children and its consequential material effects, we use the term *educator* to indicate that whomever interacts with children is engaged in care as ethical interactions within the early childhood institution.

Care as interactions

In reflecting on how to deepen an understanding of care in the early childhood institution, we could have used a term such as *relational ethics* (Moss 2014), *relational praxis* (Shin 2015), or *relational moral* (Einarsdottir et al. 2015) to emphasize that "the relational ontology of care ethics claims that relations of interdependence and dependence are a fundamental feature of our existence" (Robinson 2011: 4). While we see the advantages of these terms, we have located the relational ontology of care in interactions between people. Our decision follows Pettersen's (2012) claim that an understanding of care and care relations is enhanced when the focus is on interactions between caregivers and care receivers. In this sense, an interaction becomes the moment in which care relations and interdependence between people are actualized and enacted.

In the context of an early childhood institution, many interactions between educators and children occur throughout the day, every day. They are never absent from life in an early childhood institution. Understanding care *as* these interactions goes to and captures actual and concrete encounters and their processes as they are experienced between people who can be both caregivers and care receivers. The concreteness of focusing on care as interactions that occur during activities such as playtime, small and large group times, and routines of toileting, dressing and eating, whether indoors and outdoors, counters the vagueness that often accompanies conceptions of care. In addition, centering on interactions addresses in part the divide between care and education that persists in our field. While this divide has real political, policy, and material effects on service provision and educators, it is a false distinction in practice. If all interactions between educators and children can be potentially considered as care and all these interactions occur in all early childhood activities, then it is possible to see care and education as synonymous.

Care as ethical

Ethical interactions as care are frequently ordinary events that range from exhilarating to repetitive for both adults and children. But these events are not without tremendous ethical significance. Each interaction can be regarded as a *care-full* or *care-less* space for the educator and child that, over time, either contributes to or erodes the care relationship (Rogers 2016). Still Laugier (2015: 217) writes that care in ordinary interactions "is variously denied, undervalued, or neglected (not seen, not taken into account) in theoretical thought" because of its association with the "domestic and female." Yet, in its ordinariness, care extraordinarily "ensures the maintenance, sustainability, and continuity of the human world" (Laugier 2015: 224). For this reason, we regard everything about ordinary care interactions between educators and children, from its actual processes to its labor and beyond to its policies and politics, as ethical. We understand ethical to mean an exercise of judgment which, drawing upon Dahlberg and Moss (2005: 89), is "a provisional position taken in a particular context, a statement of value and as such incapable of closure, part of a continuing discussion rather than a finality." Therefore, our focus on care as ethical interactions does not exclude a broader social and political definition of care ethics, such as the one articulated by Tronto (2013). We also agree with Pacini-Ketchabaw et al. (2015: 175) that not only human interactions but "the materials we use in our [early childhood] centers and the multispecies places and spaces we inhabit and encounter all invite considerations of other ethical relations." However, as Tronto (2013: 21) maintains, it is possible to nest a specific understanding of care—such as care as ethical interactions that reflect a particular context, institution, and profession—within broad definitions of care. Tronto (2013: 21) states that the goal of this approach is to "see complex interrelationships" among nested caring practices. In this chapter, the focus is on interactions between educators and children but care as ethical interactions can be imagined between educators themselves and educators and families.

In the context of an early childhood institution, an educator's care interactions with children are inscribed with ethical decision-making. Taggart (2015: 383) puts it practically: "Each and every encounter with a child (of which there may be hundreds in a day) highlights the way in which ethics is embedded in the routines of play, learning, food, and sleep." Critical to ethical decision-making is an understanding that the presence or absence of care has real effects on children's flourishing and well-being (Pettersen 2012). Moreover, there are real effects on educators when their capacity to make ethical decisions is enhanced or constrained. In positioning all care interactions as ethical, we are saying that in the early childhood institution care is not natural to educators. Thus, while we agree with the aims of Noddings's (2013) description of natural caring, we do not support her distinctions between natural (sometimes understood as maternal) and ethical caring, at least not in the context of an early childhood institution. Noddings states:

> Natural caring is a decent, respectful way of meeting and treating one another that is maintained by inclination, not by rules. We treat one another with care because we want to do so—because we value a climate of care and trust within which to do our work. When natural caring fails ... we turn to ethical caring. (199)

Noddings stresses that the motivation for natural caring comes spontaneously from the emotions of love or inclination, requiring no moral effort. In contrast, we maintain that caring interactions in the early childhood institution always require ethical effort although this effort may be greater or less depending on the nature of the interaction. Thus, we regard these caring interactions as qualitatively different from, for example, those in the institution of the family. However, Noddings (2015: 73) does distinguish between *care for others* (either naturally or ethically) and *caregiving*, stating that paid and unpaid caregiving "can be engaged in with or without the care." In other words, an educator can provide care, typically custodial in nature, such as putting a child's snowsuit on because the child depends upon this assistance and will be at risk outside without adequate clothing. However, the educator can put the snowsuit on carelessly, in a brisk, impatient, uninterested, and thus uncaring manner. We would also view this interaction as uncaring but from an ethical perspective. Other care theorists, such as Held, avoid naturalizing care. Held (2006: 11) states that while care ethics values emotions and information gleaned from feelings and intuition, "we need an ethics of care" in order to subject "aspects and expressions of care and caring relations" to ethical judgments and evaluation. Drawing on Held's claim, we now turn to describing an ethics of care in interactions between educators and children.

Being and doing: Care as ethical interactions

In laying out the processes of care as ethical interactions, our focus is on both dyadic and group interactions between educators and children. While educators frequently interact with individual children, particularly very young children, they also interact with groups of children: they assist children when there are conflicts, collaborate in pursuing inquiries and projects, and lead music and movement experiences. Thinking more broadly about who receives care departs from an emphasis in some ethics of care literature on dyadic interactions (e.g., Noddings 2010). From our perspective, this rethinking is warranted given the lived experiences of being dependent on others and being responsible for others in the early childhood institution. Collins (2015), also referring to Noddings, regards an emphasis on dyadic interactions as insufficient for understanding how caregivers cannot care ethically if they do not have necessary supports in place. She points to Kittay's (1999) triad of the caregiver, care receiver, and a person (in an early childhood setting this could be a director) who, through their caring, provides the caregiver with "possibility of care" (Collins 2015: 124). However, we hasten to add that we are not suggesting that the more interactions an educator has with children, the better; on the contrary, we suggest that some interactions educators have with children may be unnecessary. For example, early childhood learning environments may not motivate and engage children who consequently exhibit misbehaviors, requiring educators to discipline children and thereby increasing paternalistic rather than caring interactions. Educators therefore need to be thoughtful about why and when to interact with children. In recognizing a need for care, a thoughtful educator may ask if that care can be undertaken by another educator and by children themselves. But when care as an ethical interaction is required, its processes are dynamic, reiterative, reciprocal, and generative. Within its processes both care givers and care receivers are subjects in their own right.

In describing care as ethical interactions, we are consistent with Held's definition of care as a practice, Noddings's notion of a care encounter, and Hamington's concept of a care performance. From Held's (2006: 36) perspective, a focus on care as a practice reveals "the work of caregiving," particularly in responding to needs, and therefore provides the means by which "practices of care can be evaluated." Noddings (2010: 49) focuses on caring for another in an encounter as a minimal care relation and an episode that is a set of encounters within a longer-term caring relation. Between these encounters, the caregiver maintains an ongoing interest and concern for the care receiver. Noddings (2010) emphasizes that it is the caregivers' actions in these encounters and episodes and their impact on others that tell them how caring they are. As Hamington (2015: 689) notes, this means that it is insufficient to declare oneself caring because "caring without action … [is] … unknown and unrealized."

Our discussion of the processes of care as ethical interactions is framed by Noddings's (2010, 2013) three-staged phenomenology of care relations in which a caregiver discerns that care is needed by the cared-for; care is given by the caregiver, and care is received by the cared-for. Within these three stages are complex emotional, intellectual, and relational processes and nuances that can be qualitatively different depending on context and children's needs. In the early childhood institution, these three stages may overlap so that, for example, the recognition of children's needs may be adjusted in dialogue with children as the care is given. Moreover, the process is not temporarily fixed, by which we mean it is possible for care to be recognized but acted upon in several interactions at different times of the day. To illustrate: an educator may notice a group of children enthralled by worms on a sidewalk after a rain shower. She mentions to the children that she has a fascinating book about worms at home, and the children ask her to bring it the next day. Another interaction follows when everyone gathers to look at the book. Similarly, based on knowledge of a child, an educator may ask a child if it would be best to discuss an issue later or collaboratively educators may meet to discuss how best to respond to children's expressions of interest. Overall, as Dahlberg and Moss (2005: 92) maintain, care as ethical interactions in the early childhood institution should not be regarded as technical practices with a locus of instrumentality. Rather they are "a locus of diverse possibilities and for the practice of an ethics of care in all of these possibilities and in all aspects of its everyday life and relations."

Care needed

Noddings (2010: 47) writes that "the carer must first of all be attentive to the expressed needs of the cared-for. These needs are not always expressed verbally." Noddings says "the carer's task is to correctly discern what is being expressed." Noddings's use of two concepts, *needs* and the *expression of needs*, as well as reference to word *correctly*, to describe the educator's discernment of needs requires further examination. With regard to the concept of needs, Kittay (1999: 133) begins with a responsibility to give care premised on "our unequal vulnerability in dependency, on our moral power to respond to others in need, and on the primacy of human relations to happiness and wellbeing." We accept then that young children have needs. In the early childhood institution, this perspective is typically based on children's corporeal vulnerability or their inability to independently carry out daily and basic activities of life, such as dressing, eating, and toileting. However, and interestingly, other developmental needs (e.g., cognitive) are perceived as requiring instructional strategies that are not classed as care, even though children in early childhood institutions are dependent on educators to provide a rich learning environment.

The differing perspectives on children's needs are, as many others have noted, a reflection of the body–mind dualism in which the body but not the mind requires care. We suggested earlier in this chapter that one way through this dualism is to focus on care as ethical interactions between educators and children. These interactions occur in all activities and therefore require educators to care-fully recognize children's expressed needs that encompass the interrelated social, intellectual, emotional, aesthetic, physical, and spiritual domains. Encompassing these domains then broadens children's needs to include their ideas, interests, inquiries, questions, and concerns. Broadening the concept of needs is consistent with other care theorists' approaches. For example, Noddings (2015: 74) maintains that children's wants and interests should be recognized and encouraged, while Held states we should aim to promote care beyond the level of needs based on necessity (Held 2006: 63). A broader concept is also consistent with new understandings of all children as competent social agents, capable of voicing a range of needs, ideas, and concerns. One objection to our broader concept is that it appears to make children "even needier" but we argue that these needs are human needs, worthy of care and respect.

However, even if we broaden an understanding of children's needs, there is a danger that an educator may rely on assumptions about these needs (Noddings 2010). While some assumptions are morally grounded (i.e., children need care and respect), *assuming* needs is prone to misinterpretation and infused with power relations. Children's needs are irregular, vary, and change; they can be unpredictable, mysterious, and expressed at different levels of intensity (Ruddick 1989). It is, therefore, necessary to listen seriously to children's expressed needs and seek clarification about them. Noddings appears to suggest that when children do express their needs, a correct interpretation of needs is possible. However, as Dahlberg and Moss (2005) suggest, any interpretation should be considered provisionally within a particular context. Similarly, Tronto (2013: 163) states that no "institution in a democratic society can function well without an explicit locus for the needs–interpretation struggle." In an early childhood institution, educators then collectively discuss their interpretations of children's needs, whether expressed or assumed, counted or discounted, in order to enhance care as ethical interactions.

According to Noddings (2015: 78), prior to interpreting children's needs "care ethics postulates the carer as receptive and feeling; she receives the other into her own mind and center of feeling: she does not project herself into the other." The caregiver assumes an other-directed disposition or attitude and listens to and cares about expressed needs. Rinaldi (2006: 78) describes a pedagogy of listening for the early childhood institution as "listening to the hundred, the thousand languages, symbols, and codes we use to express ourselves and communicate, and with which life expresses itself and communicates to those who know how to listen." Moreover, often children's caring relationships with material things such as toys need to be heard by the educator. Care-full listening also requires reflection on the particular context of a child's expressed needs because care actions are "not determined in advance by any pre-given rule" (Pettersen 2012: 378). For most care theorists, paramount to reflection on context is knowledge of the particularity of the caring relation between a caregiver and the cared-for (Pettersen 2012). The caregiver also situates her recognition of expressed needs within social and political contexts; for example, what are the limits of knowing a child's needs based on his or her social location and what are the limits of recognizing needs that are politically contentious and unresolved (e.g., a child transitioning to another gender) within the early childhood institution? However, reflection on contexts should not make a child so knowable to an educator that the educator is no longer open and sensitive to what the child is trying to tell her, particularly when expressed and assumed needs differ. Although paying attention to children's needs will vary in duration, listening well often requires time: time for educators to be attentive and reflective, and time for children to communicate, sometimes with difficulty, their questions, ideas, and requests. Often these communications are infused with a range of feelings that should be regarded of equal worth. As Pacini-Ketchabaw et al. (2015) note, an educator's respect for the emotional and bodily dimensions of children's expressed needs is important. In recognizing children's needs, educators too may experience a range of feelings from pity to anger, and struggle to act with care. Here educators must take care of themselves and each other to work through what would be ethically best to do.

In listening well, the educator also makes an ethical decision. As Pettersen (2012: 378) writes, the caregiver decides that the recognition of needs will be "dialogical rather than monological, dynamic rather than static, adjustable rather than fixed." A decision is enhanced when the educator feels a sense of responsibility and holds particular caring values (i.e., everyone is dependent at different times in their life) and motives (i.e., seeks to maintain or enhance a caring relationship) (Hamington 2015; Held 2006). In addition, Hamington (2015: 282) emphasizes that a caregiver needs to be open to the possibility of personal disruption, risk, and emotional involvement. He or she must feel competent and be able to imagine that his or her care can have an effect. Hamington (2015) adds that "the actor [i.e. caregiver] must believe that they can effectively care or they may not act even if they have a caring disposition."

Recognition of needs is therefore both affective and intellectual, with emotions and thought as well as competencies leading to the giving of care. Care scholars agree that emotions are "informative and motivating moral tools" (Engster and Hamington 2015: 4). Noddings (2015: 75) states that "to be motivated to act, we must feel something" but at the same emphasizes a high level of intellectual competence and critical thinking in caring for others. The role of thought is evident in competent and critical reflection on the context of children's needs, the weighing of the possibility of risk, and the imagining of the impact of one's care. As do other care scholars (Held 2006; Tronto 2013), we find Walker's (1998) theory of moral understanding (rather than moral knowledge, which relies on universal abstract rules and principles) useful for thinking about the recognition of needs. Walker (cited in Held 2006: 11) states that care events require the "attention, contextual and narrative appreciation, and communication" of moral understanding. Walker's statement implies that moral understanding increases as the caregiver relies less on impartiality, rules, and abstractions. For example, invoking a universal rule, "no running inside," requires no moral understanding because the rule is likely not responsive to context and individual needs. In contrast, attending to a particular child's explanation and story about how the long hallway caused them to run with exuberance requires moral understanding. This is consistent with Noddings's (2013: 25) claim that "the one caring displays a characteristic variability in her actions—she acts in a non-rule-bound fashion on behalf of the cared-for." Still the challenges of acting with variability cannot be underestimated; all educators have competing discourses of professionalism circulating in their heads, feel the pressure of adhering to rules and regulations or seek to avoid the demands of care. We must therefore appreciate the moral courage it takes educators to manage conflicting expectations and to care ethically.

Care given

One objection to our focus on care as ethical interactions may be that it glosses over the different kinds of interactions and activities in which care is given. For instance, should interactions in routines of dressing, eating, and toileting be considered different from interactions in project activities in which ideas are co-investigated by children and educators? Should the fact that some care activities, like routines, are repetitive and mundane and therefore potentially more burdensome be taken into consideration? Given that context matters in care ethics, the answer to these questions would be fundamentally, "yes." But, at the same time, all interactions within these activities, whether they involve book reading, changing a child's diaper, assisting children in problem-solving a conflict, or responding to children's requests for materials, require ethical care. In other words, we cannot say that one activity is worthy of greater ethical consideration than the other—all contribute to children's well-being and flourishing.

Nevertheless, we suggest there is an association between how a caring activity and the interactions within it are implemented and the depth of that care as an ethical interaction. To illustrate: if snack time is implemented as an opportunity for individual children to eat when they are hungry rather than as a whole-group experience, then it is possible to imagine that educators could care more deeply for children in the individualized activity. It is also possible to see how a routine could become less burdensome when it is more attuned to the needs of individual children (assuming that a sufficient number of educators are engaged in care). Similarly, complex activities, such as a discussion between educators and children about how they could investigate shadows, require deeper processes of care than an educator simply telling children what a shadow is. Activities such as toileting might be considered more procedural but still require great respect for children's expressed and bodily needs. Thus, whether care as ethical interactions is complex or procedural, it is, as Barnes (2012) says, in general "hard to do":

> It requires not only an emotional and ethical sensibility but the capacity to understand different personal, economic, social and cultural contexts, to read particular responses to acts of care and to draw from diverse sources and types of knowledge to make good judgements with others about the right things to do in situations that may be messy, confused and changing. (172)

Recognizing children's needs typically leads to decisions by educators to respond, to act, and to give care based on "what it would be morally best ... to do and to be" (Held 2006: 10). This decision-making is therefore a moment of judgment that may be clear, messy, or tentative. In giving care, the educator remains physically, emotionally, and intellectually engaged with children. As in recognizing need, the educator seeks to be responsive and present while managing distractions and maintains proximity and eye contact, where culturally and individually appropriate. Creativity and even risks and transgressions in the educator's caring actions may be necessary (Noddings 2013). Communication between educators and children continues to be dialogical and inquiry based. An educator's caregiving may become conflictual if a child's need or goal has been misunderstood, in which case negotiation of and adjustments to the care by both educators and children are required. Taggart (2011: 89) reminds us that "much of caring is reparative in nature, restoring what is fragmented and disintegrating." Resolution of mistakes and conflicts should be viewed as generative and as enhancing care relationships. In the giving of care, educators invoke a caring identity (Hamington 2015) or a caring ideal (Noddings 2013) that can motivate better caregiving. Care as reiterative action creates new knowledge about caring that can influence the caring identity and future acts of care (Hamington 2015: 282). In this way, some caring actions may become easier and require less deliberation. However, there is always the danger that in this ease, these actions become routinized and increasingly detached from context and individualization and, therefore, recalling Noddings's distinction between caregiving and caring, could no longer be regarded as caring.

The caregiving described above cannot be taken as gender neutral. Embedded in historical and social contexts of inequalities, care work in the early childhood institution is done predominantly by women. We agree with Gilligan's (2013: 23) claim that currently "within a patriarchal framework, care is a feminine ethic"; Gilligan's vision is that "within a democratic framework, care [will become] a human ethic." Therefore, a feminist analysis would ask why the giving of care is socially and culturally constructed in an early childhood institution as a women's responsibility, as women's work, and gendered labor. A feminist analysis would further ask why and how societal and institutional factors constrain the female educator's capacity to give care.

When institutional supports (i.e., insufficient number of educators in ratio to children) are not in place, the possibility of care as ethical interactions is diminished. Moreover, we regard early childhood institutions as sites of minor politics in which care as ethical interactions is fraught with power relationships implicating gender, race, class, sexuality, and disability among other social factors (Dahlberg and Moss 2005; Pacini-Ketchabaw et al. 2015; Taggart 2015). The caregiver and the cared-for cannot be separated from an understanding that each ethical care interaction is asymmetrical in terms of who has needs and who has power. Held (2006) comments that an ethics of care resists the assumption that care relationships are always entered into voluntarily and by individuals who are free and equal. In particular, relationships for children are usually not chosen by them and represent unequal access to power (the next section will address this point more). However, early childhood educators, depending on their social location, can be simultaneously powerful in relationships with the children and powerless in the relationships with others particularly with those who make decisions about their care work. Thus, educators may seek to address the absence of power to affect the nature of their care work by no longer imagining that they can affect children's lives through their care or by exercising greater control and paternalism over children. Examining how experiences of privilege and/or oppression influence the ways in which educators enact care as ethical interactions is always necessary.

It may be argued that gendered care work is so impossibly unjust that we should find another way to describe the work of early childhood educators. But care theorists argue care can be viewed as a "suppressed moral value ... capable of challenging patriarchy" and a radical "way to turn the world around" to what all human beings need—care (Pettersen 2012: 367; Tronto 2013: 182). Moreover, as Kittay (1999) contends, we cannot get away from the ontology of dependent or interdependent relationships between adults and children. Therefore, from Kittay's (1999) perspective:

> The character of the moral self, the asymmetry of the relationship, the particularity of its participants and its nonvoluntary nature make the moral demands of the dependency relationship more amenable to an ethic of care than to a rights-based or an [sic] utilitarian-based morality. (53)

However, we still need an account of care as ethical interactions that take equality and justice into consideration. Without discounting the great importance of reconfiguring care responsibilities and resources within democratic politics and policies, we focus on one such consideration at the conceptual level of care practice: Pettersen's (2012) distinction between *altruistic* and *mature* care (a term drawn from Gilligan 1982). Pettersen describes altruistic care with its origins outside of the field of feminist ethics as boundless, selfless, unconditional, and spontaneous with unreflective action, whereby the caregiver responds to anyone who comes first; and a gift that is more likely to make the care one-sided. Pettersen maintains that the features of altruistic care are more likely to make care gendered (i.e., women are assumed to be selfless and give care unconditionally) and, consequently, women unjustly assume the burdens of care. In contrast, mature care requires the caregiver to "have as much care for oneself as for others" (Pettersen 2012: 376), thoughtfully recognize needs in context, consider the limits of one's care (i.e., the caregiver is not responsible for *all* caring needs), use both emotions and reason in ethical deliberation, and encourage reciprocity in care relationships. From Pettersen's (2012: 382) perspective, these features of mature care promote a relational network in which care work is "a shared responsibility, not only by those who ethically commit to the normative value of care, it is also a matter of justice and fairness and a political responsibility." Still, this distinction between altruistic and mature care may not satisfactorily address concerns in the early childhood institution about the greater intensity and demands of care labor, the "dirty work," and staffing arrangements in which activities perceived as caring are allocated to poorly compensated and valued assistants. Moreover, there is a danger that the female educator in a conceptualization of care as ethical interactions could be essentialized as simply a carer rather than as a subject in her own right. Tronto (2013: 182) is instructive for addressing these concerns: a central task of early childhood institutions is to question and rethink who assumes caring responsibilities and under what political and institutional conditions. Until spaces for democratic and political discussions and actions are created, the caring responsibilities of educators will remain limitless, arduous, and unjust.

Care received

Children are typically viewed as passive objects of care rather than active receivers or subjects of care; care is provided because of children's "flawed condition" of being needy and dependent on others (Tronto 2013: 31). However, as Tronto (2013: 29) argues, being needy is, in reality, a human condition and all persons (including children) are "equally capable of voicing their needs." In meeting these needs, Noddings (2002: 30) explains that ethics of care "asks after the effects on recipients of our care. It demands to know whether relations of care have in fact been established, maintained or enhanced." Therefore, in the same way that children's active participation in recognizing care and in caregiving is necessary, care cannot be considered completed until a child receives or responses to the care (Engster and Slote 2015). In care ethics, a child's response is understood minimally as a right but more importantly, it is the moment in which the "moral interdependence" or the intersubjectivity of persons is recognized and care relationships are sustained (Noddings 2002: 87–88). However, Kittay (2014: 34) suggests that a response to care may still imply a certain passivity; instead she proposes that the care receiver actively "takes up the care" that has been experienced as an act of care. Whether we use the notion of response or the taking up of care, it should not be confused with a requirement that children must *reciprocate* care in a contractual sense; in other words, children should not be expected to equally give care back in that interaction (although children may certainly reciprocate or care for others in interactions of their own). Reciprocity in ethics of care is "recognition, a positive response to a carer's efforts to care. It is this response of the cared-for that completes a caring relation or encounter" (Noddings 2010: 127).

To complete care as ethical interactions, the educator checks in with children, who are regarded as capable moral agents. Checking in is required in all interactions from wiping a child's runny nose to exploring ideas about the mechanics of objects. This process of seeking children's responses to their care is, of course, varied: in some cases, children's bodily and emotional cues are read; in other cases, educators listen to children's responses. Educators may need to clarify and negotiate the meanings of children's responses. Collins (2015: 80) advises that caregivers should not be "presumptuous" about responses to care, noting that one interaction is "part of a long-term action of care, which includes both the response to the present 'encounter' and how that response carries into future 'encounters.'" The completion of care in ethical interactions is understood as open to collaborative meaning-making among all participants present and communicated potentially through pedagogical documentation. New possibilities for living and growing together in the early childhood institution are thus generated. One possibility is that children will have new needs as "past ones are met" and so the processes of recognizing, giving, and receiving care continue over time (Tronto 2013: 35). Another possibility is that within such a caring environment, children's own acts of care of others increase and deepen (Noddings 2010).

However, an educator can provide care that is not considered caring because a child's response to it is unknown or the child resists or rejects the care. It is much easier for an educator to accept children's positive responses to a caring action. In contrast, responses of resistance, rejection, grudging compliance, or discouragement indicate that an action has not been caring from the child's perspective on their experience of care. For example, children may perceive care actions as a denial of their will or feelings, insincere, or tokenistic—in this way, they judge or evaluate the other's caring actions. Moreover, all care processes are infused with power relationships and children are sensitive to caregiving (here we use Noddings's use of the term) in the guise of control and paternalism. Sometimes, educators seek to be caring but must act in the best interests of a child or in balancing group and individual needs, knowing that a child will not perceive an action as care (e.g., intervening when a child is hitting other children). For these reasons, care scholars emphasize reflection on and evaluation of care as ethical interactions. Held states plainly that relationships between persons can be judged "when they become dominating, exploitative, mistrustful, or hostile" (Held 2006: 37). Judgments about care as ethical interactions show us how to situate children's responses to caregiving in context, subject to further inquiry and dialogue, flexibility, and change. The knowledge gleaned about care through these processes by all participants advances caring relationships and contributes to greater attunement between educators and children.

The purposes of defining care as ethical interactions

In this chapter we have laid out the processes of care as ethical interactions between educators and children for a particular context—the early childhood institution. These interactions are regarded as nested in other highly interrelated care contexts such as interactions between educators and families, and between educators themselves and early childhood policies that influence their interactions in all contexts (Tronto 2013). In this section, we explore the purposes of our account of care as ethical interactions guided by Tronto's (2013: 159) contention that any caring institution requires "clear, defined, acceptable" purposes that can be discussed, debated, and evaluated by everyone within the institution. Historically, in many Western countries, the purpose of care in daycares (as they were called at that time) was to ensure the health and safety of young children whose mothers had begun to work outside of the home. As the terminology of daycare shifted to early childhood learning, the purpose of care became the promotion of self-regulation and independence so that children would be ready for formal schooling.

We suggest that what is driving our account of care as ethical interactions are three broader and deeper purposes consistent with those described by various care scholars (Moss 2014). Care as ethical interactions

1. makes care a fundamental value in the early childhood institution;
2. promotes the flourishing of children and educators; and
3. produces children and educators as different kinds of citizens.

In outlining these purposes, we acknowledge that they may be contested or in conflict with other purposes. As Dahlberg et al. (2013: 78) state, early childhood institutions should be "understood as public forums situated in civil society in which children and adults participate together in projects of social, cultural, political, and economic significance."

We agree with Held's (2006: 17) claim that "care is probably the most deeply fundamental value" and, on this basis, care provides a wider and deeper ethics for understanding human interactions. Our account of care as ethical interactions asserts this value in that we see care as integral to all interactions between educators and children, rejecting the designation of these interactions as either care or education. Furthermore, we see this value as central to all intellectual, emotional, physical, and artistic (among others) activities in the early childhood institution. However, Warin and Gannerud (2014: 196) state that "it is not enough to merely recognize and affirm this value"; it should inform pedagogy; it should change conceptions on what counts as knowledge in the moral education of children; and it should inform the professional preparation and working lives of educators.

It is not surprising that the second purpose of care as ethical interactions is the flourishing and well-being of children and educators. Human flourishing figures heavily in accounts of care as well as education. Fielding and Moss (2011: 46), for example, see "education as a process of upbringing and increasing participation in the wider society, with the goal that both the individual and the wide society flourish." When this upbringing and increasing participation in the wider society involves interactions between educators and children that are characterized by interdependence, recognition of needs, respect, and trust, children flourish. But can the flourishing of educators—their satisfaction, even happiness as caregivers—be met in the same way? We think educators can similarly flourish if certain conditions are in place. First, the caring early childhood institution is understood as a network of care relationships that involves all members of the institution so that educators are not only caregivers but also care receivers. Second, collective responsibility for a just and caring early childhood institution is assumed by everyone at the personal, political, and policy levels so that educators can care well for children. Tronto (2010) emphasizes the necessity of this condition:

> Any account of institutional care that fails to name explicitly the "care-attentives" and the "care-responsibles" allows those people, and their roles in caring, to pass unnoticed. Such not-naming contributes to the process of "naturalizing" care relations, and to blaming the caregivers who may have inadequate resources. (165)

Our third purpose of care as ethical interactions is to produce children and educators as different kinds of citizens. Noddings (2002: 223) envisions educators, through their care, modeling for children how to care, which gradually produces children who hold "an ethical ideal, a dependable caring self." Noddings (2002: 223) then imagines "a society composed of people capable of caring—people who habitually draw on a well-established ideal [moving] toward social policies consonant with an ethic of care." In our account we describe in some detail children's active participation as capable moral agents in the processes of communicating needs, in receiving care, and responding to it. We see this as the beginning of children's citizenship in a democratic and caring early childhood institution. Much is at stake in care as ethical interactions. In discussing Noddings's claims about the caring relationship, Bergman (2004: 152) writes that "in the single act of giving and receiving care, the self of each person is confirmed. One's caring is worthy, one is worthy of care." In this way, children learn not only how to care but that one must care "if the self that has been confirmed by receiving care is to be sustained." But the worthiness of educators' care as ethical interactions is undermined when care work is unrecognized and devalued by society. Educators under these conditions are not regarded as full and equal citizens worthy of good professional lives. In our account of care as ethical interactions, we envision educators engaged in care work that is rewarded, fulfilling, well received, and open to evaluation by other professionals "who know enough about caring work to make such sharing worthwhile" (Tronto 2010: 167). The contributions of educators as citizens to the flourishing and well-being of children as citizens are thus confirmed.

In outlining these three purposes for our account of care as ethical interactions we hope to have captured, at least in part feminist ethics of care's goal for the "radical transformation of society" (Held 2006: 12). In this transformative spirit, our account demands the recognition of moral significance of care, children's participation in their care, and gender justice for women who practice care ethically all day, every day.

Conclusion

The intention of this chapter has been to provide an in-depth, detailed, and rigorous account of care as ethical interactions and care relations between educators and children in the early childhood institution. We have imagined this care as continual reiterative encounters that shape educators' and children's understandings of who they are as carers and the cared-for. We have suggested that conceptualizing care as ethical interactions as flowing in and out of every interaction potentially transcends a care–education divide both discursively and in practice. We have described educators and children as both equally needy *and* capable and competent moral agents engaged in actions of care and judgment. We have envisioned care inscribed in ethical interactions as being and doing better for children and educators for, as Laugier (quoted in Gilligan 2013: 11) states, "an ethics of care cannot exist without social transformation." Thus care as ethical interactions depends upon new thinking about children's needs and participation in care, power in care relations, and institutional responsibility for creating environments that ensure care as ethical interactions can be genuinely lived and experienced by educators and children.

References

Barnes, M. (2012), *Care in Everyday Life: An Ethic of Care in Practice*, Bristol: Policy Press.

Bergman, R. (2004), "Caring for the Ethical Ideal: Nel Noddings on Moral Education," *Journal of Moral Education*, 33 (2): 149–161.

Collins, S. (2015), *The Core of Care Ethics*, Basingstoke: Palgrave Macmillan.

Dahlberg, G. and P. Moss (2005), *Ethics and Politics in Early Childhood Education*, London: Routledge.

Dahlberg, G., P. Moss, and A. Pence (2013), *Beyond Quality in Early Childhood Education and Care: Languages of Evaluation*, 3rd edn, London: Routledge.

Einarsdottir, J., A. Purola, E. Johansson, and A. Emil (2015), "Democracy, Caring and Competence: Values Perspectives in ECEC Curricula in the Nordic Countries," *Journal of Early Years Education*, 23 (1): 97–114.

Engster, D. and M. Hamington (eds) (2015), *Care Ethics and Political Theory*, Oxford: Oxford University Press.

Fielding, M. and P. Moss (2011), *Radical Education and the Common School: A Democratic Alternative*, London: Routledge.

Gilligan, C. (1982), *In a Different Voice: Psychological Theory and Women's Development*, Cambridge, MA: Harvard University Press.

Gilligan, C. (2013), *Joining the Resistance*, New York: Wiley Press.

Hamington, M. (2015), "Politics Is Not a Game: The Radical Potential of Care," in D. Engster and M. Hamington (eds), *Care Ethics and Political Theory*, 272–292, Oxford: Oxford University Press.

Held, V. (2006), *The Ethics of Care: Personal, Political, and Global*, New York: Oxford University Press.

Kittay, E. F. (1999), *Love's Labor: Essays on Women, Equality and Dependency*, New York: Routledge.

Kittay, E. F. (2014), "The Completion of Care—With Implications for a Duty to Receive Care Graciously," in A. M. González and C. Iffland (eds), *Care Professions and*

Globalization: Theoretical and Practical Perspectives, 33–42, New York: Palgrave Macmillan.

Laugier, S. (2015), "The Ethics of Care as a Politics of the Ordinary," *New Literacy History*, 46: 217–240.

Moss, P. (2014), *Transformative Change and Real Utopias in Early Childhood Education: A Story of Democracy, Experimentation and Potentiality*, Abingdon: Routledge.

Noddings, N. (2002), *Starting at Home: Caring and Social Policy*, Berkeley: University of California Press.

Noddings, N. (2010), *The Maternal Factor: Two Paths to Morality*, Berkeley: University of California Press.

Noddings, N. (2013), *Education and Democracy in the 21st Century*, New York: Teachers College Press.

Noddings, N. (2015), "Care Ethics and 'Caring' Organizations," in D. Engster and M. Hamington (eds), *Care Ethics and Political Theory*, 72–84, Oxford: Oxford University Press.

Pacini-Ketchabaw, V., F. Nxumalo, L. Kocher, E. Elliot, and A. Sanchez (2015), *Journeys: Reconceptualizing Early Childhood Practices through Pedagogical Narration*, Toronto: University of Toronto Press.

Pettersen, T. (2012), "Conceptions of Care: Altruism, Feminism and Mature Care," *Hypatia*, 27 (2): 366–388.

Rinaldi, C. (2006), *In Dialogue with Reggio Emilia: Listening, Researching and Learning*, London: Routledge.

Robinson, F. (2011), *The Ethics of Care: A Feminist Approach to Human Security*, Philadelphia, PA: Temple University Press.

Rogers, C. (2016), *Intellectual Disability and Being Human: A Care Ethics Model*, London: Routledge.

Ruddick, S. (1989), *Maternal Thinking: Towards a Politics of Peace*, Boston, MA: Beacon Press.

Shin, M. (2015), "Enacting Caring Pedagogy in the Infant Classroom," *Early Child Development and Care*, 185 (3): 496–508.

Taggart, G. (2011), "Don't We Care?: The Ethics and Emotional Labour of Early Years Professionalism," *Early Years*, 31 (1): 85–95.

Taggart, G. (2015), "Sustaining Care: Cultivating Mindful Practice in Early Years Professional Development," *Early Years*, 35 (4): 381–393.

Tronto, J. (2010), "Creating Caring Institutions: Politics, Plurality and Purpose," *Ethics and Social Welfare*, 4 (2): 158–171.

Tronto, J. (2013), *Caring Democracy: Markets, Equality and Justice*, New York: New York University Press.

Walker, M. (1998), *Moral Understandings: A Feminist Study in Ethics*, New York: Routledge.

Warin, J. and E. Gannerud (2014), "Editorial: Gender, Teaching and Care: A Comparative Global Conversation," *Gender and Education*, 26 (3): 193–199.

4

Care as Ethic, Care as Labor

Rachel Rosen

As the name suggests, *care* lies at heart of early childhood education and care (ECEC). However, the nature and status of this care has been the subject of both discomfort and contestation. In considering the low- or non-paid nature of early years work, widely circulating discourses about the low-skilled nature of early years provision, and the rendering of the very young to a quasi-natural and not-yet-fully-human state, it is not surprising that ECEC has at times been designated as less valuable and less important than formal schooling. Such assessments have not been left to fester in their own circular logics, however, but have been widely contested in academic, advocacy, and professional literature. Efforts to elevate the status of early years' provision have been pursued through the addition of the seemingly more important element of education to childcare in formulations such as *educare* and ECEC. Pseudo-neurological evidence about the importance of the first 1000 days has been mobilized to advocate for increased attention to early years provision (Bruer 1999; Edwards et al. 2015), often framed within the neoliberal terms of human capital development. Care itself has also been reclaimed from the dustbin, with attention to its social worth bolstered normatively and politically through attention to a feminist ethics of care (Davis and Degotardi 2015; Langford et al. 2017).

In the discussion that follows I suggest that an ethics of care offers promising directions for highlighting the importance of ECEC as well as the types of relationships that can be fostered both within and by ECEC. However, in the current context of global capitalism, characterized by increasing geopolitical inequities and state retrenchment from social reproduction in the name of neoliberal austerity, an ethics of care approach is likely to fall prey to or even reproduce the very problems it seeks to address without explicit politicization of key questions. What is lost or gained through invoking the concept of care, rather than other concepts? What are the social relations in which ECEC is embedded and involved in reproducing? Put simply, who cares for whom and who is recognized as providing care? How is care bound up (potentially simultaneously) with processes of accumulation, oppression, and solidarity?

These are not new questions, but they have made surprisingly little impact on discussions of ethics of care in ECEC to date, which have focused on professional identities, including surveillance and governmentality (Davis and Degotardi 2015; Gibbons 2016); the relationship between education and care (Gibbons 2016; Langford et al. 2017); relationships between parents and educators (Brooker 2010); and the place of care in producing hope, possibility, and social value (Taggart 2011). In this literature, an ethics of care has demonstrable value for reconceptualizing self and other through relational frames of interdependence. However, hiving care off from the political economy does little to challenge the unequal terrain in which these relations are lived. A different body of work takes up questions of the class relations and emotional labor involved in ECEC (Colley 2006; Rosen et al. 2017), but it can be critiqued for reducing caring relationships to those of exploitation and subordination. In many ways, this literature reflects a broader schism between treatments of care as a moral orientation to others and the world and that which considers the labor relations that lie at the heart of the political economy of care (Mahon and Robinson 2011).

These two bodies of work are not necessarily incompatible, but they do reflect disciplinary divides and differences in scalar attention. What is incommensurate, however, are variations in the political orientations that underpin theories of care, including those that might constitute themselves as feminist. These range from the gendered essentialism embedded in maternalist approaches (Ailwood 2007) to the individualism, categoricalism, and reform-orientation of liberal thought, through to those with an anti-capitalist orientation that emphasize relations of power, dispossession, accumulation, and emancipation.

In what follows, I make three key points. First, if we retain care as a key mobilizing concept, this is best conceptualized as a broad, multifaceted set of practices rather than a valorization of the emotional and intimate over and against those practices that are messy, menial, and repetitive. This more expansive understanding provides the basis for understanding the links between various acts of care, attending to the geopolitical conditions under which care labor takes place, and its links to capital accumulation in transnational contexts. This also, and here lies my second point, provides the analytic tools to counter the social stratification of such labor, which often maps on to gender, class, "race," and immigration status. Asking who does what sort of care labor likewise enables consideration of children's potential caring contributions, in contrast to much of the literature that positions children as the recipients or even objects of care. Third, I make the case for a consequentialist approach that keeps front and center questions as to the effects of diverse caring practices and caring landscapes. This necessarily implies bringing global political economic traditions together with an ethics of care. While these three points do not exhaust areas of concern, I suggest that they are particularly crucial for developing a robust and critical feminist ethics of care that is up to the task of considering the ways in which lives are made and made worth living (Narotzky and Besnier 2014) in ECEC.

Valorizing care?

Since the 1970s, there has been a proliferation of work highlighting the importance of care both as a way of understanding the interdependent character of human life and as a form of ethical action and grounds for contextually located moral and political judgment. This has countered a persistent equation of maturity and professionalism with autonomous rationality, and assumptions that acts of justice are about maximizing self-interests in an often-competitive contest of rights, both of which are emblematic of liberal political thought. Such assumptions, argues Geoff Taggart (2011: 85), continue to populate common understandings of ECEC, where "the suggestion of a need to go 'beyond caring'" is premised on linkages "between caring and female irrationality or anti-intellectualism."

In contrast, ethics of care theorists argue that ethical decision-making and action is centrally about building and sustaining relationships to ensure that no one is "left alone or hurt" (Gilligan 1982: 59). While early ethics of care scholarship has been widely critiqued for essentializing care in maternalist terms (i.e., used in reference to women's activity) and parochially situated in close personal relationships, most notably in the mother–child dyad, more contemporary theorists have countered such problems through efforts to widen and politicize care ethics. This is often through an explicitly feminist lens that centers on responsibilities toward others. Joan Tronto (1993), for example, has argued that while there is much to be learned from care work, which continues to be highly gendered, an ethics of care is a more generalized form of moral activity that is not limited to women's practices. She makes the case that "the ethic of care entails a basic value: that proper care for others is a good, and that humans in society should strive to enhance the quality of care in their world 'so that we may live in it as well as possible'" (Tronto 1995: 143). On this basis, care becomes a framework for making political decisions cognizant of people's needs, the sociocultural and institutional and political contexts in which care occurs, and power and inequalities in care relations.

Taking up an ethics of care for early childhood, Rachel Langford and colleagues (2017) argue for the "revalorization" of care. They suggest this can helpfully contest the bifurcation of care and education, where care has largely been relegated to a supporting position for education, which is in turn treated as having greater importance. Revalorizing care in such a way both recognizes its centrality to human life, and thus eliminates deficit treatments of dependency, and counters the mind–body dualism at the heart of liberal distinctions between care for the body (in ECEC) and education for the mind (in compulsory schooling). These are certainly laudable goals, and I concur with the proposal to think otherwise about affective labor and interdependence given their implications for ECEC and the status of children (about which more later).

The risk here lies in what exactly is meant by *care* in these invocations and what is rendered absent. It is precisely such concerns that prompt Rhacel Salazar Parrenas (2012) and Eleonore Kofman (2014) to argue *against* the turn to care in the effort to recognize and raise the status of all those activities we engage in to make lives and make lives worth living. Three crucial things happen in the turn to care. First, the various tasks involved, which include emotional labor as well as physical or "menial" labor that is either routine (e.g., cooking, cleaning, and feeding) or non-routine (e.g., provision of remittances, laundry, and handiwork) become disconnected. In this act of separation, care is often taken as a reference to fulfilling intimate and loving emotional engagement as opposed to the dirty and repetitive labor involved in making lives. For instance, in seeking to valorize care as being about the mind as much as the body, Langford and colleagues (2017: 315) are at pains to explain that it is "more than basic custodial activities." However, phrased in this way, it suggests that "custodial activities" are not only distinct from, but also seemingly inferior to, other aspects of care.

In Kofman's account, the separation of these various activities means that the "dirty work" is often pushed on to lower status workers, such as those coming from migrant and/or impoverished backgrounds, freeing the (relatively) privileged to engage in more valued caring practices. Such stratifications of laboring bodies are apparent in ECEC contexts where there are often sharp divisions between professionalized educators and teaching assistants, as well as in quasi-familial settings where the labor of migrant domestic workers frees up parents to engage in the more prized activities of reading bedtime stories or to love bomb[1] their children (Rosen and Newberry 2018). Such distinctions also have analytic consequences, indicative that scholarship is complicit in the process of valuing certain bodies and certain practices as a result of the way that concepts are defined and applied. Drawing on census data to compare the demographic distinctions that occur when care is conceptualized in the more limited terms of face-to-face nurturance as opposed to the broader set of tasks described above, Mignon Duffy (2005: 79) puts this in strong terms: "A theoretical focus on [care as] nurturance privileges the experiences of white women and excludes large numbers of very-low-wage-workers."

In their discussion, Langford and colleagues make it clear that caring activities are embedded in relations of power and inequality. Indeed, this important point is one that animates much of the contemporary literature on care (Bowlby 2012). Yet, it becomes difficult to contemplate such inequities or the potentially exploitative and subordinating characteristics of caring labor at the same time as seeking to valorize care. This is again a symptom of the reduction of care to acts of fulfilling nurturance, and the absenting of the more menial and dirty aspects of such labor. Perhaps more significantly here, it reflects slippages between the conditions and practices of care and care as a more generalized framework for moral decision-making, where care may be advocated as a moral good regardless of the conditions under which it manifests.

The potentials of social reproduction theory

Given the problematics of valorizing care, or indeed centering analysis on care, Kofman (2014) argues persuasively that the concept of social reproduction has greater analytic purchase for understanding the concrete labor, and often love, that goes into making lives (and see also Parrenas 2012). Indeed, social reproduction theory is having somewhat of a renaissance, as many social theorists agree that the widespread turn to cultural explanations in the 1990s is insufficient to explain the heightening inequalities and material deprivations that have followed the 2007–8 financial crisis and ensuing "global slump" (McNally 2010). More than a Bordieuan understanding of the production of the *habitus*, social reproduction refers to the processes through which the

---

[1] As advocated by psychologist Oliver James, this involves creating a short term "special emotional zone" with a child away from any regular daily routine and "bombing" them with love and fun. https://www.theguardian.com/lifeandstyle/2012/sep/22/oliver-james-love-bombing-children.

material conditions and social relations necessary for capitalist production, consumption, and accumulation are constituted. In the more specific form that Kofman takes up, social reproduction refers to "life's work" (Mitchell et al. 2003), all those activities that go into daily regeneration and generational replacement, put simply: grocery shopping, feeding, cleaning, putting to sleep, socialization, and other caring labor.

With its roots in feminist anti-capitalist perspectives (e.g., Marxist and socialist feminism), social reproduction theory emerged as an effort to understand women's subordination in capitalist societies. Social reproduction theory focuses on labor that is excluded politically, spatially, legally, and discursively from consideration within a wage calculus, in the sense that people's need to eat, rest in decent shelter, clean themselves, and engage in caring relationships remain shadowy or invisible when salaries are determined. These needs are "outlawed" (Kelsh 2013) and privatized, typically in highly gendered ways within the family where women's potential capacity to give birth is overextended to the broader realm of social reproductive labor and then naturalized (McDowell 1986). Yet, this labor is both socially and biologically necessary. It embodies, therefore, a set of crucial contradictions in its necessary accomplishment. Taking ECEC as a case in point, the increasing demand for service sector workers in advanced capitalist countries has been accomplished in part through the growing presence of women in the workforce (Gottfried 2012),[2] yet this has reduced the amount of time women have to contribute to generational replacement, including care for young children. Formal provision of ECEC can be seen as both a fix for capitalism's contradictory short- and long-term interests (for service workers in the immediate term and generational replacement for the future) and a demand from women burdened[3] by a double-day of wage labor and unwaged caring labor in contexts of increasing retrenchment (Rosen et al. 2017).

A crucial difference between the two, however, lies in capital's drive to accumulate. This includes expansion and efforts to addressing its periodic crises, such as that prompted by the easy availability of cheap credit and massive build-up of personal and national debt in the neoliberal period (Dowling and Harvie 2014:

---

[2]   This is not to suggest that service work necessarily requires women workers, simply that this sector has been constructed as highly feminized (or filled with migrant workers in the racialized division of labor).

[3]   My use of the term "burden" here is to highlight the unequal distribution and valuing of this labor. As I go on to discuss later in the chapter, children cannot be reduced to "burdens" but are often compatriots in the labor of social reproduction (Llobet and Milanich 2018) and parent–child relationship are often simultaneously experienced as fulfilling and loving, at the same time as requiring financial, physical, and emotional resources.

874). From capital's perspective, new sources of profitability are sought through shifting constellations of state and supra-state governance structures, capital, families, and civil society. For instance, there has been a spatial expansion of the sites in which social reproductive labor is accomplished (Kofman 2014). States may intervene to set up public ECEC programs, develop immigration policy to incorporate migrant domestic labor, or create the conditions for market provision. The latter is evident in the UK's prioritization of private early years' provision, with local authorities mandated to develop their own provision only in the last instance. Social reproduction is a site of direct profit-making through for-profit provision and indirectly benefits capital and the state as the direct financial costs are shouldered by families. Costs for ECEC in the UK can amount to 33.8 percent of a family's net income.[4] Capital's increasing transnational mobility also allows it to increase profits through an untethering from situated responsibility for social reproduction such as through national taxation systems (Katz 2001). The primary point here is that social reproduction theory provides the analytic tools to investigate linkages between care and capital accumulation.

A newer body of social reproduction scholarship moves away from the homogenizing and reifying focus on women's social reproductive labor to highlight that capital accumulation through social reproduction is highly differentiated. They build on Shellee Colen's (1995) argument that social reproduction is "stratified," where the same type of labor is not equally valued and rewarded. This can be seen in global care chains, as care labor is transferred from more privileged families to less privileged migrant workers, who in turn transfer their caring responsibilities in home countries to members of their extended family, with care losing value as it moves down the chain (Hochschild 2000; Parrenas 2012). Social reproduction is also stratified in its accomplishment, with some groups facing more material and normative barriers to ensuring such life-sustaining activity than others, and some groups are simply not deemed worthy of care. Drucilla Barker (2012: 588) argues that social reproduction can also be understood as an arena of social exclusion, where "young children of European ancestry are the most deserving .... The children and elderly in the sending countries simply fall out of sight like the abandoned children in the favelas and slums of the world, the impoverished elderly and sick, and all others who lack the resources to prosper in a globalized, neoliberal world." Here I would stipulate that in a globalized world, children

---

[4] This is according to data from the OECD report *Society at a Glance* 2016 available at http://dx.doi. org/10.1787/888933404933. The average amongst OECD countries is 15%.

of the wealthy may have far more in common with their peers from other countries than with those from impoverished families in their own countries, and therefore the necessity of refraining from reifying a North–South binary should be recognized. For instance, the cost of ECEC can be prohibitive in the UK, but it is especially so for families living on a low income. These families are particularly hard-hit by state retrenchment from ECEC services, such as the halving of funding for *children's centres* in the austerity climate following the global financial crisis of 2008.[5]

In my own work, I have also been concerned with the ways that social reproductive labor not only links children and women, but also differentiates and stratifies them (Rosen 2017; Rosen and Newberry 2018; Rosen et al. 2017). Women and children have often engaged together in household-based reproductive tasks, in large part due to the feminization of both social reproduction and childhood. However, the global rise in attention to ECEC has led to shifts in expectations as to where and how children and women are expected to spend their time, energy, and labor. In countries such as Indonesia (Newberry 2014) and Brazil (Rosemberg 2005), women are expected to voluntarily provide the labor required to maintain ECEC programs often mandated by the World Bank. They often do so willingly, galvanized by notions of feminine altruism, sacrifice, and concern for their communities.

Children, on the other hand, are expected to attend such ECEC programs. Much of the literature treats children as the *objects* of social reproductive labor in ECEC, burdens on their mothers due to the labor and financial costs involved in the provision of such care *and* the increased labor required in the household due to children's absence for ECEC and schooling. Children, in these accounts, are identified as the clear benefactors of "Education for All" and similar global initiatives (Rosen 2017, and for examples see Dobrowolsky and Jenson 2004; Molyneux 2006). In contrast, Jan Newberry and I make the case that children are *also* involved in social reproductive labor, both in households and ECEC (Rosen and Newberry 2018). In ECEC, such labor involves not only daily sustenance, but also the quality enhancement of exploitable labor power. In neoliberal ECEC, provision of care takes the form of human capital development tied to national competitiveness and capitalist profit (Langford et al. 2017; Rikowski 2000).

While this situation may create conflicts between women and children, benefits accrue to capital and the state in the form of reduced costs of social reproduction.

---

[5] https://www.theguardian.com/society/2018/mar/20/sure-start-funding-halved-in-eight-years-figures-show.

But this also promises increased profits through the presence of low-wage surplus labor subsidized by women's volunteerism (Newberry 2014) and, in the longer term, increased profitably through enhanced labor power. Yet, as we note, and in keeping with Barker (2012), not all children are deemed worthy of ECEC and their participation in reproductive tasks may be appropriated immediately rather than in the longer term. Importantly here, social reproduction theory helps make sense of questions about differentiation, stratification, and accumulation linked to the labor of making lives.

Theorizing care with and through social reproduction

Regardless of whether we take up Kofman's challenge to jettison care and replace it with social reproduction, it seems to me that the challenge offers some important warnings about the risks of efforts to valorize care and the challenges of taking up an ethics of care that is not adequately framed within the discussions of the global political economy. The ensuing discussion elaborates what such a theorization of an ethics of care might look like.

If we are to retain care as a key mobilizing concept, it is best conceptualized as a multifaceted and often contradictory set of practices, inclusive of those that are affective, fulfilling, messy, menial, and repetitive. Fisher and Tronto (1990: 40) provide such a definition of care as all those activities undertaken to "maintain, continue, and repair our world [including our bodies, our selves, and our environment] so that we can live in it as well as possible." In keeping with Kofman's warnings, such an expansive definition provides the basis for understanding the links between various types of activities involved in making lives worth living, including in ECEC.

This expansive understanding also allows care scholars to look across the various sites and modes in which ECEC is provided, a move that is to be welcomed if we are to understand the various interlinked contexts in which care occurs. Current literature tends toward focusing on national provision within formally regulated institutional settings. Yet this encompasses only a small range of sites where early years provision takes place, which includes public institutions, market-based provision, home-based care, programs in the voluntary sector (Rosen et al. 2017), and migrant domestic labor in household settings. Most obvious in the case of the latter, it is necessary to move away from methodological nationalism to account for the transnational character of care in ECEC. This includes the movement of care workers, the transnational families and ECEC networks they are embedded within (Baldassar and Merla 2014), flows of ECEC policy and markets across national borders (Penn 2011), and the often clashing ways that local variations of care are understood and practiced. In short, this broad conceptualization keeps in focus the breadth of ECEC sites and ways it is organized.

Such a broad focus also calls attention to who is doing what sort of caring work, if this is recognized as such, and in what ways it is accorded value. I have already discussed this in relation to the stratification of social reproductive labor. Such attention has been essential in countering the naturalization of care as women's domain and considering the ways that variations in caring labor map on to gender, class, "race," and immigration status. But here I also gesture to the importance of the question as to who does what sort of care labor in relation to children. For keeping this as an open question prompts and enables consideration of children's potential caring contributions, understood in the broader sense of tasks of making and sustaining lives.

Tronto again is instructive here in her insistence that care is defined by its reciprocity: everyone provides and receives care. "While the typical images of care indicate that those who are able-bodied and adult give care to children … it is also the case that all able-bodied adults receive care from others, and from themselves, every day … Except for a very few people in states that approach catatonia, all humans engage in caring behavior toward those around them" (Tronto 2011: 164). Yet, this point is often lost in the ECEC literature (and scholarship on gender and family that focuses on advanced capitalist countries) where care is assumed descriptively and normatively to be an adult activity. The influence of attachment theorizing in ECEC is noteworthy here as it has been widely interpreted as a dyadic relationship between educator and child in which care is undertaken by the educator (Pearson and Degotardi 2009). Discussion and debate in ECEC scholarship are important but largely adult centric in their formulation of care: critiques are leveled against policy formulations that position ECEC educators as a providing remediation in the face of inadequate parental care (James 2012) or that highlight the impact of neoliberal and exploitative conditions in which educators strive to provide quality care (Andrew and Newman 2012; Dahlberg and Moss 2005). In the bulk of ECEC literature, young children are largely reduced to a state of fundamental dependency on adult care, albeit within important efforts to resist the equation of dependency with a less-than-human status (Langford et al. 2017).

Children, in so far as they are recognized as being more than simply the object of care, are treated as learning to care, engaging in non-normative activity, or as providing care as a form of long-term, generalized reciprocity. Care in families, for example, is characterized by "the expectation that the giving of care must ultimately be reciprocated" although this can happen at "different times and to varying degrees across the life course" (Baldassar and Merla 2014: 7). Such an understanding is exemplified in the idea of a generational contract, where parents care for children who return that care as both age. In other words, children are understood to be available to care for their parents when they themselves are adults. In liberal and welfare regimes where care is organized, in part, in public or market-based sectors, generalized reciprocity may take the form of contributions to social programs (including ECEC) that create the conditions where care can be provided for different people over time.

However, a small body of literature indicates the limits of viewpoints that normatively and empirically constitute children solely as recipients of care. Needs may change over life course or context, but historical and contemporary evidence suggest that young children have the potential capacity to, and often do, engage in caring acts for themselves and others. As Magazine and Sánchez (2007) point out in their research on the Mexican community of San Pedro, Tlalcuapan, children as young as two years old are expected to contribute their reproductive labor to the household and are expected to care for younger siblings by the age of six. Children spend four to six hours on these and other household activities. Children's provision of care is not just possible but is socially expected. It is viewed as *ayuda*, or help for their families, in ways that are understood to underscore familial interdependence rather than promoting development and socialization or addressing economic necessity.

My own research in formal ECEC in the UK demonstrates the ways that children care for others in a multitude of ways, albeit that this is often not recognized as such. Aside from more familiar forms of care—such as soothing others who are upset, taking part in preparing food and cleaning up, or providing advice about how to navigate setting rules and customs—my ethnographic work on children's play about themes involving death and dying demonstrates children's capacity for "attentiveness" (Tronto 1989) to others and documents their efforts at using caring touch to convey a sense of belonging, concern, and mattering to others. While these latter caring practices occurred within the context of imaginary narratives, I argue that the desire for care from other children was evident and that the "embodied nature of imaginative play allows for the affective and haptic sensations of caring relations to traverse into players' everyday world[s]" (Rosen 2015: 171). I also suggest that children provide care for adults in the setting, including by sheltering adults from their own anxieties and helping adults feel that they were having a positive impact.

The primary point for this discussion is that children, as with adults (Sayer 2011), are socially and existentially vulnerable and are therefore reliant on others for sustenance and survival, but that the need for care does not exhaust their being. Keeping the question of care open—what it is, who does it, and how it is valued—allows consideration of such points. This is not to reject care provision for children but as a remedy for the rendering invisible of children's caring labor. When scholarship, policy, and practice do so, children's contributions are ignored and undervalued. When treated as inherently and essentially dependent beings, the category *young child* is reified and placed outside of the social in ways that decontextualize and de-historicize childhood. The rise in "child protection institutions" (Gillis 2011) in capitalist modernity comes to be seen as natural necessity rather than a manifestation of a particular social, political, and economic conjuncture in which childhood has become sacralized as a period of emotionally priceless innocence to be protected from the world rather than being treated as a part of the world (Viruru 2008). Taking seriously feminist critiques of approaches that fail to account for the contributions of unwaged reproductive labor to sustaining life and to surplus value appropriation demands that the same consideration is given to the caring practices that children may engage in.

Finally, it is also necessary to make clear distinctions between care as a moral framework and care as a set of practices bound up with inequitable social relations, power, and global capitalism. Here, scholars need to be attentive to the ways that an ethics of care may be used to justify exploitation of those working the field of ECEC. For instance, as Helen Colley (2006) documents, training for educators in the UK is geared not only toward skills development and knowledge acquisition, but also to the production of particular caring dispositions and associated emotions. Being calm, happy, and warm is cultivated, while feelings of anger or disgust are treated as inappropriate and requiring management. These certainly resonate with qualities embedded in an ethics of care perspective, which are attentiveness, responsibility, and responsiveness (Tronto 2011). However, Colley demonstrates that for ECEC students this can be stressful and disempowering because such "feeling rules" are based on middle-class notions of deportment and respectability, whereas many of those working in the ECEC field come from impoverished and working-class backgrounds. Further more, because the affective labor of managing oneself in such ways occurs in the context of marketized ECEC, emotions and subjectivities become a source of profit for someone else. While Colley focuses on the UK context, the international application of the Caregiver Interaction Scale (CIS) to measure such attributes is indicative that this is a more global phenomenon.

Borda Carulla's (2018) ethnographic research on *community mothers* who work in the Colombian government's childcare program raises a parallel set of concerns about the ways in which ethics of care principles dovetail with exploitative gendered expectations in the division of labor. The program emerged as part of the state's concern for improving children's communities and national well-being through attention to children's care. Although it was applauded by the World Bank and the Inter-American Development Bank as a "model of social development," women's labor rights were systematically violated by the program in the name of "putting the child first." Borda Carulla argues that if women's rights are not protected, it is likely that the rights of the children they care for will be violated as well. Further, it is noteworthy that to meet the impossible conditions imposed by the government program, many community mothers relied on their own children's caring labor for the other children in their care.

The concern here is that calls in the ECEC ethics of care literature, for instance for "care to re-emerge as an integral part of professional practice and professional identity" (Davis and Degotardi 2015: 1744) where caregiving involves "hands-on work that requires more conscious decision-making and dense time commitments" (Davis and Degotardi 2015: 1741), can serve as a motivation and indeed justification for exploitative conditions of caring labor if the conditions under which this labor occurs are also not simultaneously addressed. In contrast, taking an explicitly feminist and anti-capitalist approach to an ethics of care, as detailed above, can provide the tools for attending to the geopolitical conditions under which care labor takes place and its links to capital accumulation in transnational contexts. It can also provide the basis for making political judgments based on relational ontologies of social interdependency and a commitment to social and economic justice.

Conclusion

In concluding this discussion, I make the case for a consequentialist approach that keeps front and center questions as to the *effects* of diverse caring practices and caring landscapes. This is not a claim to utilitarianism or an impossible demand that we predict the unknowable outcomes of actions but an insistence that the possible, probable, and actual outcomes of approaches to care be considered. In keeping with the consequentialism put forward by Nancy Fraser (1990: 220), scholars might ask whether discursive, embodied, and structural aspects of care "disadvantage some groups of people vis-á-vis others"? Do they challenge or buttress "patterns of dominance and subordination"?

Rather than taking care as an *a priori* good, then, I am suggesting that invoking care as an ethical orientation requires unpicking the ways in which care relations may be ones of subjugation, ambivalence, concern, and solidarity, often simultaneously. In many ways, it is in the contradictory nature of care labor that its power lies. As the feminist anti-capitalist scholar Sylvia Federici (2014) explains, care has an important duality to it: necessary for capital in that it ensures workers on daily and generational basis *and* simultaneously a practice that can foment ways of being and social solidarities in opposition to the exploitative and competitive character of capitalism. For this reason alone, care—as a site of contestation, possibility, and necessity—is a powerful concept to work with.

While an ethics care may offer ways to think in morally responsible ways toward others, one that is in keeping with the interdependent character of human life, the structure and organization of caring practices raises undeniably political questions. Who is benefiting from the current arrangements of care and who is harmed? How we might achieve more socially and economically just ways of caring, of making lives worth living? These political questions also require political responses that, I would suggest, are entangled with, but cannot be reduced to, the best of responsive, attentive, and responsible care. The grounds on which such care is provided are socially structured, often inequitably. As Andrew Sayer (2011) points out, we act because things matter to us and because we care for and about others and the world, but collective social action—indeed political activism—is required to challenge and change relations of domination and exploitation.

Ultimately then, in this chapter, I have argued for the importance of developing an ethics of care for ECEC out of, or more accurately in dialogue with, feminist anti-capitalist traditions. This involves keeping both ethical and political questions about how we might ensure social and economic justice at the forefront of concern.

References

Ailwood, J. (2007), "Mothers, Teachers, Maternalism and Early Childhood Education and Care: Some Historical Connections," *Contemporary Issues in Early Childhood*, 8 (2): 157–165, doi:10.2304/ciec.2007.8.2.157.

Andrew, Y. and B. Newman (2012), "The Value of Childcare: Class, Gender and Caring Labour," *Contemporary Issues in Early Childhood*, 13 (3): 242–247, doi: 10.2304/ciec.2012.13.3.242.

Baldassar, L. and L. Merla (2014), "Introduction: Transnational Family Caregiving through the Lens of Circulation," in L. Baldassar and L. Merla (eds), *Transnational Families, Migration and the Circulation of Care: Understanding Mobility and Absence in Family Life*, 3–24, New York: Routledge.

Barker, D. K. (2012), "Querying the Paradox of Caring Labor," *Rethinking Marxism*, 24 (4): 574–591, doi:10.1080/08935696.2012.711065.

Borda Carulla, S. (2018), "When the Rights of Children Prevail over the Rights of Their Caretakers: A Case Study in the Community Homes of Bogotá, Colombia," in R. Rosen and K. Twamley (eds), *Feminism and the Politics of Childhood: Friends or Foes?*, 50–65, London: UCL Press.

Bowlby, S. (2012), "Recognising the Time–Space Dimensions of Care: Caringscapes and Carescapes," *Environment and Planning A*, 44 (9): 2101–2118, doi:10.1068/a44492.

Brooker, L. (2010), "Constructing the Triangle of Care: Power and Professionalism in Practitioner/Parent Relationships," *British Journal of Educational Studies*, 58 (2): 181–196.

Bruer, J. T. (1999), *The Myth of the First Three Years: A New Understanding of Early Brain Development and Lifelong Learning*, New York: Free Press.

Colen, S. (1995), "'Like a Mother to Them': Stratified Reproduction and West Indian Childcare Workers and Employers in New York," in F. D. Ginsburg and R. Rapp (eds), *Conceiving the New World Order: The Global Politics of Reproduction*, 78–102, Berkeley: University of California Press.

Colley, H. (2006), "Learning to Labour with Feeling: Class, Gender and Emotion in Childcare Education and Training," *Contemporary Issues in Early Childhood*, 7 (1): 15–29, doi:10.2304/ciec.2006.7.1.15.

Dahlberg, G. and P. Moss (2005), *Ethics and Politics in Early Childhood Education, Contesting Early Childhood Series*, London: RoutledgeFalmer.

Davis, B. and S. Degotardi (2015), "Who Cares? Infant Educators' Responses to Professional Discourses of Care," *Early Child Development and Care*, 185 (11–12): 1733–1747, doi:10.1080/03004430.2015.1028385.

Dobrowolsky, A. and J. Jenson (2004), "Shifting Representation of Citizenship: Canadian Politics of 'Women' and 'Children,'" *Social Politics*, 11 (2): 154–180, doi:10.1093/sp/jxh031.

Dowling, E. and D. Harvie (2014), "Harnessing the Social: State, Crisis and (Big) Society," *Sociology*, 48 (5): 869–886, doi:10.1177/0038038514539060.

Duffy, M. (2005), "Reproducing Labor Inequalities," *Gender & Society*, 19 (1): 66–82, doi:10.1177/0891243204269499.

Edwards, R., V. Gillies, and N. Horsley (2015), "Brain Science and Early Years Policy: Hopeful Ethos or 'Cruel Optimism'?" *Critical Social Policy*, 35 (2): 167–187, doi:10.1177/0261018315574020.

Federici, S. (2014), "From Commoning to Debt: Financialization, Microcredit, and the Changing Architecture of Capital Accumulation," *South Atlantic Quarterly*, 113 (2): 231–244, doi:10.1215/00382876-2643585.

Fisher, B. and J. C. Tronto (1990), "Toward a Feminist Theory of Caring," in E. Abel and M. Nelson (eds), *Circles of Care: Work and Identity in Women's Lives*, 35–62, Albany: State University of New York Press.

Fraser, N. (1990), "Struggle over Needs: Outline of a Socialist-Feminist Critical Theory of Late-Capitalist Political Culture," in L. Gordon (ed.), *Women, the State, and Welfare*, 199–225, Madison: University of Wisconsin Press.

Gibbons, A. (2016), "Playing the Ruins: The Philosophy of Care in Early Childhood Education," *Contemporary Issues in Early Childhood*, 8 (2): 123–132, doi:10.2304/ciec.2007.8.2.123.

Gilligan, C. (1982), *In a Different Voice*, Cambridge, MA: Harvard University Press.

Gillis, J. (2011), "Transitions to Modernity," in J. Qvortrup, W. Corsaro and M. Honig (eds), *The Palgrave Handbook of Childhood Studies*, 114–126, Basingstoke: Palgrave MacMillan.

Gottfried, H. (2012), *Gender, Work, and Economy: Unpacking the Global Economy*, Cambridge: Polity Press.

Hochschild, A. R. (2000), "Global Care Chains and Emotional Surplus Value," in W. Hutton and A. Giddens (eds), *On The Edge: Living with Global Capitalism*, London: Jonathan Cape.

James, A. (2012), "'Child-Centredness' and 'the Child': The Cultural Politics of Nursery Schooling in England," in A. T. Kjorholt and J. Quortrup (eds), *The Modern Child and the Flexible Labour Market*, 111–127, London: Palgrave Macmillan.

Katz, C. (2001), "On the Grounds of Globalization: A Topography for Feminist Political Engagement," *Signs: Journal of Women in Culture and Society*, 26 (4): 1213–1234.

Kelsh, D. P. (2013), "The Pedagogy of Excess," *Cultural Logic: Marxist Theory & Practice*, 20: 137–156.

Kofman, E. (2014), "Gendered Migrations, Social Reproduction and the Household in Europe," *Dialectical Anthropology*, 38 (1): 79–94, doi: 10.1007/s10624-014-9330-9.

Langford, R., B. Richardson, P. Albanese, K. Bezanson, S. Prentice, and J. White (2017), "Caring about Care: Reasserting Care as Integral to Early Childhood Education and Care Practice, Politics and Policies in Canada," *Global Studies of Childhood*, 7 (4): 311–322, doi: 10.1177/2043610617747978.

Llobet, V. and N. Milanich (2018), "Stratified Maternity in the Barrio: Mothers and Children in Argentine Social Programs," in R. Rosen and K. Twamley (eds), *Feminism and the Politics of Childhood: Friends or Foes?*, 172–190, London: UCL Press.

Magazine, R. and M. Areli Ramírez Sánchez (2007), "Continuity and Change in San Pedro Tlalcuapan, Mexico: Childhood, Social Reproduction, and Transnational Migration," in J. Cole and D. Durham (eds), *Generations and Globalisation: Youth, Age, and Family in the New World Economy*, 52–73, Bloomington: University of Indiana Press.

Mahon, R. and F. Robinson (2011), "Introduction," in R. Mahon and F. Robinson (eds), *Feminist Ethics and Social Policy: Towards a New Global Political Economy of Care*, 1–20, Vancouver: UBC Press.

McDowell, L. (1986), "Debates and Reports: Beyond Patriarchy: A Class Based Explanation of Women's Subordination," *Antipode*, 18 (3): 311–321.

McNally, D. (2010), *Global Slump: The Economics and Politics of Crisis and Resistance*, Oakland, CA: PM Press/Spectre.

Mitchell, K., S. A. Marston, and C. Katz (2003), "Introduction: Life's Work: An Introduction, Review and Critique," *Antipode*, 35 (3): 415–442.

Molyneux, M. (2006), "Mothers at the Service of the New Poverty Agenda: Progresa/Oportunidades Mexico's Conditional Transfer Programme," *Social Policy & Administration*, 40 (4): 425–449.

Narotzky, S. and N. Besnier (2014), "Crisis, Value, and Hope: Rethinking the Economy," *Current Anthropology*, 55 (S9): S4–S16, doi: 10.1086/676327.

Newberry, J. (2014), "Women against Children: Early Childhood Education and the Domestic Community in Post-Suharto Indonesia," *TRaNS: Trans-Regional and National Studies of Southeast Asia*, 2: 271–291, doi: 10.1017/trn.2014.7.

Parrenas, R. S. (2012), "The Reproductive Labour of Migrant Workers," *Global Networks*, 12 (2): 269–275.

Pearson, E. and S. Degotardi (2009), "Relationship Theory in the Nursery: Attachment and Beyond," *Contemporary Issues in Early Childhood*, 10 (2): 144–155, doi: 10.2304/ciec.2009.10.2.144.

Penn, H. (2011), "Travelling Policies and Global Buzzwords: How International Non-governmental Organizations and Charities Spread the Word about Early Childhood in the Global South," *Childhood*, 18 (1): 94–113, doi: 10.1177/0907568210369846.

Rikowski, G. (2000), "That Other Great Class of Commodities: Repositioning Marxist Educational Theory," British Educational Research Association Conference, Cardiff University, Cardiff, 7–10 September 2000.

Rosemberg, F. (2005), "Childhood and Social Inequality in Brazil," in H. Penn (ed.), *Unequal Childhoods: Young Children's Lives in Poor Countries*, 142–170. Oxon: Routledge.

Rosen, R. (2015), "The Use of the Death Trope in Peer Culture Play: Grounds for Rethinking Children and Childhood?" *International Journal of Play*, 4 (2): 163–174.

Rosen, R. (2017), "Reproductive Labour, Motherhood, and Childhood in Neo-liberal Times," Parentalidades en Chile Hoy: La Sobre-responsabilizacion de Madres y Padres y la Debilidad de los Soportes (Parenthood in Chile Today: Mother's and Father's Over-Responsibilisation and the Weakness of Support), Diego Portales Universidad, 18 July 2017.

Rosen, R., S. Baustad, and M. Edwards (2017), "The Crisis of Social Reproduction under Global Capitalism: Working Class Women and Children in the Struggle for Universal Childcare," in R. Langford, S. Prentice, and P. Albanese (eds), *Caring for Children: Social Movements and Public Policy in Canada*, 164–185, Vancouver: UBC Press.

Rosen, R. and J. Newberry (2018), "Love, Labour and Temporality: Reconceptualising Social Reproduction with Women *and* Children in the Frame," in R. Rosen and K. Twamley (eds), *Feminism and the Politics of Childhood: Friends or Foes?*, 117–133, London: UCL Press.

Sayer, A. (2011), *Why Things Matter to People: Social Science, Values and Ethical Life*, Cambridge: Cambridge University Press.

Taggart, G. (2011), "Don't We Care?: The Ethics and Emotional Labour of Early Years Professionalism," *Early Years*, 31 (1): 85–95, doi: 10.1080/09575146.2010.536948.

Tronto, J. (1989), "Women and Caring: What Can Feminists Learn about Morality from Caring?" in A. M. Jaggar and S. R. Bordo (eds), *Gender/Body/Knowledge*, 172–187, London: Rutgers University Press.

Tronto, J. C. (1993), *Moral Boundaries: A Political Argument for an Ethic of Care*, New York and London: Routledge.

Tronto, J. C. (1995), "Care as a Basis for Radical Political Judgments," *Hypatia*, 10 (2): 141–149.

Tronto, J. C. (2011), "A Feminist Democratic Ethics of Care and Global Care Workers: Citizenship and Responsibility," in R. Mahon and F. Robinson (eds), *Feminist Ethics and Social Policy: Towards a New Global Political Economy of Care*, 162–177, Vancouver: UBC Press.

Viruru, R. (2008), "Childhood Labor in India: Issues and Complexities," *Contemporary Issues in Early Childhood*, 9 (3): 224–233, doi: 10.2304/ciec.2008.9.3.224.

5

Cultivating Ethical Dispositions in Early Childhood Practice for an Ethic of Care: A Contemplative Approach

Geoff Taggart

Langford et al. (2017) argue that the care that practitioners in early childhood education and care (ECEC) offer is far more than simply "custodial." Page (2015), for example, as part of her research into "professional love," observes the following take place between a sleeping child and an adult:

> Eva was asleep on a mattress on the floor. Rainee knelt down beside Eva. She bent right down to obtain eye contact. Rainee gently stroked the back of Eva's head while quietly calling, "Hello" in a sing-songy voice. Eva reciprocated by lifting her head up, looked at Rainee, rocked back on to her knees, rubbed her eyes and moved her head from side to side before lying down again. Rainee lowered her head to maintain eye contact with Eva. Eva reached out for her teddy which was at the top of her mattress whilst Rainee continued to stroke Eva's head and talked to her until Eva was fully awake. Eva pointed to something on the other side of the room and Rainee said, "What's that?" Eva got to her knees and then stood up. Rainee remained on her knees so that she maintained eye contact. Eva said "Oh, Oh," which Rainee echoed followed by, "I'm awake, I'm awake." Eva appeared to be unsteady on her feet so Rainee, who was still kneeling, supported Eva by holding her hand. Eva sat down on Rainee's knee to drink a cup of milk, which was bought in by a practitioner. Rainee put her arm round Eva's back to support her whilst gently stroking Eva's leg. Rainee continued to talk in soft tones when responding to Eva's cues. (1)

At first sight, such an episode would seem to be both touching and unremarkable, an indication of the kind of sensitive, empathetic responses of mothers to their children the world over. Yet there is no biological connection between the two;

Rainee is a preschool teacher. So where does her "professional love" come from? In most parts of the world, the answer would be along the lines of "maternal instinct" or "feminine nurture," implying that (a) this work is restricted to 50 percent of humanity and (b) such work is not a genuine profession since this capacity for caring, being instinctive, is not part of a discrete body of skills and knowledge. Moreover, since it is domestic and natural, such work is assumed to be part of the private realm of family rather than part of the public realm of professions. A step toward professionalization could be taken by asking, if not from gender or mothering experience, where this "love" comes from. One answer is that love, caring, and empathy are expressions of innate *ethical* nature as human beings. In this regard, feminist care ethics is useful since it articulates the connection between the kind of behaviors shown by Rainee and the traditional questions of philosophical ethics, such as "what does it mean to be good?"

The implication is that if we can reconceptualize the capacity for love, caring, and intimacy as *ethical dispositions*, the way is then open toward cultivating such dispositions in professional programs. Of course, rooting a claim to professionalism in moral *emotions* may lead to doubts as to whether higher education can provide a route to this professionalism, bearing in mind education's traditional association with the refinement of logic and *reason*. The purpose of this chapter is to argue that care ethics is part of an ongoing feminist challenge to a narrow kind of epistemology in higher education that separates mind from body and feeling from intellect. Care ethics imagines a self that is embodied and relational. Connecting this philosophical model with psychological research in attachment and moral development, I propose an experiential and contemplative approach to the ethical development of teachers in ECEC.

Professional ethics and care ethics

In previous work (Taggart 2011), I contribute to the argument that for ECEC to be taken seriously as a moral, non-gendered profession (akin to teaching, nursing, social work, and ministry), the care that practitioners offer needs to be understood as a deliberately *ethical* undertaking, motivated by a sociopolitical concern to "make a difference" (Dahlberg and Moss 2005; Fennimore 2014). Where activists in ECEC have so far attempted to address the ethical nature of the work, they have understandably sought to follow other aspiring professions by drawing up a code of ethics and providing materials by which practitioners can reflect on the extent to which they embody principles in the code (Feeney and Freeman 2018). As part of this model, trainee practitioners are typically asked to consider particular ethical dilemmas and discuss them in class to try and determine the most appropriate course of action (Newman and Pollnitz 2001). Students can then be measured according to whether they made the "right" decision.

This is a common form of ethics education, borrowed from professional fields, such as business and clinical medicine. Gallagher (2013) refers to this as "fast" ethics, in contrast to a kind of "slow ethics" where a more relational, situated response is required. The fast approach can be relevant to the fields of business and medicine since the ethical dimension most commonly comes to the fore in relation to difficult intellectual decisions, whether regarding financial transparency or eliciting consent for surgery. In traditional professions, such as law, medicine, and business, it is therefore quite possible to act in a way that is ethically correct but to be impatient, judgmental, unkind, and selfish. For practitioners who are role models for young children, extending "professional love" to their charges (Page 2013), the conceptualization of ethics must necessarily be very different, leading to a different kind of ethics education.

Care ethics and ECEC

The effects of fast ethics in ECEC are clear. As I argue (Taggart 2011), we are in danger of producing practitioners who do not value or understand the complexity of their own care simply because universities find it difficult to measure this. The basis for an alternative approach can be found in *care ethics*, a term used to refer to the work of feminist writers such as Gilligan (1982), Noddings (2003), and Tronto (1994), which, rather than asking what is right and just in a universal sense, asks how to respond in particular situations and to whom one is responsible in that response. People are seen as inescapably relational, in varying degrees of dependence on one another.

Care ethics is ideally suited to the work of ECEC practitioners. This is because, although care ethics is part of a philosophical tradition of "moral sentimentalism" that emphasizes the role of feeling in ethical life, it is also part of a multidisciplinary feminist tradition that celebrates holistic, embodied forms of knowledge and behavior. The insights of care ethicists, for example, accord well with those of psychoanalytic feminists (Chodorow 1978; Hollway 2006), who trace the capacity to care back to the primordial needs and desires of infancy, producing a pleasing alignment between the standpoints of early childhood theory and those of care ethics. That is, in the same way that Piaget and Dewey demonstrate how *physical* embodiment gives rise to knowledge, challenging the dualism between body and mind, feminist approaches to morality similarly show how *ethical* responsiveness arises out of bodily life and its history, and out of the inescapable relatedness of human beings.

Such an interdisciplinary framework for the forthcoming discussion, bringing together psychology and philosophy, is inspired by the work of Govrin (2014a, b), who is concerned about the way in which care ethics, as a branch of moral philosophy, seems to be languishing in the academic backwaters. He explicitly seeks to ground it more firmly in human psychology, arguing that adult moral sense is derived from ties of dependency in early childhood. His argument, drawn from Gray and Wegner (2009), rests on the insight that, despite their complexities, moral dilemmas in adulthood seem to be understood in terms of the same primary, dyadic schema (i.e., a moral "agent" and a moral "patient") as the mother–child interactions of infancy. Recalling Noddings's (2010) metaphor of primary attachment relationships as the "incubator" of adult ethics, Govrin argues that these schemas are foundational and that the strength and security of early attachment will condition adult morality. For Govrin, the essence of care ethics lies in the importance of secure attachment to moral life.

So what might be the role of the university in preparing an ethical professional whose ethics depends as much upon psychological history as on formal intelligence? Most institutions that train preschool teachers entitle their programs "early childhood education and care." Yet, although students are asked to reflect on and analyze how young children should be *educated*, they are rarely asked to reflect upon what it means to *care* for or about those children. It is not as though practitioners are resistant to the idea. When given the opportunity, practitioners typically talk about professionalism and ethics in terms of love, care, and empathy (Campbell-Barr et al. 2015; Cousins 2015; Dalli 2008; Davis and Degotardi 2015), yet this discourse is mostly absent from the training competences and policy documents that govern their work. I would argue that this absence occurs partly because the history and structure of higher education is predicated upon an educated ideal that has never taken care seriously and that cannot accommodate itself to the broader, more embodied epistemology and ethics represented by movements in feminism. There are isolated examples where the affective dimension of ethical life is addressed in training, such as in the use of "applied theatre" (Khaner and Linds 2015) or in videoing practice (Biglan et al. 2013; Elicker et al. 2008). However, the legacy of an entrenched model that defines what it means to be moral and educated is a significant challenge for those teaching graduate-level carers.

Reflective practice and the educated ideal

Care is a holistic concept, bringing together thought and feeling, mind and body. Influential contributions to care ethics (Held 2006; Sevenhuijsen 1998) seek to show that this holistic concept is basic to human experience because of a collective susceptibility to vulnerability and dependence. Therefore, care is not something that is ever grown out of. In contrast, the hegemonic view of development, grounded in the triumph of Western science and reason, is that the role of care becomes progressively less as that of education increases and, in this way, education is assumed to be for the achievement of self-sufficiency and autonomy (Van Laere et al. 2014). Arguing that human beings are as relational as they are autonomous and as affective as they are cognitive, care ethicists are part of a broader feminist movement that challenges assumptions about the nature of knowledge and education, particularly in relation to professional education.

In the 1980s, a cadre of feminist philosophers and psychologists interpreted intellectual history to explain the way a patriarchal norm of the "educated man" had become hegemonic in higher education. Merchant (1980) shows how the arguments of Renaissance men such as Francis Bacon were used to extol a mechanistic perspective on people and the environment, perpetuating Platonic conceptions of nature as feminine and ideas as masculine. Writers such as Lloyd (1984) and Schott (1988) demonstrate that the model of the "good man," inherited from Kant, requires individuals to act purely from force of will rather than any natural feeling. The research of Gilligan (1982), which pioneered care ethics, is a reaction against the Kantian theory of moral stages that imply a natural and universal progression to moral abstraction and propositional moral reasoning, hallmarks of "the educated ideal" (Roland 1981). Some writers took a Freudian view and saw in the attempt to "rein in" the wild, disorderly, and unpredictable realm of the natural world, a kind of "reaction-formation" against the uncertainty represented by the loss of an organic, relational, medieval worldview. For example, Bordo (1987) perceives this kind of reaction-formation in Descartes's *Meditations,* the text that provides the basis for our assumption that thought is of primary importance and the external world of the senses (including the body) is secondary. Certainly, in the cultural upheaval that marked the dawn of modern science, it could be reassuring to know that at least one's thoughts are true. Yet, at the same time, Cartesian dualism legitimized an educated mindset that pushed a wealth of human experience to the margins. Care ethicist Sara Ruddick (1989: 195) notes that Cartesian reason has been idealized as "active, autonomous, controlling, progressive and socially powerful, yet exempt from unwanted social responsibilities." She contrasts this with the female experience of the birth process as "incontinent, repetitiously irregular, insufficiently individuated and vulnerable to pain, confinement and onerous responsibility" and suggests that the idealization of reason, stemming from Descartes, is a defensive reaction to human fragility. Bordo concludes her analysis of Descartes's "flight to objectivity" by contrasting his world of separate, atomized minds with the findings of Gilligan and her celebration of empathy, closeness, and connectedness as necessary features of human rationality.

Despite these challenges to an educated rationality and arguments to include care and moral emotions as knowledge, one could argue that it is not care ethics that has helped most to raise the intellectual legitimacy of qualitative knowing in the university. Instead, various kinds of phenomenology have offered alternatives to the rigid, Cartesian distinction between "knower" and "known" and have sought to show that care and relationship are inscribed at the heart of the human condition. Heidegger, for example, argues that the sheer fact of being thrown involuntarily into existence and being alive ("Being") is a state that is ontologically fundamental and that care is intrinsic to it. The perspective is summarized well by Boff (2007: 15):

> That is, to care is at the very heart of the human being: it is there before anyone does anything …. This means that we must acknowledge that the attitude of taking care is a fundamental mode of being which is always present and which cannot be removed from reality.

Care is also at the heart of Buber's (1970) phenomenology, reversing Descartes's famous dictum to something akin to "others exist, therefore I am." Buber contests the assumption that we can truly know ourselves in isolation and argues that it is only through the caring relation of "I–Thou" that the self is fully complete and understood. Despite the intellectual impact of these theories, the phenomenology that has had the most impact upon reflective practice is that of Merleau-Ponty (1945). He proposes that a caring relationship rests on more than a collection of data about the subject: it is mediated via a web of subtle perceptions understood through the body. According to Merleau-Ponty, perception has a "figure-ground" structure in the sense that, when individuals identify an object, they set it apart from the other objects in the perceptual field. The body participates in this process by becoming part of either the focal point (figure) or the background (ground). For example, when I cut my hand and put a bandage on it, my hand is the figure; when I use a pen or a knife, my hand is the ground. This movement in and out of focal attention explains how carers can offer an embodied presence to a client or patient while temporarily effacing themselves. Hamington (2004: 50) argues that the idea of "figure-ground interactions provides a useful way of framing Noddings' understanding of engrossment." That is, engrossment involves being at least temporarily other-directed, with one's thoughts and perceptions relegated to the background. Yet important perceptual data, such as a child looking pale or feeling cold, make themselves tacitly known in the background. Of equal importance is Merleau-Ponty's more esoteric metaphor of "the flesh," communicating the insight that all human knowledge is grounded intersubjectively in bodily perceptions. Human beings are both subject and object to each other, in the same way that, when I rub my hands together, they are touching and being felt simultaneously. This intersubjectivity provides a corporeal basis for an ethic of care. The relevance of these ideas to ECEC is noted by Wynn (1997), who suggests that Winnicott's holding relationship is one in which the mother is "held" and defined by the child in as much as it also occurs the other way around.

This radically intersubjective and embodied conception of the self underpins the discourse of reflective practice. This is usually seen as originating in the work of Schon (1983), which became a tool for professionalization of teaching, nursing, and social work in the 1980s and 1990s. Schon is critical of the way that professional knowledge is assumed to operate in the same way as scientific knowledge, according to objective principles that could be turned into rules. Such "technical rationality," he argues, became part of professional life as the established professions consolidated their influence in the nineteenth century, at the high watermark of Enlightenment reason. To legitimize their status, doctors and lawyers embraced a form of scientific method as their modus operandi. Yet it is clear to Schon that practitioners in caring professions do not work by applying disembodied principles to particular cases: the knowledge is far more situated and dialogical. In his famous metaphor, Schon proposes that, rather than viewing each case from the epistemological high ground, practitioners are obliged to enter the "swampy lowlands" of practice, occupied by vulnerable, unpredictable clients.

Particularly in nursing, professionalism has come to be seen as a commitment to reflective practice and a phenomenological approach to knowledge (Benner 1984). For example, Johns (2009: 3) argues that reflection "is a critical and reflexive process of self-inquiry and transformation of being and becoming the practitioner you desire to be." Self-awareness and emotional articulacy are emphasized, and practitioners are encouraged to develop a phenomenological understanding of their presence and availability to clients and patients. Such an approach to ethical practice is diametrically opposed to the ethics of Kant who argues that the very fact that an act is based on relationship rather than duty alone renders it *un*ethical. Being a "reflective practitioner" calls for more of a moral imagination than an awareness of duties, and it is here where care ethics can make the best contribution, in articulating the phenomenological dynamics of compassionate relations. For example, Benhabib (1987) demonstrates that knowledge about something seems to be a condition for care: the more people know about a person or subject discipline, the more people care about it. She argues that a key insight of care ethics is that the ethical impulse arises out of what is known in tangible and intimate terms rather than in an abstract sense: there is a "concrete other" rather than some universal, idealized other to whom we are all meant to act ethically. Dunne (1998), in his discussion of practical judgment, describes such moral practice in terms first outlined by Aristotle. This embodied practice, which requires discernment and wisdom, he calls *phronesis* and contrasts it with *techne*, the practice of making things and producing outcomes. In the field of ECEC, rather than applying rules and principles to real-life situations, it is more plausible that practitioners, as with nurses and their patients, develop an ethical *phronesis* in the course of their interactions with parents and children. But what models of relationship does care ethics draw upon, and how can they be applied to the work of practitioners?

Mothering and empathy

In the key texts of care ethics (Noddings 2003; Ruddick 1989), the figure of the mother is emblematic of the relational practice being described, and the relevance of this to the *in loco parentis* position of early childhood teachers is clear. Noddings's examples, whether responding to a child's cries or teaching the child to be gentle with the cat, center on a dyadic interaction whereby the one caring temporarily puts personal concerns to one side, becomes receptive to the needs of the cared-for, and demonstrates a responsive availability to the child. There is "motivational displacement" (Noddings 2010: 48) in that the energy of the carer flows toward the cared-for. In order for an act to be considered an act of caring, it has to be received and understood as such by the recipient.

The experiences of these acts of "natural caring," exemplified most strongly in mothering or being mothered, are what people return to at an unconscious level when responding (or not) to demands on caring capacities that are less straightforward, such as when someone falls in the street. Individuals carry within themselves a "best picture of ourselves caring and being cared for" and, in encountering the stranger, "I may reach towards the memory and guide my conduct by it if I wish to do so" (Noddings 2003: 8). Thus, mothering is the process by which ethical attitudes are cultivated and perpetuated across generations. This notion that early experience is the source of moral qualities would seem to be endorsed by no less a figure than the Dalai Lama, when pointing out the central importance of compassion:

> Compassion fosters positive conditions for survival. As soon as we leave our mother's womb, the feeling of intimacy is key to survival and the proper development of our life. Immediately after birth, the young child is like a small animal. By nature, by biology, the child senses his survival depends entirely on affection. So the child seeks immediate connection with the mother. I think mother's milk is a symbol of compassion. (Dalai Lama and Chan 2012: 101)

In her study of "maternal thinking," Ruddick (1989: 98) similarly focuses on mothering as foundational in generating an experiential sense of all that is good. In particular, she focuses on the importance of storytelling in establishing trust and imparting a sense of robust identity to children:

> Through good stories, mother and children connect their understandings of a shared experience. They come to know and, to a degree, accept each other through stories of the fear, love, anxiety, pride and shame they shared or provoked. Children are shaped by … the stories they are first told. But it is also true that story-telling at its best enables children to adapt, edit and invent life stories of their own. (98)

Ruddick argues that the ethical sensitivity demonstrated by mothers needs to be celebrated and extended to build a "politics of peace."

Understandably, the attention given to mothering as the practice that is paradigmatic of care ethics has drawn criticism. Bowden (1996: 37), for example, refers to the gender essentialism that underpins the argument and the sense that a set of "emotionally privileged, white, middle class mothering practices" are seen as representative of mothering in general. More important for the purposes of the current argument is that such an emphasis on mothering, despite the claim that men may also display these skills, does little to raise the professional standing of ECEC teachers beyond that of others doing "women's work."

Building on the philosophical insights of David Hume, Engster (2015) suggests that care behavior is not founded upon any particular social role but is more fundamental to our nature. He draws evidence from Darwinist theory, ethology, and brain chemistry to propose that care ethics is a naturalistic philosophy, rooted in biology and psychology. More particularly, the evolutionary antecedents and biological markers of care behavior can be seen to underpin the phenomenon of compassion, that empathic desire to alleviate the vulnerability or suffering of others. This is relevant to care work in ECEC (Rajala and Lipponen 2018; Taggart 2016) where practitioners routinely work empathically with vulnerable subjects.

Gilbert (2010) understands compassion as an outgrowth of the mammalian relationship of attachment and bonding, a relationship humans instinctively look for as a kind of "social mentality." That is, as an archetypal structure of the mind, compassion guides the motives and feelings of carer and cared-for in relation to each other, signals when caring is occurring, and provides positive feedback to keep it going. Within this relationship, a particular "affect regulation system" is vital, one that is often ignored. Gilbert observes that, first, humans spend a lot of time pursuing, achieving, and consuming in a driven way (an "instinctive, reason-focused system") or, second, protecting themselves in a fearful way (a "threat-focused" system). Yet there is also a "soothing–contentment" system that enables all of us to have a sense of well-being and of being at peace. The hormone oxytocin is triggered by the attachment bond, bringing feelings of softness and well-being. Gilbert articulates the heart of his argument:

> Compassion arises from the balance of the three emotion systems. In particular, it operates through care-giving, social mentality that orients us to focus on alleviating distress and promoting flourishing. We now know that this social mentality has evolved with, and is linked to, the soothing/contentment system. (202)

The findings discussed above reveal that moral capacity is more holistic than purely cognitive and that any program of ethical development needs to adopt a similarly holistic approach. Care can be seen as hardwired into human cell structure, such as in the mirror neurons that fire in response to both one's own actions and responses and those of others, allowing a foundation for empathy. Yet, if this is the case, why are human beings so variable in their capacity for care and empathy? Is this a capacity that professional education can address?

Attachment style and capacity to care

Early nurture provides clues to the variability in care and empathy, gained from research going back to the 1930s. Prior to that time, psychologists understood an offspring's bond with the mother primarily in terms of the need for food. Yet Harlow's work with monkeys and substitute mothers shows that, in fact, they prefer the softer, more comforting substitutes than the metal ones that provide the milk: emotional support seems to be as primary as nutrition (Harlow 1958). With a similar interest in biology, Bowlby (1979) theorizes that the desire for proximity to the mother is a tool for evolutionary survival and that, with a secure base, young children can become more confident and exploratory. Yet it is not only the child's care-seeking that brings this about. Ainsworth and colleagues' (1978) studies show that it is the quality of the caretaker's behavior that accounts for attachment security. Responsive attunement to the child's needs is the determining factor. By contrast, stern, authoritarian parenting seems to produce insensitivity and excessive self-reliance (avoidant attachment) in children. Vague, non-attuned and inconsistent caretaking seems to prevent children from understanding themselves and acting authentically (ambivalent attachment). The implications of these early attachments for moral development are shown by Bowlby's research into teenage criminals, which reveals the impact of "maternal deprivation."

Research over the last fifty years seems to corroborate the observation that "the attachment styles we form are predictive of how we act morally" (Music 2017: 253). Toddlers with more secure attachment are more likely to act according to their conscience and be more responsive and cooperative as they grow up (Kochanska et al. 2010). In contrast to toddlers with an experience of abuse, they are also more likely to offer support if they hear another child in distress (Main and George 1985). As adults, people with a history of secure attachment are more likely to make better life partners (Kunce and Shaver 1994), volunteer in the communities, look after their elderly parents themselves (Gillath et al. 2005a), be less susceptible to "compassion fatigue" (Tosone et al. 2010), and be more inclined to find the selflessness of child-rearing enjoyable (Volling et al. 1998). Evidence also exists that individuals with stronger attachment security are less likely to be prejudiced toward marginalized social groups (Mikulincer and Shaver 2001; Mikulincer et al. 2003). If such individuals are leaders, they are also more likely to be thought of as fair and trustworthy (Popper et al. 2000). In Gilbert's language (2010), secure individuals have a developed soothing–contentment system that allows them to feel safe enough to step outside their own perspective. Tsilika et al. (2015) note that caregivers with patterns of secure attachment are abler to give consistent emotional support to patients.

In contrast to these fortunate individuals, less positive attachment styles seem to compromise the capacity of individuals to act in altruistic, prosocial ways. Caregivers with avoidant attachment find caregiving more stressful and are less altruistic in their motives (Nicholls et al. 2014). Avoidant adults can become perfectionist and workaholic (Mayseless 1996), are reluctant to appear vulnerable, and are dismissive of vulnerability or distress (Scharf et al. 2004). Vachon (2015: 103) points out that care professionals with an avoidant attachment style are more likely to be good technicians with a less developed interpersonal ethics of care. When avoidant adults become parents, the expectations that they will be sensitive and responsive provoke unusual stress (Rholes et al. 2006), and the usual solution is to adopt a style that is either authoritarian or managerial since this kind of emotional defense helps to make caregiving manageable (De Oliveira et al. 2005; George and Solomon 2008; Simpson et al. 1996). In the typical case, such avoidance will reduce the individual's capacity for compassion, not only as it affects personal relationships but in reducing community or voluntary participation. On the one hand, therefore, it may be unlikely that individuals with this pattern choose to work with young children. On the other, avoidant adults may gain a significant amount of personal validation from their ability to control, predict, and regulate the routines of those who are especially vulnerable. If practitioners with this pattern exist, they are therefore more likely to occupy managerial positions, perhaps preferring it to the messiness of being with the children.

For adults with a contrasting style of attachment, preoccupation with relationship extends into the workplace and their interest in love, care, and support makes them ideal candidates for caring professions. Yet the realm of the personal is constantly in danger of overtaking the professional. Preoccupied adults have high tendencies to self-disclosure, particularly on social media (Oldmeadow et al. 2013) and toward dramatizing relationships: friends and colleagues are referred to in sentimental terms and may receive extravagant gifts or displays of loyalty (Bauminger et al. 2009; Collins et al. 2004; Feeney 2004). Yet when these people develop their own interests or separate relationships (e.g., with workers in a different team or organization), such adults can feel abandoned.

Relationships with children are similar. For such adults, children represent the possibility of full emotional availability: "Babies ... hold out the longed-for prospect of a relationship with someone who can be loved and who will return love without the fear of abandonment" (Howe 2011: 145). This kind of caregiver tends to act out impulsive responses in a spontaneous, inconsistent way, showering children with affection and gifts one day and wearily dismissing them the next. Irritation is likely to emerge when babies or young children begin to explore their immediate environment without the caregiver's intervention: burgeoning independence returns the adult to a sense of loneliness and poor self-worth. The existence of early years practitioners with unfulfilled emotional needs would suggest the involvement of the preoccupied style of attachment in this behavior. For example, in her research, Osgood (2012: 76) concludes that, for some of her interviewees, "becoming part of ECEC services was constructed as a form of cathartic reconciliation for the perceived shortcomings of their own childhoods." Certainly, several researchers have concluded that for disadvantaged young women working in a nursery is a passage to acceptance and "respectability" (Colley 2006; Skeggs 1997; Vincent and Braun 2010).

In the light of this overview, the relevance of psychological research in compassion to the work of ECEC practitioners is clear:

> The ability to help others is a consequence of having witnessed and benefitted from good caregiving on the part of one's attachment figures, which promotes the sense of security as a resource and provides models of good caregiving. (Gillath et al. 2005b: 9)

This could represent a rather fatalistic assessment. Apparently rigid and inflexible contrasts between different attachment styles might suggest that one's ethical capacity is predetermined through a combination of genes and environmental conditioning, allowing education and training little influence. I will argue that this is not the case.

Morality and emotional awareness

The argument I am making is that secure attachment allows for greater perspective-taking and empathy, which are key features of ethical life, and so a phenomenological approach to professional development will be necessary to help practitioners understand this. Yet, on first analysis, it would certainly seem that the idea of basing a moral theory on one's capacity for empathy is flawed. Even if we leave attachment styles out of the equation, empathy tends to falter in encounters with people perceived as outsiders (Xu et al. 2009) or if empathy is seen as potentially dangerous or uncomfortable (Davis 1996). Altruism stalls if people feel fearful and isolated. These findings echo the insights of Hume that our capacity for universal sympathy is weak and variable and underpin the arguments of psychologists such as Bloom (2018) who maintains, contrary to popular understanding, that empathy provides a very unhelpful basis for ethical behavior. Bloom offers the example that, using inherited capacity for empathy alone, people would be unfair and give preferential treatment to people with whom they feel a natural affiliation. At first sight, reasoning and judicial reflection would seem to be the tools that, once again, people fall back on in order to act morally. Yet I would argue that the pessimism about universal sympathy is unfounded. Certainly, we are all more likely to respond to one person empathetically than a hundred, even though the hundred may be more deserving. But this pattern does not indicate that empathy itself is limited, only that people fear being overwhelmed by demands of it because they wrongly believe their empathic capacity is limited (Cameron 2013: 3).

Through organizations such as the Mind and Life Institute and the Greater Good Science Center at UC Berkeley, there is increasing evidence that the capacity for care, empathy, and compassion is like a muscle that can grow stronger through practice and "that we can indeed train the brain to become more compassionate" (Davidson 2012: 118). This muscle may be underdeveloped as a result of early experience, but this does not mean that it is lost or incapable of growth. In fact, the very belief that it can grow is likely to be a self-fulfilling prophecy. For example, Schumann et al. (2014) find that, if a person holds a "mindset of empathy" in which the quality is seen as malleable and workable, they are more likely to expend greater empathic effort. Participants were offered persuasive evidence of either the fixed or malleable view of empathy: those who had been presented with the latter view were more likely to express greater willingness to be empathic over a serious disagreement. The researchers also find that those presented with the latter view spend more time listening to a personal story from someone in a different racial group and indicate that they would offer more hours volunteering in a cancer support group. The authors conclude that an effective way to cultivate moral emotions is to simply challenge the view that the capacity to have them is fixed and preset. In an objective sense, ethical characteristics certainly seem to be more adaptive and developmental than thought.

Mindfulness and caring

A central practice in "expanding the empathic bandwidth" (Cameron 2013: 1) is that of mindfulness, a secular form of present-moment, non-judgmental awareness found within most world religions but particularly within Buddhism. Originally popularized by Kabat-Zinn (1982) as a form of stress management, this practice aims to bring about this awareness by deliberately narrowing the field of attention, typically by becoming attentive to one's body and breathing. There have been a number of empirically supported studies of the effects of mindfulness that relate to prosocial behavior, in particular, better emotional regulation (Cahn and Pollich 2009; Goldin and Gross 2010). That is, by disidentifying from habitual spontaneous reactions, people can be more patient or receptive to others and build a broader repertoire of ethical behaviors. For example, in one study (Birnie et al. 2010: 10) participants were shown to have "a greater ability to adopt others' perspectives, experienced reduced distress … and were increasingly spiritual and compassionate towards themselves."

It is perhaps unsurprising that mindfulness has been shown to be effective in improving the quality of caring in work with vulnerable people and also in parenting (Coatsworth et al. 2015; Duncan and Bardacke 2010). Goh (2012) notes that mindful reflection helps social work students notice more readily when they are not listening to clients and Banks et al. (2016) affirm the use of "lovingkindness" practice to help professionals extend compassion to difficult clients. Snyder et al. (2012) suggest that the enhanced presence and availability of mindfulness practitioners makes the practice beneficial for caring professions. Studies involving parents have focused on particularly challenging situations, such as where children have mental health needs or are at risk of offending. In these intense circumstances, it is not difficult to appreciate how "the parents' activity of simply slowing down enough to notice serves an empathic function" (Reynolds 2003: 10).

Despite these benefits, as Gilbert and Choden (2013: 138) point out, "the secular mindfulness tradition has not worked with the cultivation of compassion in an explicit way." They argue that mindfulness programs need to be presented within a framework of compassion in order to deal with the self-judgment, distraction, and avoidance that are inevitable challenges. In other words, an attitude of compassion toward oneself is necessary first in order to engage mindfully and empathically with others. Engaging with the soothing–contentment system bolsters self-acceptance, and this is particularly useful in relation to insecure attachment. Mindful practice helps to reduce the stress insecure attachment causes (Cordon et al. 2009), and self-compassion practice helps to cultivate and maintain the missing internal models of attachment (Gilbert 2010; Siegel 2007). Intervention programs designed to enhance compassion in general typically involve exercises to boost compassion toward oneself, drawing upon the Buddhist notion of loving-kindness. One mindfulness exercise involves a guided visualization to imaginatively recollect or create a compassionate, benevolent parent figure or mentor. These programs have been positively evaluated in random-controlled trials (Jazaieri et al. 2013) and have been shown empirically to increase compassionate, altruistic behavior (Weng et al. 2013). As Music

(2017: 256) observes, "Ultimately, feeling safe, loved and cared for and not feeling too threatened opens up all kinds of possibilities for rich interaction and both empathic and altruistic acts."

Such self-acceptance promotes the realization of care ethics in practice. Vachon (2015: 103), for example, points out that increased self-compassion can enhance secure attachment and foster patient, attentive caregiving. More generally, Moreira et al. (2015) argue that a positive relationship with self seems to be a prerequisite for a caring, relational ethics, particularly with children. With these insights in mind, the discussion can move on to propose the kind of experiential, holistic pedagogy needed for ethical training in ECEC, which can address the psychological roots of compassion.

Contemplative pedagogy and reflective practice

The discovery of mindfulness as a powerful intervention in learning and development of care ethics has underpinned the emergence of contemplative pedagogy as a distinct field (Barbezat and Bush 2014; Ergas 2017; Lin et al. 2013; Sanders 2013) This approach focuses on the incorporation of non-Western practices, including yoga, tai chi, and walking meditation, into learning for the purposes of deepening insight and awakening ethical sensitivities. Significantly, in the light of the foregoing argument, contemplative pedagogy espouses a strongly phenomenological approach to knowledge. Roeser et al. (2014), for example, contrast the "dualistic meta-model of human development" opposing knower and known, mind and body, with a dialectical model in which the apparent opposites are synthesized. Contemplative pedagogy has had an influence upon the training of teachers (Bai et al. 2009; Kozik-Rosabal 2001; London 2013; Mayes 1998; Miller and Ayako 2005; Moss et al. 2017), building upon the insight of Palmer (1998) that "we teach who we are." It has also influenced the training of nurses (Watson 2009).

Trainees may engage in creative writing using Jungian archetypes to understand their identity as teachers or practice group exercises to develop their presence and authenticity; however, the core practice is that of mindfulness. The avowedly therapeutic intentions of this contemplative approach to professional learning are mirrored in the psychoanalytical tradition of ECEC practitioner training, typified by the Tavistock Institute with its roots in the work of Winnicott and Bion. Elfer (2014) has drawn upon this tradition to pilot an approach to work discussion for ECEC practitioners in which they can articulate the emotional challenges of attachment-based practice. In a safely contained space, practitioners consider how their own attachment styles and patterns of emotional defense may inhibit their caring practices. Similarly, Emmett's (2011: 328) intervention showed that "the inclusion of material about personal attachment history … strengthens the capacity of the participant to operationalize attachment-focused practice."

The common theme in both contemplative and psychoanalytic approaches is a radical deepening of the phenomenological reflective practice discussed earlier. Rather than an artificial technique that a practitioner may draw upon, the aspiration is that reflection will become more of a "special quality of being" (Johns 2009: 3) so that one will develop the habit of "living out of reflective practice" (Watson 2009: viii). I argue that mindfulness practice can promote this goal because it helps practitioners "unhook from autopilot" (Lombard et al. 2017: 83) and become more aware of judgments and actions. According to Watson (2009: x), a "personal wisdom practice" brings the values and dispositions of the nurse to the fore that, in turn, inform the discipline of professional caring: "The wisdom of reflective moral knowing combines with one's inner energy and the radiance of love, beauty, compassion and human presence."

In both psychoanalytic and contemplative contexts, the pedagogic process involves "clearing a space for care" (Wilde 2013: 74) with a high priority placed on listening. A secure holding space is established with clear time limits, and the minimum necessary direction is applied to the discussion. The pedagogic style is facilitative, with participants given the opportunity to articulate and explain their experiences. Elfer (2014) explains how, inasmuch as the participants discussed dealing with breaches of procedure or staff personal issues, the relatively loose structure allowed for silence to emerge between contributions and the participants gradually became more comfortable with the process. This open and bounded structure is mirrored in the "Courage to Teach" model of professional development (Palmer 1998), which draws upon the Quaker tradition of a "clearness committee." The focus of the group stays with the experience of a particular participant rather than moving back and forth. As a trainer in the process comments:

> They are fully present to the person and his or her issue, listening deeply, creating a space of deep respect. The function of the committee is not to "fix" or give advice but to help the focus person hear her own inner wisdom, claim her own authority (to literally be the author of her own story). (Hare 2013: 61)

With this in mind, participants are only allowed to reply to the speaker in the form of open, honest questions: a meditative, reflective atmosphere is maintained.

In my own experience (Taggart 2015), I endeavor to structure a safe, collaborative space as part of a module on "the professional self" in ECEC. Mindful compassion is introduced as part of a session on attachment relationships. Students are given supervision scenarios to role play and to reflect upon in terms of what they reveal about the character's attachment styles. For their assessment, they reflect upon their abilities as leaders and carers and write an assignment based on research into professional love they carried out in their settings. Evaluations of the module are often very personal and disclose how the experience has deepened their confidence in the ethical value of their practice.

Within programs such as this, an altruistic commitment to attentive and supportive care of young children can be cultivated and sustained through regular mindful exercises in which students place embodied attention on their natural reservoirs of kindness, benevolence, and compassion. By cultivating self-acceptance, practitioners can soften defenses, relax habitual attachment styles, and offer greater emotional availability and caring to children. As Siegel (2007: 86) observes, "Just as our attunement to our children promotes a healthy, secure attachment, tuning into the self also promotes a foundation for resilience and flexibility." The persuasiveness of his argument may be the reason why, in 2013, the Zero to Three organization held a US symposium that focused on the integration of mindfulness into a university-based, statewide infant mental health program (Clark et al. 2013).

Conclusion

Returning to the vignette that opened the chapter, one can more easily understand the professional state of mind and heart that Rainee brings to the interaction. She has slowed down her mind so that, rather than racing into the future, it is focused on the child in front of her, a state of engrossment. Rather than oblige the child to act and respond in ways that address Rainee's unmet needs, Rainee remains open and available. Her ethical skill, based on a phenomenological awareness of mind and body together, challenges the foundations of conventional ethics education. As Dirkx (2008) points out:

> Sustaining the ethic of the social contract implicit in professionalism requires more than a technical or rational understanding of the rules and values inherent in such a contract. Commitment to this ethic arises fundamentally from a deep sense of self, from attention to less conscious and visible forces brewing from

within. Ultimately, doing the right thing within a professional role is derived from an awareness of and deep connection with these inner forces.

Early childhood teachers are engaged on a daily basis with children who are at a formative stage in developing an attachment style, appreciating the need to work affectively and sensitively with small human beings so that they can grow up to become well-adjusted, prosocial adults. Therefore, if higher education is to take a role in the ethical preparation of practitioners for caring professions, it will need to embrace a more holistic pedagogy. If the pedagogy envisaged here can become more commonplace, teachers may recognize that, along with concepts and schemas of knowledge, adult ethical habits also stem from early "internal models" and that these habits can be developed deliberately by building and fueling a compassionate heart. In this way, compassionate teachers will be able to foster a compassionate heart in the children they serve.

References

Ainsworth, M. D., M. C. Blehar, E. Waters, and S. N. Wall (1978), *Patterns of Attachment: A Psychological Study of the Strange Situation*, London: Routledge.

Bai, H., C. Scott, and B. Donald (2009), "Contemplative Pedagogy and the Revitalisation of Teacher Education," *Alberta Journal of Educational Research*, 55 (3): 319–334.

Banks, B., T. Burch, and M. Woodside (2016), "Introducing Mindfulness and Contemplative Pedagogy as an Approach to Building Helping Skills in Human Services Students," *Journal of Human Services*, (Fall/2016): 47–60.

Barbezat, D. and M. Bush (2014), *Contemplative Practices in Higher Education*, San Francisco, CA: Jossey-Bass.

Bauminger, N., R. Finzi-Dottan, S. Chason, and D. Har-Even (2009), "Intimacy in Adolescent Friendship: The Roles of Attachment, Coherence and Self-Disclosure," *Journal of Social and Personal Relationships*, 25 (3): 409–428.

Benhabib, S. (1987), "The Generalised and Concrete Other: The Kohlberg-Gilligan Controversy and Moral Theory," in E. F. Kittay and D. T. Meyer (eds), *Women and Moral Theory*, 154–177, London: Rowman and Littlefield.

Benner, P. (1984), *From Novice to Expert: Excellence and Power in Clinical Nursing Practice*, New York: Pearson.

Biglan, A., G. L. Layton, L. B. Jones, M. Hankins, and J. C. Rusby (2013), "The Value of Workshops on Psychological Flexibility for Early Childhood Special Education Staff," *Topics in Early Childhood Special Education*, 32 (4): 196–210.

Birnie, K., M. Speca, and L. E. Carbon (2010), "Exploring Self-Compassion and Empathy in the Context of Mindfulness-Based Stress Reduction (MBSR)," *Stress and Health*, 26 (5): 359–371.

Bloom, P. (2018), *Against Empathy: The Case for Rational Compassion*, London: Vintage.

Boff, L. (2007), *Essential Care: An Ethics of Human Nature*, Waco, TX: Baylor University Press.

Bordo, S. (1987), *The Flight to Objectivity: Essays on Cartesianism and Culture*, Albany, NY: SUNY Press.

Bowden, P. (1996), *Caring: Gender-Sensitive Ethics*, London: Routledge.

Bowlby, J. (1979), *The Making and Breaking of Affectional Bonds*, London: Tavistock.

Buber, M. (1970), *I–Thou*, New York: Simon and Schuster.

Cahn, B. R. and J. Pollich (2009), "Meditation and the P3a Event-Related Brain Potential," *International Journal of Psychophysiology*, 72: 51–60.

Cameron, C. D. (2013), "Can You Run Out of Empathy?" https://greatergood.berkeley.edu/article/item/run_out_of_empathy, Accessed February, 2018.

Campbell-Barr, V., J. Georgeson, and A. N. Varga (2015), "Developing Professional Early Childhood Educators in England and Hungary: Where Has All the Love Gone?" *European Education*, 47: 311–330.

Chodorow, N. (1978), *The Reproduction of Mothering: Psychoanalysis and the Sociology of Gender*, Berkeley: University of California Press.

Clark, R., L. Gilkerson, and R. Shahmoon-Shanok (2013), "Integrating Mindfulness within Training, Supervision, and Practice with Parents and Young Children," Conference Presentation, ZERO TO THREE 2013–28th National Training Institute, December 12, 2013, San Antonio, TX.

Coatsworth, J. D., L. G. Duncan, R. L. Nix, M. T. Greenberg, J. G. Gayles, K. T. Banberger, E. Berrens, and M. A. Demi (2015), "Integrating Mindfulness with Parent Training: Effects of the Mindfulness-Enhanced Strengthening Families Program," *Developmental Psychology*, 51 (1): 26–35.

Colley, H. (2006), "Learning to Labour with Feeling: Class, Gender and Emotion in Childcare, Education and Training," *Contemporary Issues in Early Childhood*, 7 (1): 15–29.

Collins, N. C., A. C. Guichard, M. B. Ford, and B. C. Feeney (2004), "Working Models of Attachment: New Developments and Emerging Themes," in W. S. Rholes and J. A. Simpson (eds), *Adult Attachment: Theory, Research and Clinical Implications*, 121–135, New York: Guilford Press.

Cordon, S. L., K. W. Brown, and P. R. Gibson (2009), "The Role of Mindfulness-Based Stress Reduction on Perceived Stress: Preliminary Evidence for the Moderating Role of Attachment Style," *Journal of Cognitive Psychotherapy*, 23 (3): 258–268.

Cousins, S. (2015), "Practitioners' Constructions of Love in the Context of Early Childhood Education and Care: A Narrative Inquiry," PhD diss., University of Sheffield.

Dahlberg, G. and P. Moss (2005), *Ethics and Politics in Early Childhood Education*, London: Routledge.

Dalai Lama and V. Chan (2012), *The Wisdom of Compassion*, New York: Bantam Press.

Dalli, C. (2008), "Pedagogy, Knowledge and Collaboration: Towards a Ground-up Perspective on Professionalism," *European Early Childhood Education Research Journal*, 16 (2): 171–185.

Davidson, R. J. (2012), "Toward a Biology of Positive Affect and Compassion," in R. J. Davidson and A. Harrington (eds), *Visions of Compassion: Western Scientists and Tibetan Buddhists Examine Human Nature*, 107–130, Oxford: Blackwell.

Davis, B. and S. Degotardi (2015), "Who Cares? Infant Educators' Responses to Professional Discourses of Care," *Early Childhood Development and Care*, 185 (11–12): 1733–1747.

Davis, M. (1996), *Empathy: A Social Psychological Approach*, Boulder, CO: Westview.

DeOliveira, C. A., G. Moran, and D. R. Pederson (2005), "Understanding the Link between the Maternal Adult Attachment Classifications and Thoughts and Feelings about Emotions," *Attachment and Human Development*, 7 (2): 153–170.

Dirkx, J. M. (2008), "Care of the Self: Mythopoetic Dimensions of Professional Preparation and Development," in T. Leonard, and P. Willis (eds), *Pedagogies of the Imagination*, 65–82, Amsterdam: Springer.

Duncan, L. and N. Bardacke (eds) (2010), "Mindfulness-Based Childbirth and Parenting Education: Promoting Family Mindfulness during the Perinatal Period," *Journal of Child and Family Studies*, 19 (2): 190–202.

Dunne, J. (1998), *Back to the Rough Ground: Practical Judgement and the Lure of Technique*, Notre Dame, IN: University of Notre Dame Press.

Elfer, P. (2014), "Facilitating Intimate and Thoughtful Attention to Infants and Toddlers in Nursery," in L. J. Harrison, and J. Sumsion (eds), *Lived Spaces of Infant–Toddler Education and Care: International Perspectives on Early Childhood Education and Development 11*, 103–107, Amsterdam: Springer.

Elicker, J., O. Georgescu, and E. Bartsch (2008), "Increasing the Sensitivity of Childcare Providers: Applying the Video-Feedback Intervention in a Group Setting," in F. Juffer, M. J. Bakermans-Kranenberg, and M. H. Van Ijzendorn (eds), *Promoting Positive Parenting: An Attachment-Based Intervention*, 155–170, M.H. London: Lawrence Erlbaum.

Emmett, S. (2011), "Preparing Professional Caregivers as Young Children's Attachment Partners: A Longitudinal Study of a New Australian Pre-service Program," PhD diss., University of Melbourne.

Engster, D. (2015), "Care in the State of Nature," in D. Engster and M. Hamington (eds), *Care Ethics and Political Theory*, 227–251, Oxford: Oxford University Press.

Ergas, O. (2017), "Reclaiming 'Self' in Teachers' Images of Education through Mindfulness as Contemplative Inquiry," *Journal of Curriculum and Pedagogy*, 14 (3): 218–235.

Feeney, J. A. (2004), "Adult Attachment and Relationship Functioning under Stress Conditions," in W. S. Rholes and J. A. Simpson (eds), *Adult Attachment: Theory, Research and Clinical Implications*, 36–54, New York: Guilford Press.

Feeney, S. and N. Freeman (2018), *Ethics and the Early Childhood Educator: Using the NAEYC Code*, 3rd edn, Washington, DC: NAEYC.

Fennimore, B. S. (2014), *Standing Up for Something Every Day: Ethics and Justice in Early Childhood Classrooms*, New York: Teachers College Press.

Gallagher, A. (2013), "Slow Ethics: A Sustainable Approach to Ethical Care Practices?" *Clinical Ethics*, 8 (4): 98–104.

George, C. and J. Solomon (2008), "The Caregiving System: A Behavioural Systems Approach to Parenting," in J. Cassidy and P. R. Shaver (eds), *Handbook of Attachment: Theory, Research and Clinical Applications*, 833–856, London: Guilford Press.

Gilbert, P. (2010), *The Compassionate Mind*, London: Constable.

Gilbert, P. and Choden (2013), *Mindful Compassion: Using the Power of Mindfulness and Compassion to Transform our Lives*, London: Constable.

Gillath, O., P. R. Shaver, M. Mikulincer, R. E. Nitzberg, A. Erez, and M. H. Van Ijzendoorn (2005a), "Attachment, Caregiving, and Volunteering: Placing Volunteerism in an Attachment-Theoretical Framework," *Personal Relationships*, 12 (4): 425–446.

Gillath, O., P. R. Shaver, and M. Mikulincer (2005b), "An Attachment-Theoretical Approach to Compassion and Altruism," in P. Gilbert (ed.), *Compassion: Its Nature and Use in Psychotherapy*, 121–147, London: Routledge.

Gilligan, C. (1982), *In a Different Voice: Psychological Theory and Women's Development*, Cambridge, MA: Harvard University Press.

Goh, E. C. L. (2012), "Integrating Mindfulness and Reflection in the Teaching and Learning of Listening Skills for Undergraduate Social Work Students in Singapore," *Social Work Education*, 31 (5): 587–604.

Goldin, P. R. and J. J. Gross (2010), "Effects of Mindfulness-Based Stress Reduction (MBSR) on Emotion Regulation in Social Anxiety Disorder," *Emotion*, 10: 83–91.

Govrin, A. (2014a), "The ABC of Moral Development: An Attachment Approach to Moral Judgement," *Frontiers in Psychology*, 5 (6): 1–15.

Govrin, A. (2014b), "From Ethics of Care to Psychology of Care: Reconnecting Ethics of Care to Contemporary Moral Psychology," *Frontiers in Psychology*, 5: 1–10.

Gray, K. and D. Wegner (2009), "Moral Typecasting: Divergent Perceptions of Moral Agents and Moral Patients," *Journal of Personality and Social Psychology*, 96: 505–520.

Hamington, M. (2004), *Embodied Care: Jane Addams, Maurice Merleau-Ponty and Feminist Ethics*, Chicago: University of Illinois Press.

Hare, S. Z. (2013), "What Is the Clearness Committee?", in S. Z. Hare and M. LeBouttillier (eds), *Let the Beauty We Love Be What We Do: Stories of Living Divided No More*, Pawleys Island, SC: Prose Press.

Harlow, H. F. (1958), "The Nature of Love," *American Psychologist*, 13: 673–685.

Held, V. (2006), *The Ethic of Care: Personal, Political and Global*, Oxford: Oxford University Press.

Hollway, W. (2006), *The Capacity to Care: Gender and Ethical Subjectivity*, London: Routledge.

Howe, D. (2011), *Attachment across the Lifecourse*, London: Palgrave.

Jazaieri, H., G. T. Jinpa, K. McGonigal, E. L. Rosenberg, J. Finkelstein, E. Simon-Thomas, M. Cullen, J. R. Doty, J. J. Gross, and P. R. Goldin (2013), "Enhancing Compassion: A Randomised Controlled Trial of a Compassion-Cultivation Training Programme," *Journal of Happiness Studies*, 14 (4): 1113–1126.

Johns, C. (2009), *Becoming a Reflective Practitioner*, 3rd edn, Oxford: Blackwell.

Kabat-Zinn, J. (1982), "An Outpatient Program in Behavioural Medicine for Chronic Pain Patients Based on the Practice of Mindfulness Meditation," *General Hospital Psychiatry*, 4: 33–47.

Khaner, T. and W. Linds (2015), "Playing in Entangled Spaces: Exploring Ethical Know-how through Embodied Inquiry," in E. Vettraino and W. Linds (eds), *Playing in a House of Mirrors: Applied Theatre and Reflective Practice*, 97–102, Amsterdam: Sense Publications.

Kochanska, G., J. Woodard, S. Kim, J. Koenig, J. E. Yoon, and R. Barry (2010), "Positive Socialisation Mechanisms in Secure and Insecure Parent–Child Dyads: Two Longitudinal Studies," *Journal of Child Psychology and Psychiatry*, 51 (9): 998–1009.

Kozik-Rosabal, G. S. (2001), "How Do They Learn to Be Whole? A Strategy for Helping Pre-service Teachers Develop Dispositions," in B. Hocking, J. Haskell, and W. Linds (eds), *Unfolding Bodymind: Exploring Possibility through Education*, Brandon, 100–117, VT: Foundation for Educational Renewal.

Kunce, L. J., and P. R. Shaver (1994), "An Attachment-Theoretical Approach to Caregiving in Romantic Relationships," in *Attachment Processes in Adulthood Advances in Personal Relationships*, K. Bartholomew and D. Perlman (eds), 205–237, London: Jessica Kingsley.

Langford, R., B. Richardson, P. Albanese, K. Bezanson, S. Prentice, and J. White (2017), "Caring about Care: Reasserting Care as Integral to Early Childhood and Care Practice, Politics and Policies in Canada," *Global Studies of Childhood*, 7 (4): 311–322.

Lin, J., R. L. Oxford, and E. J. Brantmeier (eds) (2013), *Re-envisioning Higher Education: Embodied Pathways to Wisdom and Social Transformation*, Charlotte, NC: Information Age.

Lloyd, G. (1984), *The Man of Reason: "Male" and "Female" in Western Philosophy*, London: Routledge.

Lombard, K., S. Horton-Deutsch, and A. Davies (2017), "Creating Space for Reflection: The Importance of Presence in the Teaching-Learning Process," in S. Horton-Deutsch and G. D. Sherwood (eds), *Reflective Practice: Transforming Education and Improving Outcomes*, 65–74, Indianapolis, IN: Sigma Theta Tai International.

London, R. (2013), "Transformative Approaches to Teacher Education: Becoming Holistic Educators in 'Unholistic' Settings," in J. Lin, R. L. Oxford, and E. J.

Brantmeier (eds), *Re-envisioning Higher Education: Embodied Pathways to Wisdom and Social Transformation*, 77–94, Charlotte, NC: Information Age.

Main, M. and C. George (1985), "Responses of Abused and Disadvantaged Toddlers to Distress in Agemates: A Study in the Daycare Setting," *Developmental Psychology*, 21 (3): 407–412.

Mayes, C. (1998), "The Use of Contemplative Practices in Teacher Education," *Encounter: Education for Meaning and Social Justice*, 11 (3): 17–31.

Mayseless, O. (1996), "Attachment Patterns and Their Outcomes," *Human Development*, 36: 206–233.

Merchant, C. (1980), *The Death of Nature: Women, Ecology and the Scientific Revolution*, London: Harper Collins.

Merleau-Ponty, M. (1945), *The Phenomenology of Perception*, London: Routledge.

Mikulincer, M. and P. R. Shaver (2001), "Attachment Theory and Intergroup Bias: Evidence That Priming the Secure Base Schema Attenuates Negative Reactions to Out-groups," *Journal of Personality and Social Psychology*, 81: 97–115.

Mikulincer, M., O. Gillath, Y. Sapir-Lavid, E. Yaakobi, K. Arias, L. Tal-Aloni, and G. Bor (2003), "Attachment Theory and Concern for Others' Welfare: Evidence That Activation of the Sense of Secure Base Promotes Endorsement of Self-Transcendence Values," *Basic and Applied Social Psychology*, 25: 299–312.

Miller, J. P. and N. Ayako (2005), "Contemplative Practices in Teacher Education," *Encounter: Education for Meaning and Social Justice*, 18 (1): 42–48.

Moreira, H., M. J. Gouveia, C. Carona, N. Silva, and M. C. Canavarro (2015), "Maternal Attachment and Children's Quality of Life: The Mediating Role of Self-Compassion and Parenting Stress," *Journal of Child and Family Studies*, 24: 2332–2344.

Moss, E. E., M. J. Hirshberg, L. Flook, and M. E. Graue (2017), "Cultivating Reflective Teaching Practice through Mindfulness," in E. H. Dorman, K. Byrnes, and J. Dalton (eds), *Impacting Teaching and Learning: Contemplative Practice, Pedagogy and Research in Education*, 50–61, London: Rowman and Littlefield.

Music, G. (2017), *Nurturing Natures: Attachment and Children's Emotional, Sociocultural and Brain Development*, 2nd edn, London: Routledge.

Newman, L. and L. Pollnitz (2001), "Helping Students Make Tough Decisions Wisely: The Challenge of Ethical Inquiry," *Australian Journal of Early Childhood*, 26 (4): 39–46.

Nicholls, W., N. Hulbert-Williams, and R. Bramwell (2014), "The Role of Relationship Attachment in Psychological Adjustment to Cancer in Patients and Caregivers: A Systematic Review of the Literature," *Psychoimmunology*, 23: 1083–1095.

Noddings, N. (2003), *Caring: A Feminine Approach to Ethics*, London: University of California Press.

Noddings, N. (2010), *The Maternal Factor: Two Paths to Morality*, Berkeley: University of California Press.

Oldmeadow, J. A., S. Quinn, and R. Kowert (2013), "Attachment Style, Social Skills, and Facebook Use Amongst Adults," *Computers in Human Behaviour*, 29: 1142–1149.

Osgood, J. (2012), *Narratives from the Nursery: Negotiating Professional Identities in Early Childhood*, London: Routledge.

Page, J. (2013), "Permission to Love Them …. But Not Too Much," in J. Page, A. Clare, and C. Nutbrown (eds), *Working with Babies and Children: From Birth to Three*, 2nd edn, 192–196, London: Sage.

Page, J. (2015), "Constructions of Intimacy in Early Childhood Education and Care: Practitioners' Experiences," http://professionallove.group.shef.ac.uk (Accessed March, 2018).

Palmer, P. (1998), *The Courage to Teach: Exploring the Inner Landscape of a Teacher's Life*, San Francisco, CA: Jossey-Bass.

Popper, M., O. Mayesless, and O. Castelnovo (2000), "Transformational Leadership and Attachment," *The Leadership Quarterly*, 11 (2): 267–289.

Rajala, A. and L. Lipponen (2018), "Early Childhood Education and Care in Finland: Compassion in Narrations of Early Childhood Education Student Teachers," in S. Garvis, S. Phillipson, and H. Harju-Luukkainen (eds), *International Perspectives on Early Childhood Education and Care: Early Childhood Education in the 21st Century Vol I*, 64–75, London: Routledge.

Reynolds, D. (2003), "Mindful Parenting: A Group Approach to Enhancing Reflective Capacity in Parents and Infants," *Journal of Child Psychotherapy*, 29 (3): 357–374.

Rholes, W. S., J. A. Simpson, and M. Friedman (2006), "Avoidant Attachment and the Experience of Parenting," *Personality and Social Psychology Bulletin*, 32 (3): 275–285.

Roeser, R. W., D. R. Vago, and C. Pinela (2014), "Contemplative Education: Cultivating Ethical Development through Mindfulness Training," in L. Nucci, T. Krettenauer, and D. Narvaez (eds), *Handbook of Moral and Character Development*, 223–247, London: Routledge.

Roland, J. (1981), "The Ideal of the Educated Person," *Educational Theory*, 31 (2): 97–109.

Ruddick, S. (1989), *Maternal Thinking: Towards a Politics of Peace*, New York: Beacon Press.

Sanders, L. (ed.) (2013), *Contemplative Studies in Higher Education Special Issue: New Directions for Teaching and Learning Issue, 134*, New York: Wiley.

Scharf, M., O. Mayesless, and I. Kivenson-Baron (2004), "Adolescent Attachment Representations and Development Tasks in Emerging Adulthood," *Developmental Psychology*, 40: 430–444.

Schon, D. A. (1983), *The Reflective Practitioner: How Professionals Think in Action*, New York: Basic Books.

Schott, R. M. (1988), *Cognition and Eros: A Critique of the Kantian Paradigm*, New York: Beacon Press.

Schumann, K., J. Zaki, and C. S. Dweck (2014), "Addressing the Empathy Deficit: Beliefs about the Malleability of Empathy Predict Effortful Responses When Empathy Is Challenging," *Journal of Personality and Social Psychology*, 107 (3): 475–493.

Sevenhuijsen, S. (1998), *Citizenship and the Ethics of Care: Feminist Considerations on Justice, Morality, and Politics*, London: Routledge.

Siegel, D. J. (2007), *The Mindful Brain: Reflections and Attunement in the Cultivation of Well-Being*, New York: W.W. Norton.

Simpson, J. A., W. S. Rholes, and D. Philips (1996), "Conflict in Close Relationships: An Attachment Perspective," *Journal of Personality and Social Psychology*, 71 (5): 899–914.

Skeggs, B. (1997), *Formations of Class and Gender*, London: Sage.

Snyder R., S. Shapiro, and D. Treleaven (2012), "Attachment Theory and Mindfulness," *Journal of Child and Family Studies*, 21: 709–717.

Taggart, G. (2011), "Don't We Care?: The Ethics and Emotional Labour of Early Years Professionalism," *Early Years: An International Journal of Research and Development*, 31(1): 85–95.

Taggart, G. (2015), "Sustaining Care: Cultivating Mindful Practice in Early Years Professional Development," *Early Years: An International Journal of Research and Development*, 35 (4): 381–393.

Taggart, G. (2016), "Compassionate Pedagogy: Ethics of Care in Early Childhood Professionalism," *European Early Childhood Education Research Journal*, 24 (2): 173–185.

Tosone, C., J. E. Bettmann, T. Minami, and R. A. Jasperson (2010), "New York City Social Workers after 9/11: Their Attachment, Resiliency, and Compassion Fatigue," *International Journal of Emergency Mental Health*, 12 (2): 103–116.

Tronto, J. (1994), *Moral Boundaries: Towards a Political Ethic of Care*, London: Routledge.

Tsilika, E., E. Parpa, A. Zygogianni (2015), "Caregivers' Attachment Patterns and Their Interactions with Cancer Patients' Patterns," *Supportive Care in Cancer*, 23: 87–94.

Vachon, M. (2015), "Targeted Intervention for Family and Professional Caregivers: Attachment, Empathy and Compassion," *Palliative Medicine*, 30 (2): 101–103.

Van Laere, K., M. Vandenbroeck, and G. Roets (2014), "Challenging the Feminisation of the Workforce: Rethinking the Mind-Body Dualism in Early Childhood Education and Care," *Gender and Education*, 26: 232–245.

Vincent, C. and A. Braun (2010), "'And Hairdressers Are Quite Seedy … ': The Moral Worth of Childcare Training," *Contemporary Issues in Early Childhood*, 11 (2): 204–214.

Volling, B. L., P. C. Notaro, and J. J. Larsen (1998), "Adult Attachment Styles: Relations with Emotional Well-Being, Marriage, and Parenting," *Family Relations*, Oct, 47: 4.

Watson, J. (2009), "A Meta-Reflection on Reflective Practice and Where It Leads," in C. Johns and D. Freshwater (eds), *Transforming Nursing through Reflective Practice*, viii–x, Oxford: Blackwell.

Weng, H., A. S. Fox, A. J. Shackman, D. E. Stodola, J. Z. K. Caldwell, M. C. Olson, G. M. Rogers, and R. J. Davidson (2013), "Compassion Training Alters Altruism and Neural Responses to Suffering," *Psychological Science*, doi: 0956797612469537.

Wilde, S. (2013), *Care in Education: Teaching with Understanding and Compassion*, London: Routledge.

Wynn, F. (1997), "The Embodied Chiasmic Relationship of Mother and Infant," *Human Studies*, 20 (2): 253–270.

Xu, X., X. Zuo, X. Wang, and S. Han (2009), "Do You Feel My Pain? Racial Group Membership Modulates Empathic Neural Responses," *Journal of Neuroscience*, 29 (26): 8525–8529.

6

"I Already Know I Care!": Illuminating the Complexities of Care Practices in Early Childhood and Teacher Education

Colette Rabin

An ethic of care inspires teachers to reflect deeply about what sort of persons are being cultivated through everything teachers do. An ethic of care reveals the potential for education to foster citizens who care about the environment and one another enough to resist apathy, consider others' needs, and act on behalf of others. I became interested in an ethic of care while teaching elementary school due to its recognition of the role of schooling in socialization and cultivation of dispositions. As a teacher educator at a large urban university in an elementary teacher education program for ten years and a former early elementary school teacher for twelve years, I have explored the practical application of the philosophical framework of *an ethic of care* in early childhood education.

As a feminist–postmodern approach to moral education, care ethics makes the most sense in contrast to a traditionalist, individualistic, authoritarian ethical perspective. In this chapter, I will describe an ethic of care by comparing it to traditional moral education. I will also share several specific misconceptions about care that I have found need to be addressed in order to clarify care ethics for teacher preparation. Next, I suggest implications for teacher preparation for care ethics. Last, I put forward several pedagogies designed to teach care ethics in early childhood education.

Conceptualizing care ethics as a feminist approach to moral education in contrast to traditional moral education

The relational perspective of care ethics has been applied to moral education (Gilligan 1982; Noddings 1984, 1992, 2002, 2012). Nel Noddings, referred to as "the principal architect of the notion of education as caring" (DeStigter 2001: 302), grounds care ethics on the claim that care is a fundamental human need. Thus, our desire to be in caring relationship with one another could motivate us to learn to relate more effectively than a set of dicta based on a body of knowledge. Rather than imposing virtues or rules externally, in care ethics, moral growth occurs through the experience of enduring, reciprocal, and responsive relationships (Gilligan 1982; Noddings 1984, 1992, 2002, 2012). Ethical caring is determining another's needs and responding to those needs in relationships; such caring involves engrossing oneself in another's needs in order to respond to the need.

In contrast, traditional moral education focuses on rules with rewards and punishments to extrinsically motivate; this approach neglects the social motivation to teach morals (Kohn 1994, 1996, 1999a, b). When moral education is not grounded in the recognition of caring as an innate inclination, caring must be dictated through rules rather than cultivated through experience. Rules travel with consequences, rewards, and competition. By dictating caring, educators may miss the opportunity to draw out children's desire for connection. Without cultivating this inclination, children learn to require rules about how to treat one another.

Care ethics goes against the grain in a Western individualistic society (Foucault 1988; Gilbert 2009). Individualism cultivates competitive, isolationist dispositions (Dewey 1933; Foucault 1988). In school, one child's success defines another's failure. In stories, heroes and heroines develop strength against their social context and vanquish alone. Interestingly, despite this endemic individualism, for decades psychology has demonstrated our innate propensity to empathize with one another (Bowlby 1969/1982; Mikulincer et al. 2005), even in infants (Spokes and Spelke 2017). And early childhood education teachers frequently cite caring as their purpose for entering the profession (Goldstein and Lake 2000; Rabin and Smith 2016; Sanger and Osguthorpe 2011). Care ethics harnesses this inclination for moral education through experience in caring relationship.

Caring ethics in practice

A caring relationship is characterized by reciprocal caring actions (Noddings 2002). Caring requires attention to the cared-for's lifeworld and needs. Teachers as carers must balance a child's assumed and expressed needs in a way that sustains their relationship. For example, when a child expresses a need that conflicts with an assumed need, a teacher listens to reflect and respond from an understanding of the child's experience. In the literature examining care in the context of teaching, children deemed teachers "caring" when they persisted in believing in the children's abilities (Beauboeuf-LaFontant 1999, 2002, 2005; Noblit 1993; Siddle-Walker 1993). To practice care ethics, teachers engross themselves in their children's experience to feel with them and determine how to respond in a way that expresses solidarity with children, understanding of the larger aims of schooling, and the need to support children to succeed. In the teacher–child relationship, teachers model care so that children can learn to care for one another.

Noddings (2002) puts forth several open-ended experiences that constitute teaching morality from the perspective of an ethic of care: modeling, practice, dialogue, and confirmation. Summarized briefly here, a teacher *models* caring, creates opportunities for children to *practice* caring for others, and initiates children in a *dialogue* in which the interlocutors are more important than their arguments. Last, *confirmation* refers to recognizing the underlying best possible motive behind an outward action. Noddings (1992) describes confirmation: "Here is this significant and percipient other who sees through the smallness or meanness of my present behavior a self that is better and a real possibility" (25). Confirmation entails recognizing the best motive underlying extant behavior. In my research on teacher preparation, I found a fifth dimension to be salient, that of authenticity (Rabin 2013). *Authenticity* is conceived of as the importance of knowing and being oneself in one's role as a teacher who cares. In a case study in a large urban setting in northern California, teachers who were committed to care ethics described how caring required authenticity to avoid complying with uncaring mandates, to make choices reflective of one's beliefs, to find connections between one's self and curriculum, and to decenter one's own ways of seeing the world (Rabin 2013). Within care ethics, determining caring actions depends on the context. Care cannot be formulized and thus it differs significantly from a traditional approach to moral education based on a set of universal rules or values.

Perhaps given the desire for clear formulas for moral education or the prevalence of an individualistic perspective in education, care ethics is misunderstood by educators in several predictable ways; understanding these misconceptions elucidates care ethics so that teachers can learn to operationalize the very reasons they chose to teach (Rabin and Smith 2013).

Misconceptions about care ethics in education

As a teacher educator, I find that when my teacher candidates (I will refer to my students as teacher candidates) have the opportunity to transcend common preconceptions of caring, they come to understand care ethics (Goldstein and Lake 2000; Rabin and Smith 2013). Teacher candidates' understandings of care tend to differ from care ethics in four interrelated ways:

1. overlooking the challenge of developing caring relationships,
2. conflating the term of reference "care" with its quotidian use,
3. separating affect and intellect, and
4. tending toward monocultural understandings of care.

Given mental models persist when not recognized and challenged; articulating and explicating quotidian usage of care helps teacher candidates develop deep understandings of care ethics (Rabin 2008; Rabin and Smith 2013). Teacher education must deal with these misconceptions.

First, the relational dimension of teaching needs to be made visible. Long-time teachers who are guided by a care ethic describe the process of developing caring relationships with children as complex and critical to a learning environment where children feel safe to take the risks that real learning requires (Charney 2002; Nias 1999; Watson 2003). If teacher candidates do not have the affordances of learning a care ethics approach, they may not be aware of the need for creating caring relationships and they may rely on extrinsic control measures; compliance and control undermine the freedom and creativity that deep learning involves (Charney 2002; Hambacher and Bondy 2016; Rosiek 1994; Watson 2003). Teacher preparation needs to bring the challenges of relationship to light so that teacher candidates can recognize them and prepare to respond in caring ways.

Second, to clarify an ethic of care teacher educators must disambiguate the quotidian usage of the term *care* with what the word means in the context of care ethics. Researchers found teacher candidates' understandings of care did not extend beyond a warm-fuzzy, feminine, or static personality trait that cannot be learned but is instead associated with the feminine or maternal (Goldstein and Lake 2000). Initial understandings represent superficial, patronizing, or nice personality traits diluted in generalities, as expressed in this statement: "Of course I care" (White 2003; Goldstein and Lake 2000). As one teacher candidate said: "Just being a teacher is caring. We are just caring people." Although teacher candidates can certainly be caring in the quotidian sense here, practicing care ethics is intellectually demanding in the context of teaching. Clarifying this challenge sets teacher candidates up to learn to care.

Third, simplified or derogatory stereotypes of care derive from a Western cultural inclination to consider *affect* separate from and less valuable than *intellect* (Plato n.d.). To care in an ethical sense requires insight across differences of age, culture, race, ethnicity, language, and more in order to be present to, connect with, and support children. Despite education's traditional moral purposes (Plato n.d.), popular discourse frames the moral and social dimensions of education as superfluous and the "soft side" of teaching (Krazny 2013). Teacher candidates express this perspective with comments like, "I wasn't hired to care. I was hired to know my content." Current emphases on academic performance underscore this circumscribed view. Instrumentalist arguments often link care and academic gains with policies that advocate for programs concerned with the socioemotional needs of children because these programs seem to raise test scores (e.g., the U.S. Department of Education's "What Works" clearinghouse) (Hoffman 2009). However, justifying care's worth or measuring its quality with academic gains limits understanding of care's purposes and continues to position its worth below thought. This belies age-old philosophical arguments over the inadequacies of such binaries and neurological research showing that thought and emotion intimately color one another (Pinker 2000). Hoffman (2009) argues:

> Unless a parallel emphasis is placed on the qualities of relationship that arguably should contextualize skills and behaviors, the discourse risks promoting a shallow, decontextualized, and narrowly instrumentalist approach to emotion in classrooms that promotes measurability and efficiency at the expense of (nonquantifiable) qualities of relatedness. (539)

The interrelation of affect and intellect underscores that learning to care requires more than mastery of additional strategies; it requires a fundamental shift in teacher preparation. It asks teacher educators to teach teacher candidates that caring involves both rationality and emotionality and to encourage a willingness to take on the "emotional labour" of teaching (Hargreaves 2000; Isenbarger and Zembylas 2006).

Fourth, care can also connote monocultural White norms of politeness (Gholami and Tirri 2012; Goldstein and Lake 2000; Pang 2005; Rabin and Smith 2013; Thompson 1998; White 2003). The increasing diversity of schools heightens the importance of developing understandings of care across racial, ethnic, gender, and other differences (Delpit 2006; Knight: 2004; Wilder 1999). In order to challenge culturally bound conceptions of care, teachers need to question their implicit beliefs and assumptions given, for example, that communication styles differ (Nieto 1999) and develop cross-cultural collegial relationships. For example, in a study on cross-cultural conceptions of caring, one African American teacher opined to me that her White colleagues were incurious about her perspective (Rabin 2010). She explained that she had much to share with them but did not know how to get their attention:

> I realized the parents were telling me all kinds of stuff the White teacher didn't know. I wish the teachers and the administrator knew this. I think it's because they (the parents) were African-American. I could help to build relationships if the teachers knew to approach me or listen when I shared. You can never know how to relate if you're not Black or Latino. So, if you're White, you must learn to hear these kinds of stories from us.

Teacher candidates need opportunities to ponder how their own and children's efforts to care might be misunderstood so they are able to engage in cross-cultural dialogue. Thompson (1998) writes about the need to resist the tendency to "look for the culturally White practices and values that ... theory ... already recognize(s) as caring" (531). A deep awareness that schemas differ widely can balance our beliefs concerning how "best" to work through relational struggles. For example, teacher educators need to recognize when they teach cultural norms as taken-for-granted and unquestioned, as in the case of the cultural specificity of Western beliefs about expressing and regulating emotions through talking about them (Tobin 1995).

Teacher educators teaching care ethics must prepare teacher candidates who understand the need to engross themselves in children's perspectives to learn how to care in context, listen to children, and reflect on pedagogy from the perspective of care as an ethic. Teacher candidates need to develop eyes to see relationally. I have found that candidates learn to see care ethics through short vignettes of classroom experiences or case studies.

Teaching teachers to teach with an ethic of care

Narrative assignments support teacher candidates in unearthing common misconceptions, prior assumptions, and beliefs about care (Rabin and Smith 2013; Richert 2012; Richert and Rabin 2013; Rosiek 1994; Young 1998). Teacher candidates examine case stories and analyze what ethical caring entails. Co-developing norms for dialogue over story sets the stage for deep learning.

Co-developing norms for group work

At the beginning of my courses, I guide teacher candidates in a process over several weeks to create norms for dialogue. First, to welcome candidates to be present to the endeavor of learning together, I ask them to share their names and relate a story associated with their name. We read an excerpt from Sandra Cisneros's *The House on Mango Street* on the family origins of her name, which belonged to her grandmother. Along with this reflection on names, teacher candidates ponder what larger purpose drew them to teaching, such as to cultivate a caring and democratic citizenry, to educate for sustainability, to promote critical literacy, etc. They ask themselves how "who they are," as symbolized by their name relates to why they came to teaching and their purposes as teachers. They share their stories and look for commonalities. Before they share, I bid them consider that even when they do not share the same values, they may still share a commitment to values. I share Elie Wiesel's statement, "The opposite of morality is not immorality, but indifference."

During the second meeting, teacher candidates recall a time when they left an experience having learned something. I ask them to dig into this experience to uncover its features and how it may differ from quotidian experiences. We use John Dewey's criteria for an educative experience to analyze their experiences: continuity, end-in-view, and interaction (see Dewey 1938). These criteria uncover how learning experiences connect to children's lives in meaningful, grounded ways. Next, candidates recall a similar learning experience in the context of a dialogue; if they cannot remember taking part in a dialogue during which they learned something (many cannot), they rely on the features of their educative experience. I ask them to consider their own and others' roles; for example, I ask, what sort of moves they made as they participated in the discussion: Did they listen, did they ask questions, and what sort of questions? Can they recall their body language or the number of interlocutors involved? They ponder the features of dialogues in which they disengaged or dug in their heels.

After individually and then collaboratively reflecting in the large group, teacher candidates form small groups. They list three moves in conversation that they agree support learning through dialogue and three that undermine learning. They participate in a class session on a reading about the limits of developmental and stage theories of learning, the critical role of difficulty or liminality (Nelson and Harper 2006), and the power of a steep challenge in which learners slow down and engage in an iterative process of deep reflection toward transformational learning. They often remark how liminal experiences, such as sticky probing over real problems, were missing in their schooling. In new small groups, teacher candidates revisit a compilation of all their proposed norms. They reflect on whether or not these norms could support them through the experience of a liminal state. I ask them to ponder what each of them is willing to do to create the sort of environment in which they could all learn. They revise the list of norms.

In the third class session, teacher candidates prepare by reading a seminal piece on a philosophical exploration of dialogue, written by Nicholas Burbules along with recent empirical pieces on its application by Lefstein. They discuss what Burbules terms "the emotional factors of dialogue": concern or care, trust, respect, appreciation, affection, and hope. They have also written a personal narrative on the intersections of their race, ethnicity, gender, familial history, and their purposes for choosing the field of early childhood education. They revisit the list of norms in small groups and prepare to put them into practice, pondering where such norms might fall short. They share their narratives with one another, looking for intersections. They discuss the following prompts:

- Recall the best group dialogues. What made them so satisfying? What made the worst ones so unsatisfying? Take a few notes.
- By tables, share and listen for themes, patterns, and features of the conversations you want/don't want.
- Articulate three to four core features of the best/worst conversations and suggest three to four actions the class might take in dialogue (proposed norms) to ensure good conversations.

Next, teacher candidates revisit the norms and add what were missing and/or what they practiced, which ones they leaned on most to connect with one another while they pushed each other's thinking. Together, we condense, collate, and wordsmith these. We revisit and revise this set of norms throughout the rest of the semester. At the end of the experience, I ask them why they think I might have asked them to engage in such a protracted experience and to ponder the implications for their teaching. We discuss the need for teacher candidates to engage in democratic processes to create their own classroom structures. We map out a translation of the process for young children (described below).

Allowing the process of norm-building to take time so it can be connected to larger purposes and actual experience in dialogue, structuring ways for teacher candidates to collaborate and deliberate, and including opportunities to intentionally practice norms in dialogue supports the creation of a learning community in which teacher candidates can grapple with ethical dilemmas in order to learn care ethics.

Ethical dilemmas

In the context of having co-created norms and discussed the misconceptions of care described above, the class reads about care ethics in the chapter "Moral Education" by Nel Noddings (2002) and Anna Richert's (2012) book *What Should I Do?*. Dilemmas provide opportunities to reflect on the process of developing caring relationships with parents, children, and other teachers, as well as cultivating child-to-child relationships, which is the dyad taken up in the literature (Charney 2002; Pereira and Smith-Adcock 2011; Watson 2003; Weinstein et al. 2004). In my teacher education courses, candidates are asked to write, reflect on, and act out case stories that raise moral dilemmas. The complexity of caring becomes apparent as teacher candidates reflect on how they interpret and choose in a given situation rich in context and contingency. Teacher candidates' personal stories have addressed a multitude of scenarios, including the dilemmas of grading, balancing the needs of individuals with the whole class, and confronting societal norms and socialization around race, ethnicity, gender, and sexuality played out in the classroom.

Teaching occurs in the rushing river of moment-to-moment relational experience, and case stories allow teacher candidates to pause that river to reflect. The complexity of caring becomes readily apparent as teacher candidates improvise and reflect on how they interpret and choose in a given situation. In addition to discussing such stories, candidates can act out roles to engage in decision-making and consider multiple courses of action in light of their understandings of an ethic of care (Hamington 2010).

I briefly excerpt three examples of dilemma cases that my teacher candidates
address to provide a window into their learning. Prior to the presentation of
each case story to a class, I share the following introduction designed to orient
readers toward analyzing teaching with care ethics in ways that honor teachers'
efforts and model caring:

> The Teaching Cases were designed for use with teachers in order to practice
> applying knowledge and skills to potential real-life situations. These cases are
> hypothetical. They are condensed stories told by teacher candidates during
> their urban school placements over the last decade. The teachers in the cases
> are well-meaning novices. In these cases, they questioned how to translate the
> theory and research they were learning about into practice. Such challenges can
> surprise even the experienced veteran teachers among us, leading us question
> what other teachers would do, and why.
>
> In respect for all teachers, please be patient with the teachers in the stories.
> Given a lack of experience and necessary information, they make the very best
> choices they can and mess up to inspire us to think. The stories of these fictional
> teachers' misguided and well-meaning attempts give the reader an opportunity
> to put real life and messy and complicated classroom interactions on hold to
> have time to think together over how we can best respond to support children.

In the first example, teacher candidates explore their role with parents as well as
with children, a critical dimension of early childhood education. Research on
teacher preparation reveals the parent–teacher relationship in particular to be
sorely overlooked (Alameda-Lawson and Lawson 2012; Lee and Bowen 2006).
The case begins in a first-grade class with a teacher facilitating discussion while
parent-volunteers support small groups of children. The parents notice several
issues: one hears a child mimic an English Language Learner's accent, repeating
the way she lengthened the word *ship* until it sounded like *sheep,* and the child
who was mocked refrains from speaking for the rest of the session. Another
parent, who recently lost her job, witnesses her son's hand-me-down shirt being
called *gay.* Several parents notice children unengaged throughout the task. The
parents are concerned and raise these observations with the principal.

Teacher candidates consider the challenges of teaching children to relate and
collaborate with care. What sort of norms might be necessary in a first-grade
classroom? Here class members reflect back on their process of developing
norms and consider what that might entail for children. Teacher candidates
consider the role of parent engagement and their responsibility to involve
parents. For example, how much less likely might it be for children to make fun
of each other if the class knew all the families? What would it take to support

such community building in school? What factors might get in the way? How can teachers, let alone the children in their classes, understand these challenges without getting to know parents? Teacher candidates often respond by defending teachers against parents going behind their backs to the principal; we discuss a teacher's responsibility to cultivate a relationship in which parents would be comfortable addressing them directly. Teacher candidates also consider how to explain pedagogical choices around care (such as the time necessary to prepare children for group work in dialogue in caring ways) and empower parents and principals to support them.

In another case, cross-cultural relationship issues arise. In Carlos's story, a new third-grade child arrives from Mexico and is seated in the front of the class, near another Spanish speaker. The teacher attempts to learn about Carlos by speaking with his parents, but they don't know much English. Before the end of his first week, Carlos tries to read aloud in front of the whole class, and they laugh at his mistakes. Dialogue over Carlos's story opens reflection over specific ways to care for children. The case addresses the importance of acknowledging language divides, avoiding assumptions about Carlos's parents' interest in communicating, recognizing status in the classroom and how it might track with race and class, and the need to interrupt inequity by celebrating differences.

Teacher candidates ponder how to welcome and include diverse children, delving into how their personal racial, ethnic, and socioeconomic identities could play into their responses and how differences might shade the meaning(s) of caring actions. As one candidate put it, "When you're talking about one kid, all the seemingly small interactions, like who you call on and in what context, become important!" Candidates realize how critical it is to engage a translator to help facilitate a conversation in which they could "talk about the school community traditions, including ways for parents to get involved" and "to help uncover cultural disconnects." Candidates can recognize how authenticity plays a role in caring in that they need to act from a place of knowing their own positionality to cultivate relationships with "cultural brokers" in their children's community. As one candidate said, "I'm going to need to own that I'm a white guy and respectfully seek out the support of colleagues of color."

Teacher candidates see the need to design pedagogies for care. In one case discussion, several candidates decided to add to their classroom "jobs" a task they called the "welcoming ambassador": children would take turns supporting new class members. As ambassadors, they would design "cartoon graphics with dialogue bubbles to help English Language Learners access their classroom routines" and "tell stories of caring for one another in school." Pedagogies for care such as those described below become interesting to teacher candidates when they are confronted with real-life teaching challenges.

In this case, third-year teacher Tessa was no longer terrified to have her principal observe her because she finally made her classroom orderly with a new table point system. However, she noticed that the kids played in cliques, rolled their eyes when they were asked to work outside these groups in class, and put each other down. She introduced a "Kindness Box" and tasked children with writing notes of appreciation for the kindnesses they noticed throughout the day and place them in the box. When Tessa read the notes to the children at a morning meeting at the end of the first week, everyone noticed that only a few popular children were repeatedly appreciated. In the case, Tessa relies on disciplining the children in her class through a points system that leads them to compete to be quiet. This ends up encouraging competition while masking their underlying need to learn to care for one another.

The teacher candidates' dialogue over the Kindness Box brings to light the limits of merely telling children to care. The case explores the inclination to overlook the need to teach caring rather than just mandate caring through rules. As one candidate put it, "We can't achieve order at expense of the underlying relationship problems in our classroom." Another said, "I also find myself telling kids to 'be kind' or 'be nice.' Do they know what I mean by that?" The cases give teacher candidates the chance to discuss practical ways to teach children to care. They contrast the box practice with other practices, such as giving sentence frames for randomized appreciations. They deconstruct the practice of preset rules and how they lead to rewards or appreciation for *compliance* rather than authentic efforts of care. The class discusses the possibility of co-constructed rules or norms. Ultimately, the case shows how schooling can privilege competitiveness and individualism over generosity and kindness, which are more collectivistic characteristics. A candidate said, "We can model appreciating kids ourselves for being funny, for being different, for asking an interesting question, for slowing down to help explain to another kid."

Discussion of the Kindness Box case also affords the chance to problematize contextual factors, such as poverty, race, culture and ethnicity, gender, and other differences. I ask teacher candidates to "imagine that the praised children represent a dominant race in the classroom. Or high socio-economic status. What would you do then? Why?" This gives teacher candidates an opportunity to consider how to decenter Whiteness in the grand narrative as it plays out in schools through seemingly small moments like these.

In class, these cases can be drawn on for teacher candidates to act out scenarios and reflect on them in discussion to make visible the social and relational nature of teaching (Rabin 2008, 2009, 2010; Rabin and Smith 2013; Richert and Rabin 2013). Theatrical rehearsal of stories allows teacher candidates to reflect on their decisions in improvisations and to develop deeper learning experiences concerning the theoretical perspective of care ethics. Stories like these counteract some of the misconceptions about teaching an ethic of care by hinting at its complexity. Acting out the cases helps teachers overcome limiting preconceptions about, and understand ways to translate care theory into practice. They come to see the need for a foundation of caring relationships and how they cannot rely on formulized or predetermined responses but instead must develop artful authenticity in order to care. A teacher candidate described her learning through the case experience:

> We are not just teaching children rules of the classroom. We are teaching children how to relate to one another. Teachers can help children recognize the interrelatedness and interdependencies of people in communities. Our connectedness makes caring more meaningful to children and also helps children better understand the potential deep effect of their actions on others.

Ultimately, dramatizing stories to teach an ethic of care in teacher preparation begins to address the need for pedagogies that more closely approximate elements of practice (Grossman 2011). Once the cases raise the complexity of care ethics, teacher candidates see the need for designing pedagogies for teaching care in early childhood.

Teaching care ethics in the early childhood classroom

Early childhood teachers co-construct classroom norms for discussion and group work rather than predetermine rules, and they develop processes to teach their children to recognize, practice, and appreciate caring. Although all teaching interactions and experiences can be considered through the lens of a care ethic because teaching occurs in relationship, I have researched several interesting early childhood pedagogies designed explicitly with care ethics in mind and I describe two here.

Setting norms and intentions

Through a series of dialogues about cultivating caring classroom communities, teachers and children uncover, name, and deliberate over norms. Together they determine specific norms to practice caring. An example from one kindergarten class norm was, "We practice greeting a partner with a smile" (Rabin and Smith 2016). Rather than "rules" that assume we need to control children and suppress their negative inclinations by threatening punitive consequences, in care ethics co-constructed norms integrated into curriculum can help shift the paradigm toward teaching children to care.

At the beginning of the school year in an all-class meeting, the teacher asks the children to reflect on what kind of classroom they would look forward to coming to every day. A teacher asks children to ponder in particular how they want to feel when they think about coming to school in the morning or when they are reading or thinking about a math problem. In one second-grade classroom, children explained that they wanted to feel "happy," and their happiness was linked to being "liked" and "included." Next, the teacher asks, "What sort of actions can we take to feel this way in our classroom?" The children consider what actions are necessary to create inclusion. It is critical to note that children seem to lack a sense of their own active role in creating their environment. This is unsurprising given the likelihood that they have experienced classrooms organized by external rules and individualistic pedagogies. Based on this reflection, the children develop a class set of norms.

In an early elementary classroom, for the norms to do more than decorate the wall and to increase awareness of the connection between actions and their effects on others, children focus on one norm per week and develop an intention to take an action related to that norm. For example, in one first-grade classroom, when focusing on the norm "be a kind friend," one child intended "to accept anyone as a partner with a smile and without rolling my eyes." This process opens up opportunities for children to interpret what caring might mean in action.

Over the school year, the children complete a weekly reflective questionnaire describing an intention for the week that would contribute to classroom norms. This reflection can include reflective questions over caring; for example, one prompt was to "describe a possible scenario in which you do what you intend." Early elementary children can draw their scenario, create a storyboard, and act out their stories of caring as charades. Plans can be written as experience stories, lists, theatricals, journal entries, or essays recorded for the class to read together. With awareness of each other's intentions, children consider how they can support one another. Support can also derive from larger school and community involvement. For example, one class of third graders drafted an all-class letter to their parents and paired their classroom norms with home-related norms. One child recommended reminding the class about their intentions before break times and asking them what happened afterward. Integration with curriculum over time fosters opportunity for authenticity, modeling, practice, dialogue, and confirmation.

Rocks-in-the-basket

While the norms are co-constructed as a group, "Rocks-in-the-basket" (RITB) is a pedagogy designed to cultivate caring that is explicitly open to the children's spontaneous idiosyncratic experience in the classroom (Rabin 2014). At any time of the day and to acknowledge any act they deem "caring," children place a rock in a basket. They share a very short experience story with the class and draw and/or write in a journal kept in the basket. Each classroom contains a basket or container on a tray with about 100 rocks located in a central place. For example, in a first-grade classroom the basket and rocks sat by the rug where the class congregated for story time. Children gather rocks from local parks or bring them in from home. The following are examples of why children put rocks in the basket in a qualitative case study I conducted (Rabin 2014):

- I didn't want to play what everyone else was playing. Half the time I played what I wanted and the other half of lunch I played what everyone else wanted to play. No one seemed to feel upset, and there wasn't a big drama. I was a more caring friend than I felt like being 'cause I thought about the others.
- She was happy about her math problem. It was hard for me and easy for her. But I saw she didn't burst out and say how easy it was. That happened to me. That could have hurt, but I think she thought about it and didn't say it but kept with me while I worked.

Rocks go in the basket for very specific, grounded experiences. In addition to a pedagogy that opens opportunities for authenticity, modeling, practice, dialogue, and confirmation, RITB centers on stories of caring. Cases of caring are culled from the children's experiences (as in the short experience stories above describing compromising to play others' games and refraining from gloating over solving the math problem).

In my research I found that this recurring, collaborative, child-centered experience supports learning to care in several ways. RITB opened opportunities for *authentic* modeling, practice, dialogue, and confirmation. Rather than act out predefined rules for care, the authentic, spontaneous, open-ended structure of this practice encouraged children to think about how to care. For example, they came up with compromises during games to include one another and invited others to join games by modifying rules for different abilities. With RITB, the children themselves served as ethical models for their peers when they explained through dialogue their stories of why they put rocks in the basket; the children learn from each other's dialogue over their stories of experiences of care. Opportunities for confirmation arose. With RITB, children themselves modeled and discussed caring, and moral actions were centered in the children's experiences as narratives within reach, and therefore possible to learn from.

Given care's complexity and the ways it is often misunderstood (as described above), I have argued the importance of narrative methods to teach about care (Rabin 2008, 2009, 2010, 2011; Rabin and Smith 2013; Richert and Rabin 2013). Narrative has been long appreciated as a methodology through which we all make sense of the world (Haven 2007; Pinker 2000; Polkinghorne 1988). Stories reveal the contours of a care ethic.

Conclusion

Unearthing preconceptions of care, comparing care ethics to popular traditional approaches, raising case story dilemmas over relationships in schooling situations, and pondering pedagogies designed to cultivate a care ethic all illuminate care ethics in practice. Reflective dialogue and dramatization of narratives designed to unearth preconceptions of care supports preparation of teachers who can translate the theory of care ethics into practice in early childhood education. Practices such as Rocks-in-the-basket and co-constructed norms draw on authentic narratives of care in practice and leverage experience as the medium for learning to care. hooks (1994) reminds us of the promise of this endeavor:

> To teach in a manner that respects and cares for the souls of our students is essential if we are to provide the necessary conditions where learning can most deeply and intimately begin. (13)

References

Beauboeuf-LaFontant, T. (1999), "A Movement against and beyond Boundaries: 'Politically Relevant Teaching' among African American Teachers," *Teachers College Record*, 100 (4): 702–723.

Beauboeuf-LaFontant, T. (2002), "A Womanist Experience of Caring: Understanding the Pedagogy of Exemplary Black Women Teachers," *Urban Review*, 34 (1): 71–86.

Beauboeuf-LaFontant, T. (2005), "Womanist Lessons for Reinventing Teaching," *Journal of Teacher Education*, 56 (5): 436–445.

Bowlby, J. (1969/1982), *Attachment and Loss: Vol. 1*, 2nd edn, New York: Basic Books.

Charney, R. S. (2002), *Teaching Children to Care: Classroom Management for Ethical and Academic Growth, K–8*, Turners Fall, MA: Northeast Foundation for Children.

Delpit, L. (2006), *Other Peoples' Children: Cultural Conflict in the Classroom*, New York: The New Press.

DeStigter, T. (2001), "Affective Thought, Personalized Democracy, and the Council's Multicultural Mission," *English Education*, 33: 290–315.

Dewey, J. (1933), *How We Think: A Restatement of the Relation of Reflective Thinking to the Educative Process*, revised edn, Boston, MA: D. C. Heath.

Dewey, J. (1938), *Experience and Education*, New York: Collier Books.

Foucault, M. (1988), "The Political Technology of Individuals," in L. H. Martin, H. Gutman, and P. H. Hutton (eds), *Technologies of the Self: A Seminar with Michel Foucault*, 145–162, Amerst: University of Massachusetts Press.

Gholami, K. and K. Tirri (2012), "Caring Teaching as a Moral Practice: An Exploratory Study on Perceived Dimensions of Caring Teaching," *Education Research International*, 2012: 1–8.

Gilbert, E. (2009), "Elizabeth Gilbert on Nurturing Creativity," Retrieved from Ted Talks Website: http://www.ted.com/talks/elizabeth_gilbert_on_genius.html.

Gilligan, C. (1982), *In a Different Voice*, Cambridge, MA: Harvard University Press.

Goldstein, L. and V. E. Lake (2000), "'Love, Love, and More Love for Children': Exploring Preservice Teachers' Understandings of Caring," *Teaching and Teacher Education*, 16: 861–872.

Grossman, P. (2011), "A Framework for Teaching Practice: A Brief History of an Idea," *Teachers College Record*, 113 (12): 2836–2843.

Hambacher, E. and E. Bondy (2016), "Creating Communities of Culturally Relevant Critical Teacher Care," *Action in Teacher Education*, 38 (4): 327–343.

Hamington, M. (2010), "Care Ethics, John Dewey's 'Dramatic Rehearsal,' and Moral Education," *Philosophy of Education Yearbook*, 121–128.

Hargreaves, A. (2000), "Mixed Emotions: Teachers' Perceptions of Their Interactions with Students," *Teaching and Teacher Education*, 16 (8): 811–826.

Haven, K. (2007), *Story Proof: The Science behind the Startling Power of Story*, Westport, CT: Libraries Unlimited.

Hoffman, D. M. (2009), "Reflecting on Social Emotional Learning: A Critical Perspective on Trends in the United States," *Review of Educational Research*, 79: 533–556.

hooks, bell (1994), *Teaching to Transgress: Education as the Practice of Freedom*, New York: Routledge.

Isenbarger, L. and M. Zembylas (2006), "The Emotional Labour of Caring in Teaching," *Teaching and Teacher Education*, 22: 120–134.

Knight, M. G. (2004), "Sensing the Urgency: Envisioning a Black Humanist Vision of Care in Teacher Education," *Race, Ethnicity, and Education*, 7 (3): 211–227.

Kohn, A. (December, 1994), *The Risk of Rewards*, Urbana, IL: ERIC Clearinghouses on Elementary and Early Childhood Education.

Kohn, A. (1996), *Beyond Discipline: From Compliance to Community*, Upper Saddle River, NJ: Prentice Hall.

Kohn, A. (1999a), "From Degrading to De-Grading," *High School Magazine*, March, http://www.alfiekohn.org/article/degrading-de-grading/.

Kohn, A. (1999b), *Punished by Rewards*, New York: Mariner.

Krazny, M. (January 8, 2013), "KQED Forum: Teaching Social and Emotional Learning," Retrieved from March 30, 2013, http://blogs.kqed.org/americangraduate/2013/01/18/kqedforum-teaching-social-and-emotional-learning/.

Lawson, M. A., and T. Alameda-Lawson (2012), "A Case Study of School-Linked, Collective Parent Engagement," *American Educational Research Journal*, 49: 651–684.

Lee, J. and N. K. Bowen (2006), "Parent Involvement, Cultural Capital, and the Achievement Gap among Elementary School Children," *American Educational Research Journal*, 43 (2): 193–218.

Mikulincer, M., P. R. Shaver, O. Gillath, and R. A. Nitzberg (2005), "Attachment, Caregiving, and Altruism: Boosting Attachment Security Increases Compassion and Helping," *Journal of Personality and Social Psychology*, 89 (5): 817–839.

Nelson, C. and V. Harper (2006), "A Pedagogy of Difficulty: Preparing Teachers to Understand and Integrate Complexity in Teaching and Learning," *Teacher Education Quarterly*, 33 (2): 7–21.

Nias, J. (1999), "Primary Teaching as a Culture of Care," in J. Prosser (ed), *School Culture*, 66–82, London: Paul Chapman.

Nieto, S. (1999), *The Light in Their Eyes: Creating Multicultural Learning Communities*, New York: Teachers College Press.

Noblit, G. (1993), "Power and Caring," *American Educational Research Journal*, 30 (1): 23–38.

Noddings, N. (1984), *Caring: A Feminine Approach to Ethics and Moral Education*, Berkeley: University of California Press.

Noddings, N. (1992), *The Challenge to Care in Schools*, New York: Teachers College Press.

Noddings, N. (2002), *Educating Moral People: A Caring Alternative to Character Education*, New York: Teachers College Press.

Noddings, N. (2012), "The Caring Relation in Teaching," *Oxford Review of Education*, 38 (6): 771–781.

Pang, V. O. (2005), *Multicultural Education: A Caring-Centered Approach*, 2nd edn, Boston, MA: McGraw Hill.

Pereira, J. K. and S. Smith-Adcock (2011), "Child Centered Classroom Management," *Action in Teacher Education*, 33 (3): 254–264.

Pinker, S. (2000), *The Language Instinct*, New York: Perennial Classic.

Plato (n.d.), *The Republic*, New York: The Co-operative Publication Society.

Polkinghorne, D. E. (1988), *Narrative Knowing and the Human Sciences*, Albany: State University of New York Press.

Rabin, C. (2008), "Constructing an Ethic of Care in Teacher Education: Exploring Pedagogical Practices as Opportunities to Construct a Caring Stance," *The Constructivist*, 19, Retrieved from August 17, 2008 www.odu.edu/educ/act/journal/index.html.

Rabin, C. (2009), "The Theatre Arts and Care Ethics," *Youth Theatre Journal*, 23 (2): 127–143.

Rabin, C. (2010), "The Challenge to Prepare Teachers to Care in the Current Context: Perspectives of Teachers of Color," *Teacher Education and Practice*, 23 (3): 164–176.

Rabin, C. (2011), "Learning to Care during Story-Time in the Current Context: Moral Education from the Perspective of Care Ethics," *Journal of Research in Childhood Education*, 25 (1): 45–61.

Rabin, C. (2013), "Care through Authenticity: Teacher Preparation for an Ethic of Care in an Age of Accountability," *The Educational Forum*, 77 (3): 242–255.

Rabin, C. (2014), "Don't Throw the Rocks: Cultivating Care with a Pedagogy Called Rocks-in-the-Basket," *Journal of Research in Childhood Education*, 28 (2): 145–161.

Rabin, C. and G. Smith (2013), "Teaching Care Ethics: Conceptual Understandings and Stories for Learning," *Journal of Moral Education*, 42 (2): 164–176.

Rabin, C. and G. Smith (2016), "'My Lesson Plan Was Perfect until I Tried to Teach': Care Ethics into Practice in Classroom Management," *Journal of Research in Childhood Education*, 30 (4): 600–617.

Richert, A. (2012), *What Should I Do? Confronting the Dilemmas of Teaching in Urban Schools*, New York: Teachers College Press.

Richert, A. and C. Rabin (2013), "Preparing Teachers for Teaching Dilemmas Raised by Race and Racism: One Case Example of Teacher Education for Social Justice," in Miriam Ben-Peretz Rowman (eds), *Embracing the Social and the Creative: New Scenarios for Teacher Education*, Lanham, MD: Rowman & Littlefield.

Rosiek, J. (1994), "Caring, Classroom Management, and Teacher Education: The Need for Case Study and Narrative Methods," *Teaching Education*, 6 (1): 21–30.

Sanger, M. N. and R. D. Osguthorpe (2011), "Teacher Education, Preservice Teacher Beliefs, and the Moral Work of Teaching," *Teaching and Teacher Education*, 27 (3): 569–578.

Siddle-Walker, V. (1993), "Interpersonal Caring in the 'Good' Segregated Schooling of African American Children: Evidence from the Case of Caswell County Training School," *Urban Review*, 25 (1): 63–77.

Spokes, A. C. and E. Spelke (2017), "The Cradle of Social Knowledge: Infants' Reasoning about Caregiving and Affiliation," *Cognition*, 159: 102–116.

Thompson, A. (1998), "Not the Color Purple: Black Feminist Lessons for Educational Caring," *Harvard Educational Review*, 68 (4): 522–546.

Tobin, J. (1995), "The Irony of Self-Expression," *American Journal of Education*, 103 (3): 233–238.

Watson, M. (2003), *Learning to Trust*, San Francisco, CA: Jossey-Bass.

Weinstein, C., S. Tomlinson-Clarke, and M. Curran (2004), "Toward a Conception of Culturally Responsive Classroom Management," *Journal of Teacher Education*, 55 (1): 25–38.

White, B. (2003), "Caring and the Teaching of English," *Research in the Teaching of English*, 37 (3): 295–328.

Wilder, M. (1999), "Culture, Race, and Schooling: Toward a Non-Colorblind Ethic of Care," *The Educational Forum*, 63 (4): 356–362.

Young, L. (1998), "Care, Community, and Context in a Teacher Education Classroom," *Theory into Practice*, 37 (2): 105–113.

7

Ripples: The Absence and Presence of Care amid Social Injustice in the Elementary Classroom

Maria Karmiris

The purpose of this chapter is to present feminist care ethics, critical disability studies, and Black feminist thought in a dialogue about the limits, fragility, and tenuous nature of care as teachers and students encounter one another in the public education classroom. There are three significant contributions I hope to make in this chapter. First, I want to consider the simultaneous absence and presence of care between teachers and students amid the power imbalances that continue to disproportionally impact disabled, Black, and poor members of school communities. Of particular interest here will be a consideration of how care connects to some bodies more than it does to others, and how those subsequent attachments justify turning away from those marked with differences (Ahmed 2004, 2012). Second, I want to consider how care requires both the sustenance and unraveling of a self deeply complicit in institutional injustices by considering the ways Western epistemologies such as feminist care ethics continue to be embedded in a framework that sustains social injustice in our schools. Third, I intend to show how adopting an interdisciplinary–intersectional approach might contribute to a reconfiguration of feminist care ethics in ways that might guide our teaching and learning relationships in turning toward one another rather than turning away.

Throughout this chapter, I will reference the work of feminist care ethics scholars and critical disability studies scholars, as well as scholars of Black feminist thought. In addition to relying on the work of these scholars to both analyze and question the rhetoric of care that impacts teaching and learning in elementary classrooms, I draw inspiration from the picture book *Each Kindness* (Woodson 2012) as well as some of my experiences of teaching in Canadian elementary schools since 2002. Thus, my intention in this chapter is to explore the ways that teaching and learning require attending to how practices of care continue to implicate both teachers and students, in a simultaneous turning away from and toward difference in ways that intensify the ethical conundrums encountered in the middle of caring.

The dilemma of care: Turning toward and away from kindness

"Each kindness—done and not done. Like every girl somewhere—holding a small gift out to someone and that someone turning away from it" (Woodson 2012). In this quote from a picture book entitled *Each Kindness,* well-known children's author Jacqueline Woodson evokes the metaphor of ripples in a pond (Woodson 2012). In a turning point Chloe, the story's main character, drops stones into a pond and considers the events of the last several months of school where she repeatedly turned away from, avoided, and ignored the new girl Maya who had joined the class (Woodson 2012). Throughout the story, Chloe must choose to continue to belong to her group of friends who ridicule Maya for her appearance because her clothes seem already worn and never seem to quite fit right (Woodson 2012). Maya is depicted as reaching out toward her classmates as her classmates repeatedly turn away; continually leaving Maya isolated and alone (Woodson 2012). Chloe is clearly troubled by the apparent either/or decision framed within desiring to sustain her own social inclusion rather than risking social exclusion by turning toward Maya and the potential gift of a new friendship (Woodson 2012). One day during class, Chloe's teacher encourages the students to think about their small acts of kindness as reverberating in the lives of others by having each student drop a pebble in a pail of water (Woodson 2012). Haunted by her own exclusions of Maya, Chloe refuses to drop a pebble into the water. Ultimately, Maya moves away, and Chloe remains haunted by her, caring about inclusion in ways that constrain her ability to care for and with others.

Woodson's story, which foregrounds both the presence and absence of care, leaves its mark in the way it emphasizes both the ubiquity and seemingly unresolvable nature of Chloe's and Maya's dilemma. Teaching and learning in the elementary classroom entails confronting numerous instances where students and teachers are in the middle of Chloe's and Maya's conundrum: turning toward and away from others when the possibilities for inclusion remain conditional, limited, and constrained by a version of care structured to preserve exclusions. Who, when, where, what, and how each of us engages in caring about, with, and for one another invariably leads to a consideration of how caring is shaped and shapes the power imbalances that generate an uneven distribution of care and inclusion (Ahmed 2004, 2012). In Woodson's story, the power imbalance that marks Maya as someone to be excluded foregrounds the import of class in the Othering of a subject that is both close enough to be noticed for her difference and yet kept far enough away that her difference both shapes and refuses to shape the contours of care encountered in this classroom. Chloe is troubled by Maya's presence because Maya's presence requires her to confront the limits and constraints of who, when, where, and how she cares for and with others.

This story does not just merely depict the challenges children encounter when trying to care amid one another; I would also contend that Woodson's story metaphorically represents the limits of care as they are encountered by teachers, administrators, and indeed in the articulation of educational policies and practices. For example, in the elementary classroom, the power imbalances foregrounded in Woodson's story are evident in tactics of conditional inclusion through which teachers are complicit in assessment and evaluation practices that determine who and to what degree students belong to the category of "normal" as outlined in standardized curriculum (Baker 2002: 663–703, 2015: 168–197; Slee 2008: 99–116, 2013: 895–907). At the level of district school boards such as the one in Toronto, Ontario, care is implicated in the ways students and teachers find themselves among intersecting vectors of race, gender, class, and disability that disproportionately mark some bodies with more difference than others, as well as in the ways that geography impacts the distribution of material and social resources (Brown and Parekh 2013). An oft-cited pattern in the data collected in several Canadian school boards, including the Toronto District School Board, reflects ongoing injustices that impact disabled, Black, and poor students in ways that continue to preserve hierarchies of marginalization and exclusion (Annamma et al. 2013: 1–31; Brown and Parekh 2013; Collins et al. 2016: 4–16; Connor 2008; Erevelles and Minear 2010: 127–145). Thus, the story of the absence and presence of care represented in both Chloe's and Maya's dilemmas remains representative of the way care manifests itself in the small moments of daily classroom life. Maya and Chloe's story of confronting the conditional nature of care and inclusion is emblematic of and implicated in larger sociocultural practices. The injustices embedded in sociocultural practices are mirrored in educational policies and practices.

The matter of how care is defined, distributed, and encountered is a matter that directly impacts teaching and learning relationships in every elementary classroom, including the numerous classes I have taught since the formal beginning of my teaching career in 2002: the boy in my first year of teaching who kept his head down and cried as he told me he wanted to kill himself; "Parvana" and "Onika" [pseuds.] who had smiles for everyone, yet almost always played alone at recess because their classmates read them (and knew the teachers also read them) as different from "normal"; "Yousuf" [pseud.] who was diagnosed with a visual impairment yet refused to use his CCTV. "I don't want the kids to know I am different," he would say.

The small sampling of provocations listed here have embedded and enmeshed themselves in my teaching and learning experiences. Like Chloe, I remain haunted by my failings, my complicities, and the indelible impressions countless children have left on my understanding of the limits, risks, and inadequacies of care. The notion that if we all could only figure out a way to be more caring and/or care differently that the world would be a better and more socially just place for all remains both alluring and elusive. Eminent scholars in the ongoing debates related to defining care remark on the challenges of agreeing on any firm definition of the term (Held 2004: 141–155, 2010: 115–129; Kittay 2009: 606–627; Kittay and Carlson 2010; Kittay et al. 2005: 443–469; Robinson 2006: 5–25; Robinson 2011: 845–860).

The three central tenets that are generally evoked in feminist care ethics include valuing care as a public good that can potentially mitigate and diminish social injustice, care as embedded in all forms of social relations where human subjects are considered vulnerable and dependent upon one another, and the relationship of care with the ever-vexing problem of inequality and the power imbalances that sustain hierarchies of exclusion and marginalization (Held 2004: 141–155, 2010: 115–129; Kittay 2009: 606–627; Kittay and Carlson 2010; Kittay et al. 2005: 443–469; Robinson 2006: 5–25; Robinson 2011: 845–860). Within both formal and informal educational policies and practices, the notions of care so much espoused in feminist care ethics are present throughout schools and classrooms.

Despite the ubiquity of the rhetoric of care in public education, care not only remains elusive for many, but contributes to the barriers that sustain policies of conditional inclusion and the ever-present risk of exclusion. Disability scholars have been pointing to the way the rhetoric of care continues to sustain mechanisms of exclusion for students marked with disability and how race and class continue to disproportionally impact the labeling of disability (Baker 2002,

2015; Erevelles and Minear 2010; Parekh and Underwood 2015; Rogers 2016; Rogers and Weller 2012). The way that care remains conditional is also evident in Woodson's story. Maya and Chloe (as representative of countless other children) drift in and out of possible encounters with care largely due to the risks of belonging (Woodson 2012). Care, while ostensibly present and simultaneously absent in the public space of the elementary classroom, shapes relationships in ways that foreground the partialities and limits of becoming human with and amid other humans.

Who, when, where, and to what degree and how a student is conditionally included/excluded remains bounded by sociocultural norms that implicate the limits of how care manifests itself amid teaching and learning practices. Disability studies scholars who apply the methodological and analytical tools of a variety of scholarly disciplines have expressed significant concerns with the ways policies and practices in elementary public schools sustain exclusions that disproportionately impact those who find themselves at the intersection of race, gender, class, and/or disability (Annamma et al. 2013; Baker 2002: 663–703, 2015; Connor 2008; Erevelles and Minear 2010; Slee 2008, 2013).

For example, in a scholarly field termed DisCrit, Annamma and colleagues apply critical race theory to disability studies to analyze "the role of the liberal, White middle class in maintaining structures and practices of privilege within education" (Annamma et al. 2013: 7). Elsewhere, Collins and colleagues analyze the ongoing rationalizations of assessment and evaluation practices that sustain the labeling and segregation of disabled students into special education (Collins et al. 2016). "DisCrit recognizes the shifting boundary between normal and abnormal, between ability and disability and seeks to question ways in which race contributes to one being positioned on either side of the line" (Annamma et al. 2013: 10). Significant here in both the analysis and questioning of education policies and practices is how the rhetoric of spatial inclusion that is ubiquitous in current policy documents has done little to substantively transform or shift how students marked as different encounter the process of teaching and learning (Annamma et al. 2013; Baker 2002, 2015; Connor 2008; Erevelles and Minear 2010; Slee 2008, 2013). Though distinct from the work of Annamma and colleagues and Collins and colleagues, Rogers offers her own contribution to demonstrating how disability, education, care, and inclusion intersect. When analyzing how intellectually disabled people encounter care, Rogers also considers who and under what conditions humans count as human (Collins et al. 2016; Rogers 2016; Rogers and Weller 2012).

While the work of DisCrit scholars, such as Annamma and colleagues and Collins and colleagues, justifiably foreground how assessment and evaluation practices in schools disproportionately impact immigrant and racialized communities, Rogers seeks a demonstrable transformation in curriculum goals (Collins et al. 2016; Rogers 2016; Rogers and Weller 2012). In an effort to make the case for the inclusion of varying embodiments of difference, such as "a girl that dribbles so much that she wears a rolled-up hanky in her mouth or a boy who bangs his head with his hand when distressed," Rogers suggests that constraining and limiting educational curricular goals are overdetermined by concerns of the neoliberal economy (Rogers 2016: 5). "Simply to say education is the pathway to employment is not nearly nuanced enough and certainly not caring or ethical" (Rogers 2016: 59). Significantly here, Rogers's work applies care ethics and disability studies in a way that foregrounds the limits of current educational policies and practices that continue to engage in the labeling and categorizing humans as economic producers and consumers. Thus, the way we come to care with and for one another in educational settings remains constrained by who counts as human and how that accounting is enmeshed in preserving the hegemony of White, liberal, middle-class sociocultural and economic norms. These constraints continue to leave their mark on those labeled with disabilities that point to the limits of care amid encounters with teaching and learning for both students and teachers.

To be in the world is to both mark and be marked by the world in ways that implicate how we all care with, for, and about one another. Chloe refuses to drop a stone into the pail of water her teacher is using to represent the power kind acts can have in her life and in the lives of others. Chloe refuses Maya's overtures of friendship. Chloe repeatedly turns away. Maya moves away. Seemingly untouched by one another, the refusal of care leaves its own mark. The impressions of care's absence, paradoxically, intensify the desire for care's presence. As a teacher, I remain haunted by both the absence and presence of care amid the hundreds of students I have encountered over the years of teaching and learning. I still wonder what happened to the boy and his refrain of self-harm. I wonder what happened to both Parvana and Onika. I wonder too if Yousuf ever embraced his difference instead of trying to fit in with all his classmates. In keeping with Rogers's articulations of "care 'ful' and care 'less' relations" (Rogers 2016: 6), I regret, too, that in moments when care has seemed the most necessary, that somehow it has also appeared to fail in ways that leave me persistently wishing that if I had said or done something/anything differently, maybe just maybe care would have made more of a difference.

Within the context of teaching and learning, there is an apparently hopeless hope about care that is encountered as both alluring and elusive. While foregrounding the alluring possibilities of care, scholars of feminist care ethics often represent care as a solution to the dilemmas of social injustice (Held 2004, 2010; Parekh and Underwood 2015; Robinson 2006, 2011; Rogers 2016; Rogers and Weller 2012). According to Held, "With better and more extensive practices of care, the needs for law and the enforcement mechanisms of the state could shrink. With better care in childhood and adolescence, fewer persons would turn to crime" (Held 2004: 147). Elsewhere, Robinson states that "care and caring are undervalued and under-resourced globally and this contributes significantly to gender, racial and North-South inequality" (Robinson 2006: 8). Robinson and Held suggest here that it is the absence and/or diminishment of care within the public sphere that leads to the harshness and cruelty encountered by those who continue to experience marginalization and exclusion (Held 2004; Robinson 2006).

This premise is distinct from what I intend to convey in this chapter. Through a dependence on the work of disability studies scholars, feminist scholars, and my own teaching and learning experiences, it is my contention that it is indeed care's presence that limits, confines, and embeds our social interactions within the complicities of injustice. A "self" among many selves, that is steeped in the constraints of the domineering logics of Western epistemologies that shape lived encounters with difference, remains oriented toward preserving the boundaries of belonging that sustain regimes of marginalization and conditional inclusion. Thus care, and the ways in which teachers and students turn toward and away from one another while invoking care, comes to be inescapably enmeshed in the ethical dilemmas of social injustice between you and I and us.

At the end of *Each Kindness*, Woodson leaves her readers wondering about what happened to Chloe and Maya. How did the absence and presence of care, in their particular encounter, both shape and refuse to shape their efforts to sustain, inhabit, and generate caring relations with others? To what extent was either of these characters, able to learn from and/or heal from the failure of care, to care enough and/or too much? When care encounters injustice at the intersections of race, gender, class, and or disability, it remains mired in the uncertainties that are entailed in unbalanced relations of power.

Robinson contends that "from the perspective of care ethics, the goal is not simple 'inclusion' of the previously excluded into a system, community or dialogue that may in fact lead to further isolation. Rather, moral recognition and responsibility require a long-term commitment to listening to those who are excluded, marginalized or exploited" (Robinson 2011: 853). Along with Robinson, Hankivsky suggests the need for feminist care ethics to consider how other perspectives and impressions might support the reconfiguration/reorientation of care amid the ongoing injustices that pervade our social relations (Hankivsky 2014: 252–264; Robinson 2011). Hankivsky goes further to contend that "care ethics is not an inherently intersectional perspective" and encourages scholars to adopt a more intersectional approach in order to more critically consider the role of care amid injustice (Hankivsky 2014: 252). In an effort to respond to the provocation posed by Hankivsky and Robinson, the next section of this chapter will consider the ways that scholars of Black feminist thought work within and against feminist care ethics scholars and disability studies scholars to simultaneously sustain and unravel a version of the subjective self that confronts care's complicities in injustice.

The limits of care and belonging as an everyday practice embedded in the enactment of Western epistemologies

My best friends that year were Kendra and Sophie. At lunchtime, we walked around the school yard, our fingers laced together, whispering secrets into each other's ears .... The weeks passed. Every day, we whispered about Maya, laughing at her clothes, her shoes, the strange food she brought for lunch. Whenever she asked us to play, we said no. (Woodson 2012)

In *Each Kindness*, what is evident is that Chloe cares in a way that can be identified as ordinary and commonplace within the everyday events of contemporary public schools. She cares about her friends and about sustaining her relationship with those friends, inevitably turning toward them. Chloe and her friends care about Maya, too. They care enough to notice her difference. They care enough to preserve the line dividing them from Maya. Maya cares, too. Despite the numerous occasions when her classmates turn away from her, she keeps trying to reach out. Care here is involved in the process of both creating and disrupting enclosures of human relations in ways that foreground how the seemingly small moments are mired in the larger sociocultural mechanisms of injustice. Both Chloe and Maya care, yet, the evident power imbalance between them sustains the conditions of marginalization and exclusion encountered by countless students in elementary classrooms.

Anzaldúa reminds us that the "us/them dichotomy" and indeed "the process of marginalizing others has roots in colonialism" (Anzaldúa et al. 2003: 10–14). Spelman outlines a concept she calls the "economies of attention" and how the domineering logics of colonialism shape the ways we all relate to one another to sustain the hegemony of the liberal subject (Spelman 1997: 5–10). In her analysis of American race relations, Spelman offers a critique of empathy and considers how the "paradigm out of which the understanding of 'I am You' was shaped historically are ones of domination and imposition" (Spelman 1997: 130). Spelman's evidence for pointing toward the limits of empathy and indeed the fact that it has little to no effect on systemic inequality can be found in her analysis of the ways dominant White culture engages in the appropriation of the pain of others, specifically in the foregrounding of guilt over the ways American society has been rooted/routed through slavery (Spelman 1997: 125–132). She states: "Feeling for others in their suffering can simply be a way of asserting authority over them to have a view about what their suffering means, what the most appropriate response to it is" (Spelman 1997: 70). What is significant in Spelman's analysis of how emotions like empathy are deeply embedded in unbalanced power relations and ongoing injustices is the way in which care's declared presence is simultaneously complicit in its continued absence (Spelman 1997: 70). Care in its focus on difference remains constrained in its ability to make a difference.

Chloe is constrained by the care she experiences in her friendships. Even as she recognizes the possibility for a new friendship with Maya, she engages in laughing and whispering with her best friends (Woodson 2012). She chooses her own inclusion amid her friends while participating in the exclusion of another. Chloe cares in ways that leave her in the middle of complicity. Chloe's encounter with difference reverberates because of its ordinariness. In her story, I recognize my own as a teacher who cares about students but is simultaneously tethered to policies and procedures that sustain hierarchies of conditional inclusion and/or outright exclusion. I remain haunted by the countless ripples that have moved out and away in my own pond but continue to reverberate in my teaching and learning journey.

In an analysis and conceptualization of what they term "epistemological racism," Scheurich and Young (1997: 4–5) contend that current teaching, learning, and researching methodologies are racially biased. Citing the dominating and domineering presence of modern Western civilization, Scheurich and Young state: "All of the epistemologies currently legitimated in education arise exclusively out of the social history of the dominant White race" (1997: 8). Civilizational racism from which epistemological racism is both rooted and routed reverberates in social, institutional, and individual forms of biases (Scheurich and Young 1997: 8). Though the analysis and contention of the embedded nature of epistemological racism offered by Scheurich and Young is twenty years old, it remains remarkably relevant and salient in the contemporary moment for two reasons. First, they point to data in 1997 that demonstrated a "higher percentage of students of colour are currently more likely to be 'at risk,' 'learning disabled,' or 'emotionally disturbed'" (Scheurich and Young 1997: 6). Twenty years later, and as mentioned earlier in this chapter, race, gender, and class are factors that continue to disproportionately impact processes of identifying and labeling disability in our public schools (Annamma et al. 2013; Brown and Parekh 2013; Collins et al. 2016; Connor 2008). Second, in pointing to the depth and breadth of the ways all are implicated in sociocultural, institutional, and civilizational levels of racism, Scheurich and Young (1997) inevitably implicate feminist ethics of care as well as policies and practices in elementary education as part of the epistemological branches that sustain the unjust edifice of modern Western civilization.

Like the ripples in the water that leave Chloe haunted by her choices to exclude another (Woodson 2012), the work of Scheurich and Young serve as a reminder that caring relations are embedded and indeed complicit in unjust Western-centered civilizational framework (Scheurich and Young 1997). Chloe laces her hands with those of her friends as she repeatedly turns away from another. To acknowledge and confront how social relations and thus the relations through which we all come to care with, for, and about one another are enmeshed in ways of knowing and sensing the world that perpetuate and sustain injustice and marginalization is also to question the subjective self from a posture of both humility and complicity. Scheurich and Young, Spelman as well as Woodson, serve to shake us as both scholars and educators out of complacency and/or certainty that care in social relations can make things better without the necessary considerations of the ways in which care remains constrained by its exclusions (Scheurich and Young 1997; Spelman 1997; Woodson 2012).

Within the setting of the elementary classroom, educators must ask themselves how caring is implicated in the simultaneous inclusion of some while others encounter care in the classroom as conditional and precarious. Although we all remain embedded in a Western onto-epistemological framework that perpetuates social injustice, by adopting an intersectional approach, feminist care ethics might contribute to a reconfiguration of elementary school policies and practices by both acknowledging and confronting the ways caring relations remain mired in injustice. The next section of this chapter intends to consider some methodological tools from feminist scholars, including those who inhabit the intersection of disability studies as well as Black feminist thought, in ways that might support scholars of feminist care ethics in re-imagining caring relations with one another both in and out of the classroom.

Confronting a commitment to care amid complicity in social injustice

Rather than offering care as a solution to the problems encountered in our elementary classrooms, Woodson's story *Each Kindness* exemplifies the ways that care is in the middle of and mired in the problem of unjust social relations. Chloe's choice to exclude Maya is entangled in her desire to care with and about lacing her hands with those of her best friends. Caring about inclusion simultaneously generates exclusions in ways that leave us all complicit in social injustice. Instead of turning away from our complicit relationship with social injustice, I contend that feminist care ethics would benefit from confronting the inequities embedded in our caring relations. For example, Probyn-Rapsey considers the ways in which complicity (as distinct from guilt) can work to decenter the liberal subject so as to open distinctly different possibilities amid efforts to care through social relations as well as to persist in the theorization and application of critical researching–teaching–learning methodologies (Probyn-Rapsey 2007: 65–82). Within her own context and research interests of relations among the Australian colonizer, Indigenous peoples, and immigrants, Probyn-Rapsey states that "complicity is a structural relationship that cannot be expiated fully because it exists in multiple networked forms" (Probyn-Rapsey 2007: 68). She goes on to consider the ways that unbalanced power relations effect the degree and implications of complicity amid the vectors of gender, race, and class (Probyn-Rapsey 2007: 68). The intent of complicity is a refusal to turn away so that "the feeling of not being able to move because of the ramifications of always treading heavily in the problem itself, rather than stepping beyond it" (Probyn-Rapsey 2007: 79). Probyn-Rapsey here accurately attunes to the desire of modern Western civilization for "progress"—to keep moving up and on rather than admitting and confronting how the domineering logics of colonialism keep every human stuck in the middle of injustice that detrimentally shapes the lives of some humans more so than a few fortunate others (Probyn-Rapsey 2007: 79).

In provoking scholars and researchers to bridge the divisions colonialism has generated, Anzaldúa substantiates Probyn-Rapsey's contention that the emphasis on moving on in fact conceals the moment of stasis in our unjust human relations (Anzaldúa et al. 2003; Probyn-Rapsey 2007). As long as Western society remains mired in continued rationalizations to exclude and marginalize those among us perpetually caught in social misfits (Garland-Thomson 2011: 591–609), Western liberalism's story of moving on and up remains illusory. This is also aptly articulated by disability studies scholar McRuer (2006: 182) who states: "Paradoxically since efficiency simultaneously signifies that a dynamic system is moving forward but that it is also decidedly not being jarred or redirected, we could say that ... progress is essentially going nowhere." Rather than moving on, acknowledging and confronting complicity offers all of us an opportunity to feel how the ripples of both caring too much and not enough have marked us, impressed and pressed upon us. Thus, perhaps our differences can embolden each of us to distinctly and collectively care differently through, with, and in the middle of becoming human with other humans.

Probyn-Rapsey (2007: 75) states, "Awareness of complicity is, can be, the very starting point of White feminist engagement with racial domination." This provocation is in keeping with Spelman's work as well as recent critical perspectives of the potential role of feminist care ethics by Robinson and Hankivsky (Hankivsky 2014; Robinson 2011; Spelman 1997). Robinson implores scholars and researchers to listen with intention and sincerity to those who disproportionately encounter exploitation and marginalization (Robinson 2011). Ahmed (2004), in her contribution to the analysis of emotions as social rather than psychological, considers ways of listening that refuse modes of appropriation that perpetuate domination. "Our task is to learn how to hear what is impossible. Such an impossible hearing is only possible if we respond to a pain that we cannot claim as our own" (Ahmed 2004: 35). The intention here is to refuse to perpetuate the hegemony of Western subjective self by foregrounding that care ethics and its most profound dilemmas of conditional inclusion occur amid the intersections of race, gender, class, and disability.

Here we might consider the work of Rogers and Kittay within disability studies and feminist ethics of care (Kittay 2009; Kittay and Carlson 2010; Kittay et al. 2005; Rogers 2016; Rogers and Weller 2012). Rogers and Kittay have foregrounded considerations of the intellectually disabled and their continued marginalization from the current social context that overvalues productivity as a commodity rather than valuing long-term and short-term dependencies upon one another. We might also consider one of Garland-Thomson's contributions to feminist materialism and disability studies: "Shape structures story" (Garland-Thomson 2007: 113). "We use the cultural story that we call normalcy to structure our shapes" (Garland-Thomson 2007: 114). The resilience of the cultural story of normalcy implicates everyone (including you, I, and us) in the processes of exclusion and marginalization that continue to constrain care in social relations and therefore makes Probyn-Rapsey's foregrounding of complicity significant in the ways it refuses the mantle of progress as a rationalization for the injustice of sameness.

In evoking the work of Probyn-Rapsey, as well as disability studies scholars McRuer and Garland-Thomson, my intention here is to consider the fruitful possibilities amid a feminist care ethics that confronts the ways it is mired in the dilemmas of unjust social relations (Garland-Thomson 2007; McRuer 2006; Probyn-Rapsey 2007). To admit our limits and how care is constrained amid those limits are also to refuse the imposition of a solution upon another. Admitting our limits leaves space for others and leaves you and I and us confronting one another and the dilemmas of the social injustices that persist in shaping relations of care.

Ahmed asserts that "emotions shape the very surfaces of bodies, which take shape through the repetition of action over time, as well as orientations towards and away from others" (Ahmed 2004: 4). When Ahmed's insights are considered alongside those of Garland-Thomson and Probyn-Rapsey, it might also be possible to consider the ways that a subjective self that foregrounds its complicity and its vulnerability amid its social relations with other humans paradoxically offers opportunities for transforming the self and what it means to become human with other humans (Garland-Thomson 2007, 2011; Probyn-Rapsey 2007). This is in keeping with the work of scholars such as Rogers who have provoked the fields of feminist care ethics and disability studies to consider what it might mean to displace the normative demands of the neoliberal, independent self that eschews human dependence (Rogers 2016; Rogers and Weller 2012). A self that is constrained, bound, and tethered to other selves attends to the binds of those social relations. Caring about how we are bound to one another thus entails considering how a vulnerable self is complicit in the power imbalances that sustain ableism, classism, racism, and gender biases. If the contributions of feminist care ethics scholars as they relate to foregrounding the vulnerabilities and dependencies of the self are viewed alongside scholars of Black feminist thought such as Coloma (2008: 11–27) and Weheliye (2014), we can engage in a form of care to "try to overturn the destructive perceptions of the world that we have been taught through our cultures" (Anzaldúa et al. 2003: 19). Both Coloma and Weheliye provoke all of us to consider the ways in which the self is messy, tangled, and contingent amid unjust relations of power. They offer the possibility of recognizing the self as multidimensional, complex, and vibrant in ways that hold out fruitful possibilities for scholars in both disability studies and feminist ethics of care. In addition to its theoretical contribution, foregrounding a self that is messy, contingent, vulnerable, and complicit amid caring relations with others also has the potential to transform everyday classroom encounters with one another. No longer framing her choice to care about and with her best friends as an automatic exclusion of Maya, perhaps Chloe can accept herself as contingent and vulnerable in ways that generate the possibility of extending her hand toward rather than away from the differences of another.

For example, Coloma (2008) applies the work of scholars in the field of Black feminist thought to post-structuralism to posit the concept of constitutive subjectivity. He considers the image of a prism and suggests that subjectivities "operate within multiple planes ... that enable subject positions to refract within and through each other in various unpredictable ways" (Coloma 2008: 20). He offers numerous examples of his own research encounters that demonstrate various subject positions he embodies in differing contexts and how these embodiments implicate the self in varying degrees of complicity and vulnerability (Coloma 2008: 20). As a conceptual tool, constitutive subjectivity is significant for the way it foregrounds the import of contextual variables as they relate to the shifting power imbalances the subjective self encounters while engaging in social relations. Coloma's insights here resonate because they implicate elementary teachers and students, showing how varying encounters with difference generate moments of (dis)connection that echo across time, space, and circumstance with varying degrees of intensity. Significantly, Coloma's insights also consider a version of selfhood no longer mired in the binaries of us–them, where power flows in unidirectionally.

Just as Chloe is haunted by Maya's absence long after she leaves, as a teacher, I am also haunted by the numerous student encounters whereby care's presence also amplified its subsequent absence. Coloma's conception of constitutive subjectivity is significant as well when applied to the elementary context more broadly. His work provokes a reexamination of curricular goals, assessment, and evaluation practices so as to refuse sustaining the hegemonic narrative of Western liberal ableism that insists upon a universal ideal of what becoming human with other humans entails. Thus, in confronting how the self is displaced through being marked and impressed upon by a network of social relations (Coloma 2008: 20), feminist care ethics can work with and alongside scholars of Black feminist thought to substantively shift the onto-epistemological routes–roots of our teaching, learning, and researching practices.

Conclusion

The scholarship of Black feminist thought and disability studies amplify the need to engage in caring relations both despite and because of the risks of the power imbalances. These scholarly fields respectively call on all of us to engage in teaching, learning, and researching relationships amid an acknowledgment of our own vulnerabilities alongside other humans who at any given moment may depend on us or alternately we might turn toward as dependents. Constitutive subjectivity as articulated by Coloma amplifies the dilemma of self, representation, and the ethical demand to care for and with one another (Coloma 2008: 20). Similarly, Probyn-Rapsey's conceptualization and application of complicity offers feminist care ethics scholars as well as elementary school teachers a method to confront and turn toward the ongoing conditional inclusion/exclusion of children labeled with disabilities (Annamma et al. 2013; Baker 2002, 2015; Collins et al. 2016; Connor 2008; Erevelles and Minear 2010; Probyn-Rapsey 2007; Rogers 2016; Rogers and Weller 2012; Slee 2008, 2013).

When feminist ethics of care meets disability studies and Black feminist thought at the intersections of a vulnerable self amid other vulnerable selves, perhaps we can all be encouraged as educators, learners, and researchers to step more humbly, gently, and with less conviction with and through each other's lives. Within the elementary classroom, this entails an acknowledgment of the pervasiveness of teaching and learning practices that exclude and marginalize children in ways that implicate how we all come to care for and with one another. Woodson's story of the absence and presence of kindness between children (Woodson 2012) who have already absorbed the sociocultural cues of how some humans count more than others resonates for its ubiquity. Just as Chloe and Maya are tainted by the sociocultural processes that impede encounters with care, as an elementary teacher since 2002, I, too, have been tainted through my complicity in the social injustices that pervade the educational system. I remain both haunted and delighted by the countless children like Parvana, Onika, and Yousuf whom I have encountered within a context in which caring was both absent and present. Because of my ongoing encounters with racism, ableism, classism, and gender biases, I can no longer turn away. Although like Woodson's character Maya, my students drift out and away, their stories still ripple through my own.

In focusing on the contributions of disability studies scholars and scholars of Black feminist thought, my intent in this chapter has been to respond to the provocation of feminist care ethics scholars such as Hankivsky and Robinson in order to consider how elementary teaching and learning practices are steeped in the dilemmas of both care and social injustice (Hankivsky 2014; Robinson 2006, 2011). One significant matter this chapter has attempted to address is how the hegemony of a Western liberal onto-epistemology implicates care in sustaining mechanisms of exclusion and marginalization. I have also considered how the contributions of disability studies scholars as well as scholars of Black feminist thought might endeavor to shift and hopefully transform the onto-epistemological routes and roots through which social relations are embedded. In part, this has entailed an acknowledgment of and confrontation with the ways the subjective self is both complicit and vulnerable amid social relations that remain mired in unbalanced and unjust relations with power. Through the work of disability studies scholars and scholars of Black feminist thought, I have also attempted to demonstrate how feminist care ethics might be substantively enriched through adopting a genuinely intersectional approach to its methodological framework. If feminist care ethics intends to transform the teaching and learning practices in elementary classrooms, it will require numerous helping hands to ultimately transform the unjust power dynamics that continue to pervade this sociocultural institution. I hope that you and I and we can ultimately turn toward one another without turning away.

References

Ahmed, S. (2004), *The Cultural Politics of Emotion*, New York: Routledge.

Ahmed, S. (2012), *On Being Included: Racism and Diversity in Institutional Life*, Durham, NC: Duke University Press.

Annamma, S. A., D. Connor, and B. Ferri (2013), "Dis/Ability Critical Race Studies (Discrit): Theorizing at the Intersections of Race and Dis/Ability," *Race Ethnicity and Education*, 16 (1): 1–31.

Anzaldúa, G. E., S. J. Ortiz, I. Hernández-Avila, and D. Perez (2003), "Speaking across the Divide," *Studies in American Indian Literatures*, 15 (3/4): 7–22.

Baker, B. (2002), "The Hunt for Disability: The New Eugenics and the Normalization of School Children," *The Teachers College Record*, 104 (4), 663–703.

Baker, B. (2015), "From 'Somatic Scandals' to 'A Constant Potential for Violence'? The Culture of Dissection, Brain-Based Learning, and the Rewriting/Rewiring of 'the Child'," *Journal of Curriculum and Pedagogy*, 12 (2): 168–197.

Brown, R. S. and G. Parekh (2013), "The Intersection of Disability, Achievement, and Equity: A System Review of Special Education in the TDSB," (Research Report No. 12–13–12), Toronto, Ontario, Canada: Toronto District School Board.

Collins, K. M., C. Connor, B. Ferri, D. Gallagher, and J. F. Samson (2016), "Dangerous Assumptions and Unspoken Limitations: A Disability Studies in Education Response to Morgan, Farkas, Hillemeier, Mattison, Maczuga, Li, and Cook (2015)," *Multiple Voices for Ethnically Diverse Exceptional Learners*, 16 (1): 4–16.

Coloma, R. S. (2008), "Border Crossing Subjectivities and Research: Through the Prism of Feminists of Color," *Race, Ethnicity and Education*, 11 (1): 11–27.

Connor, D. J. (2008), *Urban Narratives: Portraits in Progress, Life at the Intersections of Learning Disability, Race, and Social Class*, New York: Peter Lang.

Erevelles, N. and A. Minear (2010), "Unspeakable Offenses: Untangling Race and Disability in Discourses of Intersectionality," *Journal of Literary & Cultural Disability Studies*, 4 (2): 127–145.

Garland-Thomson, R. (2007), "Shape Structures Story: Fresh and Feisty Stories about Disability," *Narrative*, 15 (1): 113–123.

Garland-Thomson, R. (2011), "Misfits: A Feminist Materialist Disability Concept," *Hypatia*, 26 (3): 591–609.

Hankivsky, O. (2014), "Rethinking Care Ethics: On the Promise and Potential of an Intersectional Analysis," *American Political Science Review*, 108 (02): 252–264.

Held, V. (2004), "Care and Justice in the Global Context," *Ratio Juris*, 17 (2): 141–155.

Held, V. (2010), "Can the Ethics of Care Handle Violence?" *Ethics and Social Welfare*, 4 (2): 115–129.

Kittay, E. F. (2009), "The Personal Is Philosophical Is Political: A Philosopher and Mother of a Cognitively Disabled Person Sends Notes from the Battlefield," *Metaphilosophy*, 40 (3–4): 606–627.

Kittay, E. F. and L. Carlson (eds) (2010), *Cognitive Disability and Its Challenge to Moral Philosophy*, New York: John Wiley & Sons.

Kittay, E. F., B. Jennings, and A. A. Wasunna (2005), "Dependency, Difference and the Global Ethic of Long Term Care," *Journal of Political Philosophy*, 13 (4): 443–469.

McRuer, R. (2006), *Crip Theory: Cultural Signs of Queerness and Disability*, New York: New York University Press.

Parekh, G. and K. Underwood (2015), "Inclusion: Creating School and Classroom Communities Where Everyone Belongs. Research, Tips, and Tools for Educators and Administrators," (Research Report No.15/16–09), Toronto, Ontario, Canada: Toronto District School Board.

Probyn-Rapsey, F. (2007), "Complicity, Critique and Methodology," *ARIEL*, 38 (2–3): 65–82.

Robinson, F. (2006), "Care, Gender and Global Social Justice: Rethinking 'Ethical Globalization,'" *Journal of Global Ethics*, 2 (1): 5–25.

Robinson, F. (2011), "Stop Talking and Listen: Discourse Ethics and Feminist Care Ethics in International Political Theory," *Millennium*, 39 (3): 845–860.

Rogers, C. (2016), *Intellectual Disability and Being Human: A Care Ethics Model*, New York: Routledge.

Rogers, C. and S. Weller (2012), *Critical Approaches to Care: Understanding Caring Relations, Identities and Cultures*, New York: Routledge.

Scheurich, J. J. and M. D. Young (1997), "Coloring Epistemologies: Are Our Research Epistemologies Racially Biased?" *Educational Researcher*, 26 (4): 4–16.

Slee, R. (2008), "Beyond Special and Regular Schooling? An Inclusive Education Reform Agenda," *International Studies in Sociology of Education*, 18 (2): 99–116.

Slee, R. (2013), "How Do We Make Inclusive Education Happen When Exclusion as a Political Predisposition?" *International Journal of Inclusive Education*, 17 (8): 895–907.

Spelman, E. V. (1997), *Fruits of Sorrow: Framing Our Attention to Suffering*, Boston, MA: Beacon Press.

Weheliye, A. G. (2014), *Habeas Viscus: Racializing Assemblages, Biopolitics, and Black Feminist Theories of the Human*, Durham, NC: Duke University Press.

Woodson, J. (2012), *Each Kindness*, New York: Nancy Paulsen Books.

8

The Controversy of Ravza's Pacifier: In Search of Embodied Care in Preschool Education

Katrien Van Laere, Griet Roets, and Michel Vandenbroeck

Over the last forty years, early childhood education and care (ECEC) has gained recognition by governments, parents, employers, local communities, and researchers for various reasons. The importance of ECEC provision has been stressed, supported by the argument that it enables the early learning of children as a foundation for reaching higher educational attainment and productive employment in later life. Longitudinal studies in the United States and the United Kingdom have demonstrated, for example, that high-quality preschool can improve outcomes in terms of children's cognitive development, socioemotional functioning, and educational performance, especially for children from low socioeconomic backgrounds and children with migrant backgrounds (see reviews of Lazarri and Vandenbroeck 2013; Melhuish et al. 2015; Leseman and Slot 2014; Bennett 2012).

In the international realm, it is therefore argued that ECEC is increasingly conceptualized as a preparation for compulsory schooling since children are expected to acquire (pre-)literacy, (pre-)numeracy, and (pre-)scientific skills from a young age, and this development has been called *schoolification* of preschool education (Moss 2013; OECD 2006; Woodhead 2006). Preschool education is increasingly constructed as a prep school with a significance in later stages of life (Ang 2014; Vandenbroeck et al. 2010). According to critical scholars, the emphasis on schoolification indeed shows that children are considered autonomous and rational human beings who need to be made ready for future economic, social, political, and cultural life (Lynch et al. 2009; Noddings 1984).

In this chapter, however, we want to scrutinize the interpretations of learning in preschool arrangements that tend to limit the attention given to the *caring* dimension of education (Alvestad 2009; Forrester 2005; Kyriacou et al.

2009; Van Laere and Vandenbroeck 2017). The debate so far has focused on conceptualizations of care and education in ECEC, and it has been argued that a divide and hierarchy between care and education have been constructed in which caring is subordinate to learning (Cameron and Moss 2011; Garnier 2011; Kaga et al. 2010; Löfdahl and Folke-Fichtelius 2015). By increasingly emphasizing the future employability of children, some scholars believe that schoolification of the early years contributes to intensifying Cartesian rationalism, signifying a further disembodiment of education (Fielding and Moss 2011; Tobin 1997; Warin 2014). We focus on the idea that this hierarchy between care and education stems, in theoretical terms, from an underlying notion of a mind–body dualism that might have implications for how children are approached by professionals following ECEC policies and practices (Van Laere et al. 2014).

In what follows, we first explain how contemporary feminist thinkers have framed this mind–body dualism in care arrangements as problematic. To go beyond this hierarchical binary between care and education, we elaborate on the work of Hamington (2004, 2014, 2015a, 2016), an ethics of care theorist whose work is rooted in phenomenological ontological notions. Second, we frame our research methodology, inspired by a video-cued, multi-vocal conversation that was organized during ten focus groups with parents and four focus groups with diverse preschool staff in the Belgian cities of Ghent, Brussels, and Antwerp. During the focus groups, a movie of a so-called typical day in a preschool class was discussed. Third, we engage in a qualitative analysis that is inspired by a specific storyline in the video (see Van Laere 2017). During this research project and analysis, the interactions with Ravza, a two-and-a-half-year-old Turkish girl in preschool, evoked a lot of discussion and controversy among the research respondents. By analyzing the meanings that respondents attribute to the situation of Ravza, we consider conceptualizations of care and education and make a plea for professionals who might learn to embrace differentiated manifestations of interdependency, underpinned by notions of difference and solidarity in our societies, that allow for such practices in early childhood settings.

A mind–body hierarchy in care

An essentialist mind–body dualism

From a perspective of contemporary feminist theory, it is argued that discourses and practices in Western societies often implicitly embody an underlying mind–body dualism that is constructed on the basis of essentialist claims that the body is ontologically separate from the mind (Braidotti 2006, 2013; Gatens 1996; Haraway 1991). This so-called Cartesian error in Western cultures, which refers to the assumption that there exists a dualism of mind and body, "a mind somehow cut off from matter" (Grosz 1994: 86), was challenged by feminist theorists in the 1980s and 1990s. These early third-wave feminists asserted that European modernist ideals, idealizing rationality and progression, are founded in the impossible separation of the body and the mind (Braidotti 2006, 2013; Price and Shildrick 1999). Feminist scholars have rejected these essentialist ontological assumptions (Braidotti 1991; Butler 1990; Gatens 1991; Grosz 1994; Haraway 1991) and challenged dominant and historically rooted essentialist discourses and practices of care since those who *give* and *receive* care are perceived as marginal bodies (Hughes et al. 2005; Wolkowitz 2006). In the case of ECEC arrangements, the disembodiment of education not only affects children and parents, but the staff's bodies also tend to be denied or marginalized.

Implications for those who receive care

For those who receive care, the mind–body dualism means that they have often been considered as a burden to society since they do not meet the ideal of the rational and self-managing citizen/subject involved in self-determination, free choice, and self-reliance (Clarke 2005; Williams 2001). Reindal (1999: 354) asserts the ideal of "independence and the ability to govern oneself" in rational ways is a widely accepted and frequently promoted basis for care policies and practices. This ideal of rational autonomy is nonetheless problematic. A dependence–independence dichotomy (see Reindal 1999; Williams 1999) is easily created and might have deep implications for people such as children, disabled people, elderly people, and all people who are unable to choose and control their lives independently without significant others (Dean 2015; Dowse 2009; Lister 1997; Reindal 1999; Watson et al. 2004; Williams 2001). It has been argued that those policy and practice rationales paradoxically and easily mark people out as different in kind and devalued in their humanity (Williams 2001). In that sense, those who receive care seem to belong to the private sphere of the "household of emotions" in Western societies and disappear as a concern from the public sphere, where issues of social justice and solidarity prevail (Hughes et al. 2005).

Implications for those who give care

For those who give care, the mind–body dualism implies that certain types of care will continue to be relegated to the private domain of human activity (Hughes et al. 2005). In that sense, *body work* (bodies' work on other bodies), a concept of Wolkowitz (2006), can be considered as inferior and "dirty work," as workers have to negotiate the boundaries of the body (Douglas cited in Twigg et al. 2011).

Inspired by the notion of "leaky bodies," caring is predominantly about the containment, in its material form, of bodily fluids and, in its symbolic form, of bodily difference that is perceived as a burden to the social order (Hughes et al. 2005). Dealing with leaky bodies and boundaries cannot be avoided (Shildrick 1997) and breaks down the modernist myth of the rational (or becoming-rational) subject, signaling a world of relational transactions of caring and mutual recognition. A similar, slightly different concept introduced by Hochschild (2003) is *emotional labor*. Feminists have criticized dominant assumptions in which care, being perceived as emotional labor, is expected to happen in the shadows of the symbolic order (Hughes et al. 2005). Emotional work, such as caring, therefore involves devalued work (Hochschild 2003; Twigg et al. 2011).

From this perspective, it is argued that caring work is consequently gendered, yet also classed and racialized. The gendered nature of care constructs women as natural subjects: caring work is seen as the duty and responsibility of women, being considered as unpaid work that women naturally do in the private sphere (Lister 1997). And when caring work is paid, the wages tend to be low and the recognition for employment poor, which reinforces already existing inequalities in the labor market (Rake 2001). Tronto (1993), for example, shows how the concrete giving and receiving of care is, in a male imaginary, left to the least powerful in society (Cockburn 2010; Tronto 1993). Moreover, the Cartesian division between mind and body appears not solely as a strongly gendered construction, but also a classed and racialized construction that implies that body work and emotional labor carry a stigma and will be done by the lowest in the pecking order (Isaksen et al. 2008; Twigg et al. 2011; Wolkowitz 2006).

The body matters

An anti-essentialist corporeality

In search for alternative understandings that go beyond this mind–body dualism, feminists have argued for anti-essentialism as an alternative basis for feminist politics and collective concerns for women and men. From the perspective of third-wave feminist theory, rather than reducing the body to an unspoken being in Western societies, the body matters (Witz 2000), and not just to women, as "an open-ended, pliable set of significations, capable of being rewritten, reconstituted, in quite other terms than those which mark it" (Grosz 1994: 61). Their central argument is that the mind is always embodied or based on corporeal relations and that the body is always social, political, and in-process rather than natural, thus referring to a non-unitary vision of the subject whose mind and body are intrinsically interrelated (Braidotti 2006; Vandekinderen and Roets 2016).

In third-wave feminism, definitions of care are accordingly placed within broader social and political concerns rather than within an essentialist, individual-gendered psychology (Cockburn 2010). The caring relationship is valorized for its potential to symbolize the very embodiment of care in our societies; the interpretation of caring as marginal work is challenged and claims for dignity and respect for both the giver and receiver of care can be made (Hughes et al. 2005). In that vein, those who *give* and *receive* care are perceived as *bodies that matter*.

Implications for those who receive care

The underlying interpretations of subjectivities of those who receive care, underpinned by biological essentialism, are challenged, and the notion of corporeality—or embodied subjectivity—is introduced (Braidotti 2006). These extended interpretations of the body assert new figurations of embodied rather than purely rational subjectivity (Braidotti 2006, 2011; Lather 1991). Making sense of corporeality suggests a relational rather than purely rational approach to the autonomy of the human subject (Dowse 2009; Goodley and Roets 2008; Goodley et al. 2014; Vandekinderen and Roets 2016), one that embraces interdependency rather than in-dependency as "an indispensable feature of the human condition" (Reindal 1999: 354). From a life course perspective the interdependent need for care is intrinsically a universal feature of the human condition that tends to be more or less intense but remains as a continuum (Lister 1997) and requires that we all embrace a notion of relational autonomy for *all* citizens (Williams 2001). As Lister (1997: 114) argues aptly, *relational autonomy* refers to an autonomous self that "does not have to be set in opposition to notions of interdependency and reciprocity, provided that it is understood that this autonomy, and the agency that derives from it, is only made possible by the human relationships that nourish it and the social infrastructure that supports it." This feature of interdependency can, however, be considered as a universal feature of the human subject. In that sense, *all* human subjects require or give care during the course of their lives: "The giving and receiving of care is imperative to human existence but is experienced differently at various points in the life course" (Watson et al. 2004: 333).

Implications for those who give care

From a third-wave feminist perspective, an ethics and politics of care implies an embodied ethics (Braidotti 2013). In that vein, here we mainly rely on Maurice Hamington's (2004, 2012, 2014, 2015a) theory of embodied care as a suitable theoretical backbone for the deconstruction of the Cartesian dualistic tradition that values the mind over the body. For Hamington, care permeates the human condition and is about who we fundamentally are as human beings. Hamington (2012, 2015b, 2016) argues that, on an ontological level, human beings are fundamentally relational and embodied beings. On an ethical level, this means that people are confronted with choices to be made in order to "do the right things." Rather than prescribed caring behaviors, the normative caring response is a product of openness and attentiveness to the questions that emerge in a particular relationship in a specific context (Hamington 2016).

Research methodology

Research context

The Flemish community of Belgium is historically characterized by a split childcare system consisting of care services for children from zero to three years old (*kinderopvang*) under the auspices of the minister for Welfare and preschool institutions (*kleuterschool*) for children from two-and-a-half to six years old that are part of the educational system (Oberhuemer et al. 2010). Every child is entitled to free preschool from two-and-a-half years onward. Despite almost universal enrolment in preschool education, there is an unequal attendance—children from migrant and/or poor families are slightly more often absent from preschool than their more affluent peers—that causes policy concerns, as it is allegedly associated with school failure in later years (Department of Education 2015). According to the latest studies by the Programme for International Student Assessment (PISA), Belgium is one of the countries with the most pronounced educational gap between children with high socioeconomic status (SES) and low SES and between children with and without migrant backgrounds (OECD 2013, 2016).

Video-cued multi-vocal conversation

The studies "pre-school in three cultures" (revisited) and "children crossing borders" of Joe Tobin and colleagues are an important source of inspiration for our qualitative study (Tobin 2009, 2016; Tobin et al. 1989, 2013). Tobin stimulates and evokes a multi-vocal conversation. This makes use of visual materials as a powerful tool to evoke genuine, spontaneous reactions. Research respondents are considered as subjects who can understand, even enjoy and find a movie provocative or meaningful, and are therefore invited to participate in focus groups (Tobin and Hsueh 2007).

To enable this multi-vocal conversation during the focus groups, a movie of a typical day in preschool was compiled. The movie shows how nineteen children, with and without migrant backgrounds, experienced a half- or full-day in a reception class (*instapklas*) of the Duizendvoet preschool in Lokeren, a small town in Belgium. The footage includes parents bringing and fetching their children, teacher-guided and free activities in class, free time at the outdoor playground, toileting, snack time, and lunchtime. We edited the movie in different stages and discussed these edited versions with the staff and parents of the children portrayed in the movie.[1]

Focus groups

The movie is not considered as data. Yet, 24 minutes movie was used to evoke reflection of staff members and parents on ECEC practices. We conducted ten focus groups with sixty-nine parents in the cities of Ghent, Antwerp, and Brussels. We decided to invite the participation of parents who are objects of policymaking, which entails a focus on a diversity of parents with a migrant family history. We conducted four focus groups with forty-two preschool staff members (preschool teachers, teacher's assistants, after-school care workers,

---

[1] The final movie can be viewed for research purposes at the following link: https://vimeo.com/199802331 (password: katrien).

and supervisory staff) in the cities of Ghent and Brussels. These cities are characterized by a higher than average concentration of poverty and having a larger than average proportion of inhabitants with migrant backgrounds.

Data analysis

The overarching data analysis of the focus groups corresponds with principles of abductive analysis, which is "a creative inferential process aimed at producing new hypotheses and theories based on surprising research evidence" (Timmermans and Tavory 2012: 170). The starting point is identifying surprising facts that cannot be simply explained by induction or deduction.

In our study, the majority of the research participants feel emotionally touched and disturbed by the movie footage in which Ravza, a little girl with a pacifier, cries a lot. Quite surprisingly, even staff members that do not consider care as part of their professional repertoire, identify possible care needs of this child. As parents and professionals watch the movie, most of them problematize that Ravza is sitting alone most of the time, that she cries, and that she does not play by herself or with others. For some, it breaks their hearts, as they say in their own words, to see Ravza crying in the movie. Many participants were trying to figure out what is going on with Ravza, and what could be done by the professionals in the classroom to deal with the girl. A lot of the discussions concerning the situation of Ravza focus on the observation that Ravza is holding a pacifier,[2] and this causes some controversy over whether or not children should be allowed to have a pacifier in preschool.

Research findings

In what follows, we address the different standpoints concerning the pacifier, not with the intent of defining whether a pacifier is desirable or not, but in order to understand explicit or underlying thoughts on education and care in the early years. The majority of participants attribute a negative connotation to the pacifier, feeling that it functions as an obstacle to the learning of Ravza and

---

[2]   We note that the search for a translation of pacifier into English is already an interesting cultural inquiry as this object has different cultural connotations and names. In Dutch, we say *tut* or *fopspeen*, which addresses the suction need of a baby without giving them food or letting them drink. In English, other words exist such as *soother, comforter,* etc. We have chosen to use the word *pacifier*, knowing that this term is not a neutral term.

the other children in preschool, while other parents and professionals attribute a more positive connotation to the pacifier as it could compensate for the care dimensions that seem to be missing in the preschool system.

Pacifier as an obstacle for education

Pacifier as a hindrance for speaking and learning the dominant language

In our study, many parents and preschool staff share experiences about children like Ravza, who do not master the dominant language and have not attended childcare before. According to them, these children have a higher risk of experiencing adaptation problems in preschool. Although participants underline the importance of a caring and attentive teacher, many parents and professionals seem to agree that eventually these children have to adapt to the preschool system. This was a particular concern in the view of preschool teachers, who view Ravza's crying as somewhat normal behavior since Ravza is transitioning from the home to the preschool environment, and, therefore, they argue that this behavior should be gone by the fifth week of starting preschool. In that sense, many parents and professionals express their concern that the pacifier might hinder Ravza from speaking up in the class and communicating with the teacher and the other children.

> *After-school care worker: I think it is a pity that the girl is holding on to her bookbag and her pacifier the whole time. The teacher should encourage her to remove the pacifier. If you remove the pacifier, she will be able to talk with the other children. Now she seems lost. (FS 4)*

Moreover, the opinions of parents are that it is a task of the teacher to make this clear to the parents.

> *Parent 1: If she cries, she can't learn and if she has the pacifier, she can't learn. I will know before my baby comes to the school that I have to do exercises to stop this, and then she will become cleverer in the school to contact another person. If they have a pacifier at three or four years, they are a little disabled … If children of five years old have a pacifier, it is difficult to speak and then they look for contact and receive no answer.*
>
> *Parent 2: They indeed say that, but I don't think so. I know so many children. They always said about my children that a pacifier is not good for the teeth and not good for talking.*
>
> *Parent 1: The child will not become clever if she cannot speak.*

Parent 2:	*I don't think so because my son had a pacifier. Super, his teeth were good, and his talking was also good. From he was two-and-a-half years old, he spoke really well. The same applies to his cousins.*

Parent 3:	*Without pacifier, it is much better. They will talk Dutch a lot and play well. (FP4)*

The main concern of the first mother seems to be that Ravza won't be able to talk and, therefore, will not be able to learn because of having a pacifier. The mother perceives the pacifier as a hindrance for learning in the sense that Ravza is not able to communicate, and consequently, she may not develop properly. The second mother in this fragment questions the view that a pacifier is not good for the teeth and the development of the child. Most parents in this focus group agree with the first mother that children should not have a pacifier in class. The first mother states that it is the task of the teacher to ask the parents to stop using the pacifier as it is the task of parents to prepare the child for preschool. This mother also emphasizes the importance of learning Dutch so that a child is prepared to become clever in school and also in life. For a majority of the parents, learning Dutch is the most important function of preschool; their children need Dutch in order to be able to follow primary school to succeed in school life and later in work life. Some parents, for example, express the hope that their children will become doctors or civil servants. Therefore, succeeding in school is important and in parents' view, this is only possible when children master the Dutch language as soon as possible. A common belief of many parents is that differences in dealing with children will disappear once the children know Dutch.

Banning pacifiers so children will become self-reliant

Although her child desperately wants to hold on to a pacifier in preschool, one mother explains that children should stop using the pacifier because they are not babies anymore. The idea that a pacifier does not belong in preschool is also a predominant view of the teachers.

Preschool teacher 1:	*While seeing this child in the movie, I'm thinking that I'm a hard teacher for toddlers. In my case, the "pampering," such as washing hands are things that they need to do themselves. Like the pacifier. For me the pacifier has to be removed from the child. The pacifier belongs to home, in the schoolbag, or for sleeping and so on. I think that these children are kept very small. But, maybe it is because I'm hard.*

Preschool teacher 2:	*She will not be able to come out of her state in which she is really nestled now. (FS1)*

In this example, the pacifier symbolizes "staying small." This seems to imply that children need to "grow up" the moment they enter preschool. By banning a pacifier, children won't be kept small anymore by the teacher or the system. Some parents also allude to this meaning by reporting that they say to their child that they are not babies anymore so they have to stop holding a pacifier in preschool. In this fragment, the teacher connects "staying small" with children who don't do things themselves. It also became clear in the focus group that stimulating self-reliance in children is an important function of preschool, according to the teachers and some childcare workers. The teacher in this citation identifies herself as having a "hard" approach, which implies that the approach the teacher in the movie uses is too "soft." The teacher uses the verb "pampering" when referring to the children to problematize this approach.

The underlying assumption here is that, once children arrive in preschool, it is time for them to take responsibility for growing up and doing things themselves, especially when it comes to their own bodily and emotional caring needs. In this "hard" approach focused on stimulating self-reliance, teachers state that there is not much time for individual attention because they are responsible for collective education. Both parents and preschool staff acknowledge that young children are in the process of dealing with bodily needs, such as eating, drinking, blowing their noses, using the toilet, and sleeping. Nevertheless, several teachers view supporting these processes as subordinate to preschool learning. Other teachers express the expectation that parents, in the home environment, or childcare workers, in the childcare center, should have already taught the children to be self-sufficient in their physical needs before entering preschool at the age of two-and-a-half. Being disciplined in controlling bodily and emotional functions, reflected in the ideal of not carrying a pacifier, is seen as a prerequisite for early learning in preschool. Some parents concur with this idea as they are afraid that their children will not receive appropriate attention from the teacher in the early learning processes if they are not able to manage their bodily needs by themselves.

Pacifier as a small act of disobedience

Teachers attribute another meaning to the pacifier, connecting the pacifier to the phenomena of children who keep their jacket on in the beginning of school or want to keep their schoolbags with them.

> Preschool teacher: *Children who keep the schoolbag, their jackets on, and hold on to a pacifier, give me somehow the feeling that they want to*

> *push through their opinion. So, they feel like "ok, the teacher*
> *can listen a little bit to me." But this should only be in the first*
> *day or week. (FS 1)*

The teacher perceives this action as children wanting to challenge the teachers by making him or her listen to them. Children need to learn fairly early that they cannot force their opinion in the class. This implies that children have to learn to obey to the teacher and the school system and let go of their personal needs, desires, and questions. Many professionals and parents understand discipline and obedience to the teacher as important aspects of education; it is assumed that a well-behaved child will do better in preschool and eventually in later schooling and will even be better prepared to work for a boss in later life. In line with this, it is remarkable how, for some professionals, having objects from the home environment like the pacifier and the schoolbag is a non-desirable practice, as it would hinder the child's adaptation to the school system. Or, as one of the after-school workers in the focus group says:

> *I understand you have to comfort her, but if you allow the pacifier from home, they*
> *start bringing everything from home.*

Having objects such as a personal pacifier seem to represent small acts of disobedience from the child (and parents) toward the teacher, the school system, and the broader society. Or, as a preschool teacher who was responsible for thirty children between two-and-a-half and four years old, expresses:

> *In the beginning children are more like anarchists. They do not know how things*
> *are going in school and what the rules are. I let them be for a couple of days, and*
> *then they really have to start listening.*

Pacifier as a compensation for the lack of embodied care

Pacifier as emotional comfort

Several parents understand the pacifier as way to make Ravza more relaxed and to bring peace to her.

> Parent 2:   *When children cry and you give them a pacifier, they become calm*
> *and relaxed.*
> Parent 4:   *That is just a habit …*
> Parent 2:   *The pacifier means a lot to the child, maybe not for us. But for the*
> *child, if you all of a sudden take this away like the teacher who would*
> *say, "noooo, no pacifier, pacifier out," the child becomes internally ….I*
> *don't know.*

Researcher:	What do the others think?
Parent 5:	*No pacifier in school!*
Parent 2:	*But I'm not telling you that a pacifier is something good. I know this is nothing special. But after a while, this becomes a habit of the child. She comes to the school and comes from home, somewhere else. And then, all of a sudden, the pacifier needs to be removed. I don't know, I think the child feels different. (FP4)*

For this mother, the pacifier represents a comfort that can make Ravza more relaxed. As she concludes further on, children won't be able to learn if they don't feel good and relaxed. According to her, feeling emotionally safe in the class is a condition for education. This mother explicitly expresses that individual and emotional care should come prior to learning. Several parents, teacher's assistants, and teachers perceive the pacifier as a connection to home since children are in the process of being separated from the home environment. They question the abrupt transition between home and school, which can cause a lot of anxiety, sadness, pain, and insecurity within the child. Ravza may even experience a kind of "culture shock" in the meaning of feeling totally disoriented due to the rapidly changing social and cultural environment. Many parents and teachers state that it is hard for a child to say goodbye for the first time when he or she is separated from his or her mother, especially in situations where children have never been in contact with the Dutch language or gone to childcare. A pacifier could mediate this transitional shock "so she can feel a bit more at home" in the preschool. Although most teachers are convinced that children should not have pacifiers in school, a few teachers are aware of the possible difficulties in the transition between home and school. For example, one teacher allows the children to bring a pacifier or their own stuffed animal. They have to put this in a visible hanging basket so they can see their pacifier and stuffed animal as a kind of emotional comfort, yet they cannot take it.

In that sense, the pacifier might symbolize a lack of embodied care for children in the preschool system. Many parents connect this with a teacher who has to be a "mother-like" person, in the sense of being a person who is available for the children, a person who gives warmth and emotional comfort, and as a person that children can trust. In the focus group of the teacher's assistants, it becomes apparent that they see their job as providing individual attention and emotional care as compensation for the collective education from the teacher in which individual care and attention is lacking.

Remarkably, some parents also underline the importance of both children and adults who are able to care for each other, which indicates a sense of interdependency. In the stories of these parents and teacher's assistants, it becomes clear that caring and learning cannot exist independently: caring activities like eating, drinking, toilet training, sleeping, and comforting are educational in nature; supporting cognitive, social, motor, and artistic learning processes requires that the educators have a caring attitude.

Pacifier as a compensation for the impossibility of offering embodied care in preschool education

Although many teachers find the individual attention for children time-consuming—they are responsible for the collective education, three teachers who recently became mothers state that becoming a mother has changed their viewpoint. They refer to how the mothers must feel when their toddler starts preschool. It is remarkable that one teacher questions the "hard" way in which Ravza's teacher reacts to Ravza's crying.

> Preschool teacher 1: *I thought it was a weird moment with Ravza. The way the teacher says, "stop crying," I don't know if she understands Dutch, but it must be hard for the mother that her daughter is sad. I would do it differently. On that moment, I found the teacher a bit hard, "Now you have to stop crying because you have a pacifier."*
>
> Researcher: *What do the others think?*
>
> Preschool teacher 3: *I think it depends on how long this is going on. Because I sometimes dare to say like, "Now it has been enough."*
>
> *(Other teachers agree verbally and non-verbally) (FS1)*

According to this participant, the teacher in the movie uses the pacifier as a way to prevent Ravza from crying because it would disturb the desirable class practice, and therefore tries to take distance from the child.

Despite the contentious relationship between learning and caring, the story of Ravza clearly demonstrates that the caring needs of children do not simply disappear. The majority of preschool staff members identify the physical and emotional caring needs of Ravza but have different ways of coping with the alleged impossibility of dealing with these needs as an underlying and evident assumption in preschool. Preschool staff members develop strategies for restraining their caring responses and for not fully utilizing their embodied potential to care. However, some teachers state that they found it important to engage in care in preschool. They legitimize their caring responses either as part of their own caring personalities or attribute them to the fact that they are mothers themselves. Irrespective of whether or not teachers engage in care, there is a clear consensus that care in preschool education does not fundamentally belong in the professional repertoire of teachers.

Conclusion

The story of Ravza and her pacifier illustrates the relationship between caring and learning as a productive topic in preschool, as it evokes many questions and caused uncertainty, discomfort, and controversy among the participants of our study. Many parents and preschool staff feel that children like Ravza, who do not master the dominant language and have not attended childcare before, have a higher risk of experiencing adaptation problems in preschool, which in turn could hinder their early learning opportunities. Despite the omnipresent fear of exclusion, they assume that children have to adapt to the preschool system, irrespective of the abrupt transition they experience from home/childcare to preschool at a very young age. The question they do not explicitly raise, is how the preschool staff and system could adapt to the different experiences and starting positions of children.

In that vein, the pacifier symbolizes a problematic conditionality of the acceptance of an embodied human being with bodily and caring needs. On a more abstract level, preferably the body should be disciplined before the start in preschool or as soon as possible in preschool in order for children to be supported and able to learn. At the same time, the pacifier is used to question the divide between caring and learning in preschool, being sensitive to the embodied care that children might require. Bloch and Kim (2015) problematized the introduction of a formal notion of "readiness" in the Head Start programs in the United States in which, for example, children's needs for emotional stability and security are increasingly reframed as competences or skills within a developmental hierarchy that children need to possess and demonstrate. If the child cannot sufficiently self-regulate and demonstrate the required skills, it becomes the child's problem instead of the teacher's problem or that of the preschool or the curriculum (Bloch and Kim 2015). In this line of thinking, Lehrer et al. (2017) point out how implicit ideas and practices of readying children for Canadian preschools have paradoxically contributed to marginalizing and stigmatizing children.

The discussions, therefore, illustrate the vital tension between adhering to a dominant mind–body dualism, resulting in a hierarchy of education over embodied care, and the idea that the body does exist and matter in preschool education. In our study, the participants underline the importance of early learning in terms of learning the dominant language, learning to be self-reliant and independent, and learning to obey. To this end, Lynch (2016) stated that Cartesian rationalism has actually slightly changed the hegemony of the *homo sapiens* to the hegemony of the *homo economicus* (the self-sufficient, rational, and economically productive citizen) in education. Both concepts deny the existence of the *homo sentiens* (the interdependent, affective, relational human being) contributing strongly to the invisibility of affective and caring relations among human beings in education (Lynch 2016; Lynch et al. 2007). Scholars like Hamington (2012, 2015a, 2016) indeed argue that, on an ontological level, human beings are fundamentally relational and embodied beings, and therefore human bodies are made to give and receive care.

Our study suggests that the human subject as a *homo sentiens* should be valued in preschool education. Kurban and Tobin (2009) report the statement of a five-year-old girl of Turkish descent in a German preschool who says, "They do not like our bodies." The authors hypothesize that it is an expression of a young child's awareness of otherness, alterity, and feelings of alienation in terms of race and identity. The girl feels that she is viewed as "less then fully human" (Kurban and Tobin 2009).

Our study suggests that the ways in which care and education are conceptualized significantly impact on inclusion and exclusion mechanisms in preschool. Professionals tend to suppress their caring responses. Many preschool teachers view caring not as part of their professional identity and expertise. This needs to be understood in the context of an ECEC split system in which the caring and learning of young children are attributed to different types of services (childcare or preschool) and professionals. This can also be related to the fact that care signifies a devaluation of the preschool teacher profession, as care is historically associated with lower-qualified women assumed to "naturally care" for children (Van Laere et al. 2014).

In relation to the theoretical debates on ECEC professionalism, arguments have been made for a holistic view in which education and care are intrinsically the same, and the concept *educare* has been introduced (Cameron and Moss 2011; European Commission 2011; Kaga et al. 2010). In countries with an integrated ECEC system or with a social pedagogical tradition like the Nordic countries and Germany, this *educare* view is more prevalent than in countries with a split system of separate childcare services and preschools (Kaga et al. 2010). In that vein, we argue that the development of a professional, reflective language of educare might be very fruitful and enable staff to utilize their embodied potential to care.

Our study also reveals that we need to take distance from decontextualized pleas for "holistic development" if we want to do justice to a humane educational praxis (Roets et al. 2017). The label "holistic" does not prevent professionals from accommodating individualistic meanings or a relativism of critical value positions, or to "become detached from fundamental political and ethical questions of justice and equality" (Lorenz 2016: 6). Building further on the theoretical work of Hamington makes us aware that much more is needed to combat social inequalities in preschool.

Professionals should learn to embrace differentiated manifestations of interdependency and difference, underpinned by the value of solidarity in our societies as a matter of public concern (Lorenz 2016; Roets et al. 2017). According to Lorenz (2016: 14), this requires "building and respecting reciprocity beyond the personal sphere, ... as the subject of reflexive negotiations." This is not a simple challenge and endeavor since *care* has been used for a long time as a means of disciplining and keeping women docile in patriarchal structures (Canella 1997). This might explain why professionals in our study who emphasize that care is vital, mainly adopt "mother-like" assumptions borrowed from their experiences in the private sphere in their caring attitude. Instead of simply "introducing" care into what previously seemed to be low-care situations (e.g., preschools in ECEC split systems), we underline that embodied care is crucial and can be enriched by stimulating staff's caring imagination, thereby promoting their critical reflection about the solidarity they can shape as belonging to their public mandate (Hamington 2014).

References

Alvestad, M. (2009), "Early Childhood Education and Care Policy in Norway," *European Early Childhood Education Research Journal*, 17 (3): 416–424.

Ang, L. (2014), "Preschool or Prep School? Rethinking the Role of Early Years Education," *Contemporary Issues in Early Childhood*, 15 (2): 185–199.

Bennett, J. (2012), *ECEC for Children from Disadvantaged Backgrounds: Findings from a European Literature Review and Two Case Studies, Final Report*, Brussels: SOFRECO—European Commission.

Bloch, M. N. and K. Kim (2015), "A Cultural History of 'Readiness' in Early Childhood Care and Education: Are There Still Culturally Relevant, Ethical, and Imaginative Spaces for Learning Open for Young Children and Their Families?" in J. M. Iorio and W. Parnell (eds), *Rethinking Readiness in Early Childhood Education: Implications for Policy and Practice*, 1–18, New York: Palgrave Macmillan.

Braidotti, R. (1991), *Patterns of Dissonance*, Cambridge: Polity Press.

Braidotti, R. (2006), "Posthuman, All too Human—Towards a New Process Ontology," *Theory Culture & Society*, 23 (7–8): 197–208, doi:10.1177/0263276406069232.

Braidotti, R. (2011), *Nomadic Subjects: Embodiment and Sexual Difference in Contemporary Feminist Theory*, New York: Columbia University Press.

Braidotti, R. (2013), *The Posthuman*, Cambridge: Polity Press.

Butler, J. (1990), *Gender Trouble: Feminism and the Subversion of Identity*, New York Routledge.

Cameron, C. and P. Moss (2011), "Social Pedagogy: Current Understandings and Opportunities," in C. Cameron and P. Moss (eds), *Social Pedagogy and Working with Children and Young People. Where Care and Education Meet*, 7–32, London: Jessica Kingsley Publishers.

Canella, G. (1997), *Deconstructing Early Childhood Education: Social Justice and Revolution*, New York: Peter Lang.

Clarke, J. (2005), "New Labour's Citizens: Activated, Empowered, Responsibilized, Abandoned?" *Critical Social Policy*, 25 (4): 447–463.

Cockburn, T. (2010), "Children, The Feminist Ethic of Care and Childhood Studies: Is This the Way to the Good Life?" in S Andresen, I. Diehm, U. Sander, and H. Ziegler (eds), *Children and the Good Life. New Challenges for Research on Children*, 29–39, Dordrecht: Springer.

Dean, H. (2015), *Social Rights and Human Welfare*, London: Routledge.

Department of Education (2015), *Kleuterparticipatie: inschrijvingen en aanwezigheden [Toddler Participation: Subscribed and Present]*, Brussels: Flemish Government.

Dowse, L. (2009), "'Some People Are Never Going to Be Able to Do That': Challenges for People with Intellectual Disability in the 21st Century," *Disability & Society*, 24 (5): 571–584.

European Commission (2011), "Early Childhood Education and Care: Providing All Our Children with the Best Start for the World of Tomorrow," European Commission, Accessed August 1, 2011, http://eur-lex.europa.eu/LexUriServ/LexUriServ.do?uri=COM:2011:0066:FIN:EN:PDF.

Fielding, M. and P. Moss (2011), *Radical Education and the Common School*, London: Routledge.

Forrester, G. (2005), "All in a Day's Work: Primary Teachers 'Performing' and 'Caring'," *Gender and Education*, 17 (3): 271–287, doi:10.1080/09540250500145114.

Garnier, P. (2011), "The Scholarisation of the French Ecole Maternelle: Institutional Transformations Since the 1970s," *European Early Childhood Education Research Journal*, 19 (4): 553–563, doi:10.1080/1350293x.2011.623539.

Gatens, M. (1991), *Feminism and Philosophy: Perspectives on Difference and Equality*, Cambridge: Polity Press & Indiana University Press.

Gatens, M. (1996), *Imaginary Bodies: Ethics, Power and Corporeality*, London and New York: Routledge.

Goodley, D. and G. Roets (2008), "The (be)comings and Goings of 'Developmental Disabilities': The Cultural Politics of 'Impairment,'" *Discourse: Studies in the Cultural Politics of Education*, 29 (2): 239–255, doi:10.1080/01596300801966971.

Goodley, D., R. Lawthom, and K. Runswick-Cole (2014), "Posthuman Disability Studies," *Subjectivity*, 7 (4): 42–361.

Grosz, E. (1994), *Volatile Bodies: Towards a Corporeal Feminism*, London: Routledge.

Hamington, M. (2004), *Embodied Care: Jane Addams, Maurice Merleau-Ponty, and Feminist Ethics*, Urbana: University of Illinois Press.

Hamington, M. (2012), "Care Ethics and Corporeal Inquiry in Patient Relations," *International Journal of Feminist Approaches to Bioethics*, 5 (1): 52–69.

Hamington, M. (2014), "Care as Personal, Political, and Performative," in G. Olthuis, H. Kohlen, and J. Heier (eds), *Moral Boundaries Redrawn: The Significance of Joan Tronto's Argument for Professional Ethics*, 195–201, Leuven: Peeters Publishers.

Hamington, M. (2015a), "Care Ethics and Engaging Intersectional Difference through the Body," *Critical Philosophy of Race*, 3 (1): 79–100.

Hamington, M. (2015b), "Politics Is Not a Game: The Radical Potential of Care," in D. Engster and M. Hamington (eds), *Care Ethics and Political Theory*, 272–292, Oxford: Oxford University Press.

Hamington, M. (2016), "A Performative Theory of Care," *Care Ethics and the Body*, Utrecht, January 25, 2016.

Haraway, D. J. (1991), *Simians, Cyborgs, and Women: The Reinvention of Nature*, London: Free Association Books.

Hochschild, A. R. (2003), *The Managed Heart. Commercialization of Human Feeling*, Berkeley: University of California Press.

Hughes, B., L. McKie, D. Hopkins, and N. Watson (2005), "Love's Labours Lost? Feminism, the Disabled People's Movement and an Ethic of Care," *Sociology—The Journal of the British Sociological Association*, 39 (2): 259–275, doi:10.1177/0038038505050538.

Isaksen, L. W., S. U. Devi, and A. R. Hochschild (2008), "Global Care Crisis a Problem of Capital, Care Chain, or Commons?" *American Behavioral Scientist*, 52 (3): 405–425, doi:10.1177/0002764208323513.

Kaga, Y., J. Bennett, and P. Moss (2010), *Caring and Learning Together. A Cross-National Study on the Integration on Early Childhood Care and Education within Education*, Paris: UNESCO.

Kurban, F. and J. Tobin (2009), "'They Don't Like Us': Reflections of Turkish Children in a German Preschool," *Contemporary Issues in Early Childhood*, 10 (1): 24–34.

Kyriacou, C., Tollisen Ellingsen, P. Stephens, and V. Sundaram (2009), "Social Pedagogy and the Teacher: England and Norway Compared," *Pedagogy, Culture & Society*, 17 (1): 75–87.

Lather, P. (1991), *Getting Smart. Feminist Research and Pedagogy with/in the Postmodern*, New York: Routledge.

Lazarri, A. and M. Vandenbroeck (2013), "Accessibility of ECEC for Children from Ethnic Minority and Low-Income Families," Accessed June 22, 2018, http://en.calameo.com/read/001774295780e9c56e158?authid=lunFhaVetzQ6.

Lehrer, J. S., N. Bigras, and I. Laurin (2017), "Preparing to Start School: Parent and Early Childhood Educator Narratives," in S. Dockett, W. Griebel, and B. Perry (eds), *Families and Transition to School. International Perspectives on Early Childhood Education and Development*, Cham: Springer.

Leseman, P. P. M., and P. L. Slot (2014), "Breaking the Cycle of Poverty: Challenges for European Early Childhood Education and Care," *European Early Childhood Education Research Journal*, 22 (3): 314–326.

Lister, R. (1997), *Citizenship: Feminist Perspective*, Basingstoke: Macmillan.

Löfdahl, A. and M. Folke-Fichtelius (2015), "Preschool's New Suit: Care in Terms of Learning and Knowledge," *Early Years*, 35 (3): 260–272.

Lorenz, W. (2016), "Rediscovering the Social Question," *European Journal of Social Work*, 19 (1): 4–17.

Lynch, K. (2016), "Care, Education and Resistance: Why Affective Equality Matters," "Care and Carers in Education" conference, University of Roehampton, London, September 5, 2016.

Lynch, K., M. Lyons, and S. Cantillon (2007), "Breaking Silence: Educating Citizens for Love, Care and Solidarity," *International Studies in Sociology of Education*, 17 (1–2): 1–19.

Lynch, K., J. Baker, and M. Lyons (2009), *Affective Equality: Love, Care and Injustice*, Basingstoke: Palgrave Macmillan.

Melhuish, E., K. Ereky-Stevens, K. Petrogiannis, A. Ariescu, E. Penderi, K. Rentzou, A. Tawell, P. Leseman, and M. Broekhuisen (2015), "A Review of Research on the Effects of Early Childhood Education and Care (ECEC) on Child Development," WP4 Accessed November 3, 2015, http://ecec-care.org/fileadmin/careproject/Publications/reports/CARE_WP4_D4__1_review_of_effects_of_ecec.pdf.

Moss, P. (2013), "The Relationship between Early Childhood and Compulsory Education: A Properly Political Question," in P. Moss (ed.), *Early Childhood and Compulsory Education: Reconceptualising the Relationship*, 2–50, London: Routledge.

Noddings, N. (1984), *Caring: A Feminine Approach to Ethics*, Berkeley: University of California Press.

Oberhuemer, P., I. Schreyer, and M. Neuman (2010), *Professionals in Early Childhood Education and Care Systems. European Profiles and Perspectives*, Farmington Hills, MI: Barbara Budrich Publishers.

OECD (2006), *Starting Strong II. Early Childhood Education and Care*, Paris: OECD Publishing.

OECD (2013), *PISA 2012 Results: Excellence through Equity (Volume II)*, Paris: OECD Publishing.

OECD (2016), *PISA 2015 Results (Volume I). Excellence and Equity in Education*, Paris: OECD Publishing.

Price, J. and M. Shildrick (1999), *Feminist Theory and the Body: A Reader*, Edinburgh: Edinburgh University Press.

Rake, K. (2001), "Gender and New Labour's Social Policies," *Journal of Social Policy*, 30: 209–231.

Reindal, S. M. (1999), "Independence, Dependence, Interdependence: Some Reflections on the Subject and Personal Autonomy," *Disability & Society*, 14 (3): 353–367.

Roets, G., P. Smeyers, M. Vandenbroeck, M. De Bie, I. Derluyn, R. Roose, B. Vanobbergen, L. Bradt, and A. Van Gorp (2017), "Du choc des idées jaillit la lumière: Thinking with Eric Broekaert's Integrated and Holistic Paradigm of Education," *Therapeutic Communities*, 38 (3): 169–176.

Shildrick, M. (1997), *Leaky Bodies and Boundaries. Feminism, Postmodernism and (Bio)ethics*, London: Routledge.

Timmermans, S. and I. Tavory (2012), "Theory Construction in Qualitative Research: From Grounded Theory to Abductive Analysis," *Sociological Theory*, 30 (3): 167–186.

Tobin, J. (1997), *Making a Place for Pleasure in Early Childhood Education*, New Haven, CT: Yale University Press.

Tobin, J. (2009), "Children Crossing Borders: Including the Voices of Migrant Families in ECEC Programmes," Unpublished document.

Tobin, J. (ed.) (2016), *Preschool and Im/migrants in Five Countries. England, France, Germany, Italy and United States of America. Vol. 1, Early Childhood and Education. New Perspective on Early Childhood Education and Care*, Brussels: P.I.E. Peter Lang.

Tobin, J. and Y. Hsueh (2007), "The Poetics and Pleasures of Video Ethnography of Education," in R. Goldman (ed.), *Video Research in the Learning Sciences*, 77–92, New York: Lawrence Erlbaum Associates.

Tobin, J., A. Arzubiaga, and J. K. Adair (2013), *Children Crossing Borders. Immigrant Parent and Teacher Perspectives on Preschool*, New York: Russell Sage.

Tobin, J., D. Y. H. Wu, and D. H. Davidson (1989), *Preschool in Three Cultures. Japan, China, and the United States*, New Haven, CT and London: Yale University Press.

Tronto, J. C. (1993), *Moral Boundaries: A Political Argument for an Ethic of Care*, London: Routledge.

Twigg, J., C. Wolkowitz, R. L. Cohen, and S. Nettleton (2011), "Conceptualising Body Work in Health and Social Care," *Sociology of Health & Illness*, 33 (2): 171–188, doi:10.1111/j.1467-9566.2010.01323.x.

Van Laere, K. (2017), "Conceptualisations of Care and Education in Early Childhood Education and Care," Doctoral Dissertation. Promotor Prof. Dr. Michel Vandenbroeck., Department of Social Work and Social Pedagogy, Ghent University.

Van Laere, K. and M. Vandenbroeck (2017), "Early Learning in Preschool: Meaningful and Inclusive for All? Exploring Perspectives of Migrant Parents and Staff," *European Early Childhood Education Research Journal*, 1–15, doi:10.1080/135029 3X.2017.1288017.

Van Laere, K., M. Vandenbroeck, G. Roets, and J. Peeters (2014), "Challenging the Feminisation of the Workforce: Rethinking the Mind-Body Dualism in Early Childhood Education and Care," *Gender and Education*, 26 (3): 232–245.

Vandekinderen, C. and G. Roets (2016), "The Post(hu)man Always Rings Twice: Theorising the Difference of Impairment in the Lives of People with 'Mental Health Problems," *Disability & Society*, 31 (1): 33–46.

Vandenbroeck, M., F. Coussee, and L. Bradt (2010), "The Social and Political Construction of Early Childhood Education," *British Journal of Educational Studies*, 58 (2): 139–153, doi:10.1080/00071001003752237.

Warin, J. (2014), "The Status of Care: Linking Gender and 'Educare'," *Journal of Gender Studies*, 23 (1): 93–106, doi:10.1080/09589236.2012.754346.

Watson, N., L. McKie, B. Hughes, D. Hopkins, and S. Gregory (2004), "(Inter) dependence, Needs and Care: The Potential for Disability and Feminist Theorists to Develop an Emancipatory Model," *Sociology*, 38 (2): 331–350.

Williams, F. (1999), "Good-Enough Principles for Welfare," *Journal of Social Policy*, 28 (4): 667–687.

Williams, F. (2001), "In and beyond New Labour: Towards a New Political Ethics of Care," *Critical Social Policy*, 21 (4): 467–493.

Witz, A. (2000), "Whose Body Matters? Feminist Sociology and the Corporeal Turn in Sociology and Feminism," *Body & Society*, 6 (2): 1–23.

Wolkowitz, C. (2006), *Bodies at Work*, London: Sage.

Woodhead, M. (2006), "Changing Perspectives on Early Childhood: Theory, Research and Policy," *International Journal of Equity and Innovation in Early Childhood*, 4 (2): 1–43.

9

Nurturing Hope to Support Autonomy: The Role of Early Childhood Educators

Amy Mullin

Theorists writing from many different perspectives routinely emphasize the importance of respecting people's autonomy and, just as routinely, argue or more commonly assume that young children have no autonomy. In this chapter, I define personal autonomy, explain why it is desirable in a wide variety of cultural contexts, and argue that children can, if properly supported, demonstrate autonomy in specific contexts.

I further argue that hope is a neglected but key condition for autonomy and that early childhood educators can nurture and sustain the hope of young children, including those aged three to eight. In order to do this, early childhood educators need to be aware of, attentive to, and responsive to individual children's varying capacities and goals so that they can help the children hope for goals that are both personally meaningful and toward which they can make progress.

Personal autonomy

I understand personal autonomy as the ability to self-govern in the service of personally meaningful goals and commitments. Autonomy is relational and not only are other people required to help develop autonomy but also other people can either sustain or thwart the ongoing exercise of it. In order to be autonomous and self-governing, there must first and foremost be a *self*—by this, I mean individuals can hold some relatively stable and personally meaningful commitments, rather than entertaining a series of frequently shifting impulses or a series of goals that are imposed externally. Most broadly, I describe relatively stable goals and commitments as what individuals care about—these could be own and other people's well-being, relationships with people and animals, development of new skills, acquisition of knowledge, time spent with favorite objects or in favorite contexts, or contributions to joint projects such as acting with others in a play or helping reduce negative impacts of human behavior on the environment.

While I speak of personally meaningful goals as key to autonomy, Colin Macleod talks about authentic goals and argues that an authentic goal is one that we can "represent to ourselves as choice-worthy in the sense that we recognize considerations that recommend its adoption" (Macleod 2003: 321). I disagree, and I distinguish between having a personally meaningful goal, commitment, or project and being able to reflect upon and articulate the worth of that goal, commitment, or project. The two can depart from one another in two different ways. First, there can be reasons why a certain project, ideal, or commitment may be worthy without an individual being personally motivated to pursue it. For example, it is not enough to think that playing the viola is a worthy activity because music is enjoyable to many people. One will not find playing the viola to be a personally meaningful goal if one does not like listening to viola music or making music, or if one does not think that the goal of making music is enough to make one spend a lot of time practicing the viola. Second, one may care deeply about a person or spending time in a favorite place without being able to articulate what makes that person or place especially valuable and without being able to explain what it means to value something. Individuals may just know that they want to be with the person and like it when that person smiles and laughs or that being in that place feels really good.

Barriers to autonomy

Individuals cannot be autonomous if there are barriers to achieving personally meaningful goals. External barriers occur either when the situation is so unpredictable that plans have little chance for success (e.g., while living in a chaotic home or a refugee camp), when there is not enough opportunity to understand an unfamiliar situation, or when other people deliberately or indifferently place obstacles in the way, for example, by limiting access to knowledge or by coercively preventing individuals from acting in preferred ways. When scholars think of barriers to acting autonomously, it is perhaps these external barriers that we think of first as we might imagine someone lying to or threatening us or taking for themselves the resources we need to achieve our ambitions.

There are also many internal barriers to autonomy. One type of internal barrier exists when individuals either do not understand their situation and resources well enough to make strides toward achieving goals or cannot imagine how they might make progress. Another internal barrier exists when individuals cannot depend upon themselves—for instance if impulses overpower the ability to persevere in the face of obstacles.

A final internal barrier is a lack of hope—the belief or an unarticulated assumption that progress toward achieving goals is not possible, even in situations in which there are no external barriers and when understanding and impulse control exist. This lack of hope could be because of experiences of external or internal barriers, because there is little in the way of imaginative resources that would help the finding of pathways to realizing goals, or because individuals have little self-confidence in their ability to negotiate the world and/or to work collaboratively with others toward mutual goals. Lack of hope might be because social recognition of worth and capacities is rarely received.

When individuals have personally meaningful goals and, rather than the above barriers, there are supportive others who help them imagine, understand, and persist, and who work collaboratively toward goals, then individuals can be autonomous in particular domains of their lives. I call this *local autonomy*, and in order to have it people must understand their options, and know their personal and social resources, and how they might be able to make progress toward their goals within a given domain, such as family life, or work, school, or in leisure time with friends.

Cross-cultural need for autonomy

My understanding of local autonomy as self-directed agency in service of personally meaningful goals is very similar to the account of autonomy offered in "Self Determination Theory" as initially developed by psychologists Edward Deci and Richard Ryan. According to self-determination theory, autonomy is one of the most important psychological needs people have cross-culturally, along with the need to be able to interact skillfully in local settings and have relationships with people that include mutual understanding and warmth (Deci and Ryan 2008: 15). People are autonomously motivated either when engaging in activities that they find interesting and enjoyable in themselves, or when they engage in activities for the sake of goals or values that they have internalized and accepted, as opposed to when they feel controlled by others.

Why might people want personal autonomy—for themselves and the people they care about? Autonomy is positively associated with finding activities to be meaningful and rewarding—either because the activities are rewarding in themselves or because there is a connection between activities and a chosen goal. Autonomy understood in the broad way I have sketched above, rather than in more narrow ways that associate it with independence from others and distance from and critical reflection upon priorities, is valued in a wide variety of cultures, both individualist and collectivist (Deci and Ryan 2008: 15–16). This is unsurprising because a lack of autonomy involves either a failure to be motivated toward any personal goals or feeling controlled by others because under threat of punishment or at risk of not having needs met if others do not approve of activities. It is clearly valuable for all people—including children—to find their activities to be either intrinsically rewarding or undertaken in pursuit of goals they freely embrace.

Children and autonomy

While personal autonomy is widely valued, it is also widely associated with adult status. Paternalism, or overriding another person's wishes with the goal of serving that person's interests, is routinely thought to be appropriate and, indeed, required for children but inappropriate in most circumstances for autonomous adults or older teens who qualify for adult status (discussed in Mullin 2014). Denial of any degree of autonomy in young children is routine—and rarely involves much in the way of argument. For example, Paul Benson observes that "the normal conditions of young childhood" are like Orwellian social conditioning, extreme abuse, and mental illness in interfering with autonomy (Benson 2005: 107). John Christman similarly writes: "Lacking autonomy, as children do, is a condition which allows or invites sympathy, pity, or invasive paternalism" (Christman 2018).

It is true that there are times and contexts in which children do not understand their situation or what will advance or undermine their interests, and times as well when they cannot control their impulses enough to act to achieve goals they care about. However, I think that widespread denial of autonomy in children fails to recognize the extent to which children can care deeply about things, especially other people and relationships with them (Mullin 2007). I have also argued that the fact that children typically depend considerably upon others to help them meet their needs does not undermine their autonomy so long as those others do not stand in the way of children making progress toward their goals by belittling, ignoring, or deceiving them (Mullin 2007). I believe the same is true in the case of adults with significant needs for help from others. Need for others' assistance only undermines autonomy when those others fail to respect the perspective and commitments of the person with the needs, whether adult or child.

I therefore consider young children, including those of an age to still be in early childhood education, as capable of local autonomy and believe they should be supported in acquiring and exercising it. My focus is on the period just after the infant and toddler stages of early childhood education—from ages three to eight. These children often have passionate attachments—especially to people in their lives as well as other things that they care stably about—and their attachments can provide them with personally meaningful goals. Children in this age range are also capable—albeit not always—of governing their actions in accordance with their goals, especially when they are not overly tired, hungry, or stressed. When their environments are not so chaotic as to prevent them from being able to make reasonable predictions about the potential outcomes of their efforts, and when they have sufficient experience of a particular domain of their lives, such as familiarity with the routines, personnel, and possibilities of their early childhood education context, then they can also imagine and explore feasible ways to achieve their goals within that domain.

It is hardly novel to recognize that autonomy requires people to understand their situation and that people cannot be autonomous if there are significant external barriers in the way of the pursuit of goals. Mackenzie has written persuasively about the importance of one potential internal barrier. She argues that people must be able to imagine how things could be otherwise because without that ability it is impossible to conceive of outcomes that are worth working toward (Mackenzie 2000). However, it is not enough for people to be able to imagine alternatives; people must also think that those alternatives might be realized. They must have hope.

Hope

The importance of *hope* has not been discussed in the literature about autonomy. If people do not have hope that valued relationships can be maintained or repaired, that they can protect and promote the well-being of people they care about, work cooperatively with trusted people to achieve shared goals, make progress toward acquiring skills and knowledge, and have experiences that make them happy, then it doesn't matter if they have goals and could make progress toward them if they tried because they won't try.

What do I mean by *hope*? How can it be distinguished from closely related concepts like optimism and self-efficacy (or the idea that goals can be achieved by working on one's own)? I begin by giving an account of a minimal philosophical account of hope, indicate how it fails to distinguish between hope and despair, and then survey several accounts of hope that attempt to make that distinction before introducing my own understanding of what I term *engaged hope*. I then indicate how engaged hope is similar to the way hope is understood in hope theory, developed in psychology by Snyder (2002). Finally, I distinguish engaged hope from wishful thinking, optimism, and self-efficacy.

Hope vs. despair

Day argues that hope is not an emotion but instead is the combination of a desire for an outcome with a belief that the outcome is neither certain to occur nor impossible (Day 1969: 98). However, Meirav (2009) points out that if hope is defined solely as desiring a good and believing it to be neither certain nor impossible to occur, then it cannot be distinguished from despair. Those who despair may desire an outcome and think it possible to achieve that outcome but assign it such a low probability that they despair of it coming to pass. Meirav attempts to distinguish hope from despair by suggesting that one who hopes must believe that aspects of the situation beyond one's control are well-disposed toward one. This seems implausible, as one can hope in the absence of information about the attitudes of others and might hope precisely because one believes others to be neutral rather than hostile.

There are several other attempts to differentiate hope from despair by emphasizing the extent to which hope involves a more-positive-than-not assessment of the possibility of achieving a desired outcome or involves an orientation toward action. Pettit, for instance, argues that hoping involves giving the desired outcome a "galvanizing and orientating role" while "setting aside doubts about the possible nonoccurrence of the prospect and acting accordingly" (2004: 152). I agree that hope characteristically involves readiness for action but not that it requires setting aside doubts or avoiding the development of backup plans. People can hope for the best but plan for the worst—or simply hope and yet doubt and keep alternatives open.

Engaged hope

Engaged hope is similar to Smith's analysis of hope, involving readiness for action and understanding the future as something one can shape (Smith 2008: 17), but goes beyond it to include actual exploration of pathways to achieving one's goal. If one is merely ready for action in support of a goal but does not explore any means of achieving that goal, one is not experiencing engaged hope. What I mean by engaged hope is in keeping with how hope has been characterized and measured in hope theory, which was developed in the 1990s by Snyder and extended since by him and others. According to hope theory, hope has three dimensions: goals, pathways, and motivation. Engaged hope requires an individual to have some goals, have thought about pathways to realizing these goals—ideally multiple pathways—and have some motivation to pursue them.

Given the way engaged hope is oriented toward action and planning in accordance with goals for the future, it does not include hoping that past events, whose outcome is still unknown by the person hoping, have gone well. It is distinct from the kind of hoping or wishful thinking that involves no planning or motivation toward action, such as hoping the weather will be fine tomorrow. It also differs from the kind of daydreaming that children often engage in— imagining outcomes they would like to see happen without actually expecting those outcomes to be realized as a result of any efforts of their own or with others and without exploring any realistic way in which the outcomes might come to be.

Engaged hope also differs from a generally optimistic attitude. The latter need not involve exploring means to achieve one's goals but instead merely assumes things will turn out for the best. Optimism may lead one to remain in risky situations or neglect opportunities that involve personal effort. General optimism may actually discourage one from taking action or exploring paths to achieving one's desired outcomes. McNulty and Fincham (2012), for instance, argue that optimism, or generalized expectation of positive future outcomes, is not inherently valuable (101). They show that optimists are more likely to gamble even when they experience negative consequences (103) and are less likely to seek to remedy their problematic behavior than those who are less optimistic (105).

Engaged hope may also be confused with beliefs about self-efficacy or believing one can accomplish goals alone. Both engaged hope and self-efficacy assume one can actively influence one's environment, however, self-efficacy is narrower, focusing on what one can achieve only through one's own actions

(Maddux 2009: 1). Engaged hope can involve recognition of circumstances and people beyond one's control as factors required to achieve goals. Engaged hope is exploratory, often more tentative than believing one can control a situation, and frequently involves working collaboratively with others to make progress toward one's goals.

When hope is defined and measured according to hope theory—involving goals, pathways, and motivation—it is clearly distinguished from despair but need not involve assuming high probability of a good outcome. In many cases, young children will have no clear or even vague estimation of the probability of desired outcomes when they hope. Engaged hope also differs from Bovens's understanding, according to which those who hope must engage in "mental imaging" of what it would be like if one were to achieve the hoped-for outcome. He writes: "Mental imaging is no less a necessary condition for hoping than the proper belief and desire" (1999: 674). Engaged hope goes beyond Bovens in requiring some motivation on the part of the one who hopes to pursue the goal rather than merely daydreaming about a world in which the goal is attained without one's efforts, or idly considering pathways without any intention of pursuing them. Engaged hope may also involve less than what Bovens requires as one can plausibly have a goal without devoting much attention to imagining what it would be like when the goal is realized. Children may have very little specific idea of what it would be like to attain a long-term goal but simply think it would be better than the present and focus on what it would be like to make progress toward it.

Engaged hope requires one to think that there is enough chance of a good outcome to make it worth exploring pathways to that goal and to be motivated to take steps along one of those paths should circumstances permit. It involves, as McGeer says, "taking an agential interest in the world" (McGeer 2008: 246). Hope can be highly unrealistic, depending on the person's temperament and knowledge about their situation and is particularly likely to be unrealistic when young children hope, as they may not have the information they need to assess their situation and prospects with much accuracy. Yet evidence from a large study of older children reveals that being hopeful does not keep children from attending to negative information and hence learning to accurately assess their odds.

A study of Chinese teenagers in Hong Kong suggests that youth high in hope focus more on positive information than those low in hope, but there is no correlation between high hope and inattention to negative information. Using a measure of children's hope called the Children's Hope Scale, the researchers found that hope positively correlated with attention to positive information and ability to reframe an event but had no correlation with attention to negative information (Yeung et al. 2015: 100). This means that those who hope are typically still alert to negative information that can lead to caution—or reversal— in pursuit of hopes, allowing those who hope to take risks while being aware of dangers.

Hope and children's autonomy

Having discussed engaged hope, I move on to connections between hope and autonomy. In what follows, when I refer to hope, I have engaged hope in mind. By autonomy, as discussed above, I mean the capacity to guide one's actions to pursue goals one finds personally meaningful.

When young children have goals they care about and can control their momentary impulses to achieve those goals, they can be autonomous in situations related to their goals, so long as they are not blocked from making progress, either by direct control or misdirection. Children's self-control can be undermined by stressors such as being ill, hungry, or very tired; their belief that they can make progress toward their goals can be undermined if they regularly face insurmountable obstacles or see the hopes of people they love regularly thwarted. If children cannot imagine alternatives to the present, they will not be able to hope and therefore attempt to pursue their goals.

Engaged hope already includes having goals and skills such as imagining situations being otherwise and exploring pathways to one's goals, both important to autonomy. Since engaged hope also includes being motivated to pursue goals, it presupposes that those who hope take their goals as reason for action. Thinking about hope can illuminate the extent to which being motivated to pursue one's goals is affected by circumstances that undermine hope. It is hard to hope and explore pathways to goals in the absence of some predictability in one's environment, or if one knows that others, such as parents or educators with the power to control one's options, will block attempts. Children who hope are responsive to features of context, like the presence or absence of supportive others and presence or absence of resources necessary to move toward their goals, which are important for autonomy.

In hope theory, hope is measured by what one believes or assumes about one's self. Therefore, one might hope without actually being able to act in ways that are in keeping with autonomy when the hope is based on self-deception about having the personal resources to pursue one's goals or because of failure to recognize obstacles in one's way. Hope is therefore no guarantee of autonomy but is necessary for it. This connection between hope and autonomy is reinforced by research that shows that being high in hope correlates strongly with finding meaning in life (Rand and Cheavens 2009: 7).

As individuals make progress toward the goals they have by virtue of hoping and as they face obstacles to progress, they have opportunities to learn more about what they care about and how to pursue their goals. Learning more about what they want and what they can do to work toward goals is an opportunity to learn more about who they are. Children in particular can learn about their skills, capabilities, and what they might need to develop, as well as what it feels like to achieve a goal or to be thwarted in its achievement, as they hope. This kind of self-understanding and experience of the world is an important resource for developing further areas of autonomy.

Rand and Cheavens show that people high in hope respond better to stressors than those lower in hope. People with hope generate more strategies in response to those stressors and are more likely to use them (Rand and Cheavens 2009: 97). Hope enables children to respond positively to challenges and view mistakes as opportunities to learn to better pursue their goals. Researchers often think that children are naturally high in hope but sometimes children may merely be optimistic or involved in imaginative play akin to wishful thinking.

Early childhood education and hope

Engaged hope can be a challenge to develop and sustain. Parents can certainly help their children develop hope and maintain it in the face of challenges, but early childhood educators have resources that parents do not, in that they have professional experience with many children in a certain age range, in a way that most parents who are not also early childhood educators do not. The educators therefore have more familiarity with what it is reasonable to expect of children at particular stages of development than their parents may have, and educators also have opportunities to connect the children they teach and care for with potential collaborative partners—children's peers for achieving their goals.

Moreover, education is important in sustaining and enabling hope because of its potential to increase opportunity. Clearly, parents have very different personal and social resources depending on their circumstances, and educators in schools and early childhood settings might be able to provide resources and expertise that parents living in poverty or otherwise very stressful circumstances do not have. Of course, educators will only be able to do this if institutions with high concentrations of at-risk children are adequately resourced, and if educators are taught how best to encourage and sustain hope in the children.

What kinds of opportunities to nurture hope are available to those who care for and educate young children? Shade argues that teachers can "generate a context of hope by having students work in small groups where the goal is to cooperatively overcome an obstacle to attain some specific end (such as learning about a new topic or ... solving problems)" (Shade 2006: 207). I take this as a very important reminder that hope is not the same as self-efficacy and that one of the most important lessons children can learn is that they can work toward common goals with others—both their peers and supportive adults like teachers.

Shade's remarks about teachers helping students work cooperatively in small groups to overcome an obstacle are not specific to any particular age group and may be thought to be more applicable to children older than those aged three to eight. However, I would argue that children in this age range are indeed capable of working together to solve problems, especially when they are supported by an educator. Moreover, an example Shade gives of a more personal and less collaborative goal—learning to read—is something that most children acquire in precisely this age range (Shade 2006: 208). He is certainly right to observe that reading is a complex skill that requires children to persist—and that reading aloud to others requires not only having a goal of learning to read and willingness to persist in the face of obstacles and frustrations, but also requires children to be courageous and risk embarrassment when they read aloud to others and make public mistakes. Children's responses to one another as they stumble and err as they learn to read also shows how even a relatively personal goal like learning to read benefits from a supportive community of fellow learners and can be undermined by a more critical response from other children. This gives their educators another way to inspire and support children's hope—by finding ways to foster a supportive attitude and actions from children's peers.

The role of stories

Both before children can read on their own and afterward, early childhood educators can incorporate stories into the curriculum that inspire hope and demonstrate protagonists overcoming obstacles—but the stories must resonate with the children to whom they are told. It is important for children to learn that they will face obstacles to achieving their goals, that those obstacles can be both internal and external, and that very often they will need to work with others to overcome the obstacles. Learning to recognize barriers to effective cooperation, like jealousy, resentment, and an unwillingness to appear vulnerable before others, as well as learning about strategies to overcome these barriers can be crucial for hope.

Educators need to strike a delicate balance between finding stories that inspire children with goals that are ambitious and avoiding stories that depend upon unlikely resources or assistance from others or which suggest that all children need to succeed is a positive attitude. Having dreams come true because there is a fairy godmother does not teach a child to hope but instead to wish. It is also not useful to teach children that all they need to achieve what they hope to achieve is a positive attitude, like the little engine who thought he could and so he could. Children, like adults, face far more barriers to realizing their dreams than needing to have a positive attitude—and a positive attitude is actually something they are already likely to have when very young. If educators teach children that they can accomplish their goals simply by believing in themselves, then children are not learning when they need to work with others, when they need to acquire new skills, how to navigate a system that does not make it easy for them to make progress without feeling stupid, and when they might need to find a way to retain while nonetheless modifying important goals.

Educators need to listen to the children in their care and discover what goals the children have for themselves, what achievements they are proud of, and what obstacles they have overcome before selecting stories that can inspire and support hope in their listeners. One excellent way of doing this can be to have children tell stories, scaffolded by their educators, about what they'd like to achieve in the near future and when they are grown, as well as stories about what they have already achieved. Educators can model the idea that achievements can be the work of a group and can include helping others, growing plants, and taking care of the environment rather than only solo and competitive activities.

Teaching children to hope is not primarily about teaching them to work toward goals in a distant future, although it can be important to help them make connections between short-term and long-term goals. Children from three to eight have plenty of opportunities to strive for important goals that can be achieved during that period and to recognize how those short-term goals can be meaningful not only in the short term but also as part of long-term plans. It can be important to recognize that achievements that most children will realize between three and eight, like learning to read or do simple math, are both hard to achieve and worthy of celebration.

Educators can help young children see how larger goals can be broken into small goals so that meaningful progress can be made. Learning the alphabet is part of learning to sound out words, and learning to sound out words is part of learning to read both words that make sense phonetically and those that need to be memorized. Getting good at reading *Captain Underpants* books is part of becoming a good reader who may one day become a writer or teacher or any of the other professions that depend upon being a good reader. Similarly, learning to recognize numbers and learning how to count are part of being able to divide piles of toys fairly, pay for items and receive the right amount of change, become good enough at math to build bridges as an engineer, or order the right amount of food as a manager in a grocery store. Learning how some goals can be nested inside others can be part of being inspired to persevere. Educators, in turn, can best learn how to relate smaller goals to larger ones in children's lives by listening to the children's hopes for themselves not only for when they grow up, but also for when they are just a little older than they are right now.

Collaboration to nurture hope and achieve goals

One of the most important ways to nurture hope in children is to regard them as people who not only have the potential to accomplish things in the future but who can also make positive contributions to their own and others' lives now, while they are still very young. Child-centered education, in which children share direction with their teachers, not only allows children to shape their daily activities in ways that reflect their interests, but also teaches them that they have ideas worth listening to and goals worth respecting. Headteacher Kate Nash describes Silverhill Primary School in the UK as offering just such child-centered education (Warwick et al. 2018). The school stresses care for the self, care for others, and care for the environment and encourages children to develop ways of contributing to these goals. Teachers work collaboratively with one another to teach their young students how to work with one another and with people in communities both close and distant as they partner with schools in India and Africa and learn from scientists at a research station in Antarctica. The children routinely spend unstructured time in nature, have plenty of opportunities for self-directed play, are encouraged to ask open-ended questions, create books together with their teachers as learning tools for themselves and future students, and also brainstorm and carry out mutually formed plans for respecting the environment.

Another preschool, this one located in a socially disadvantaged Australian community attended by many children from low-income families and run cooperatively by their families, shows that child-centered education can take place in schools that are not very well resourced. Arthur and Sawyer describe Indigo Preschool (a pseudonym) as founded on collaboration and partnerships with a focus on respecting children as active social participants with insights into their own experiences and ideas worth acting upon (Arthur and Sawyer 2009). Teachers, family members, and children all have input into what happens at Indigo, from the daily curriculum to what goes into children's portfolios. Sharing ownership of their portfolios encourages children to reflect upon their own achievements and demonstrate the work of which they are most proud to others, reminding them of what they worked toward in the past, and that they are capable of further achievements going forward—in other words, nurturing hope. One example of the way children shape their curriculum involves the fact that one boy's interests in lessons about dinosaurs and extinction led to his eager learning about the nest of a species of endangered bird encountered while on a family vacation. He then came back to share this with his class, who then researched more about the birds and animals currently endangered in Australia (Arthur and Sawyer 2006).

Early childhood educators can only nurture hope in children when they have good relationships with them. Nurturing someone else's hopes requires listening to and learning from that other person, and children will only disclose their hopes when they trust their teachers. Robin Dillon's concept of *care respect* can be helpful here in outlining the appropriate attitude for early childhood educators to have toward the children in their care. Too often, we think of respect as something owed only to adults who are relatively independent and capable of interacting and cooperating with others as equals. While it is true that children typically need more assistance in achieving their goals than adults do, to a large extent this is only a matter of degree, as we all need help from others in achieving our goals. Moreover, dependence on others should be no barrier to respect. I have argued above that children are capable of directing their behavior to accord with personally meaningful goals in certain situations when they understand their situation and their options and have the personal resources to overcome conflicting impulses and doubts that may arise in response to obstacles, in other words that children are sometimes autonomous. Therefore, I also think there should be no sharp distinction between respecting children's autonomy and respecting adults' autonomy, even though typically adults will have more areas in which they are capable of local autonomy than children have.

Nonetheless, Dillon draws our attention to a way in which all people, whether dependent or not, whether autonomous or not, deserve respect by pointing to a kind of respect that involves providing care and support rather than refraining from intruding upon one another. For Dillon, care respect involves directing attention toward the person for whom we are caring and seeing that person as worthy of close attention (Dillon 1992: 108–109). Care respect has three core features:

1. response to and valuing of others in their particularity,
2. recognition that each person has their own perspective, and
3. recognition that each person depends upon others and yet is also separate from them (Dillon 1992: 115).

Care respect for others therefore requires being attentive and humble. Early childhood educators should not assume that they know what children want and need and what they are capable of but instead should seek to discover these in dialogue. Educators should be open to learning from those they teach and care for, including young children. Educators should also be aware that the people in their care need to trust the educators before they will disclose their needs and interests, what they fear, and what they long for. It is therefore very important for early childhood educators to work on their relationships with the children they teach and care for.

In fact, teachers' perceptions of the quality of their relationships with young children in kindergarten and grade one are strongly predictive of children's development of important skills like writing. The more conflictual the relationship, the lower the performance on independently scored samples of writing, even controlling for the quality of children's receptive language and grade level (White 2013: 172). In addition, at-risk children who have supportive relationships with their teachers perform as well in reading as children who are not at risk while their at-risk peers who do not have supportive relationships do not (White 2013: 167). While it may seem vague to encourage teachers to work on their relationships with the young children in their care, White notes that teachers identified as supportive are those who allow children to shape the kind of writing that they do and show understanding of the choices that children make in their writing (White 2013: 168). Dillon's account of care respect can also serve as an important guide, with its stress on recognizing that children have their own perspectives. To this I add that vulnerability and dependence are perfectly compatible with the ability to make contributions (Mullin 2011).

Children's educators can nurture children's hopes by having hopes for them and attending to children's hopes for themselves. Educators can model respect for a variety of kinds of lives and achievements so that children do not feel that there is only one way to succeed. Educators can show how they sustain their own hope by demonstrating how they respond to obstacles to achieving their own goals with continued hope and exploration of new pathways to achievement— or by developing new goals. Educators can show that supportive others can help to achieve one's goals. Educators can encourage children to have a variety of hopes so that the children are not demoralized when they don't reach one of those goals.

Children's educators can help children think about different pathways to their goals and encourage hopes that involve making progress rather than competing with others. To this point, I have been stressing young children's academic accomplishments, such as reading, writing, and learning about the world and math. However, early childhood education also has a great deal to do with helping children develop physical skills. When children engage in physical activities like running, jumping, manipulating scissors, and turning cartwheels, they can be inspired to take delight in their accomplishments, even if they are not particularly physically deft at the outset or one of the first people in their program to master a new skill, rather than thinking they should only persevere if they are better than others around them. Children are far more likely to have their hopes sustained and nurtured when they focus on newly acquired physical skills rather than when they focus on what they can or cannot do in comparison with others. Even the children who fare well in such comparisons become vulnerable to seeing their accomplishments as valuable only when they are better than others. This makes their sense of self-worth, which is key for hope, dependent on how they fare in competition. Moreover, a competitive attitude makes collaboration and cooperation, of the sort that is required to make progress in most areas of life more difficult.

Besides academic and physical accomplishments, children in early childhood education frequently have opportunities for artistic accomplishments, both ones they do on their own (or with an educator's assistance) and group accomplishments like painting a wall in a classroom or putting on a puppet show, dance performance, or play. These are another source of accomplishments that need not be competitive and can be shared with an appreciative audience, whether of family members who display their children's artistic creations, or peers who watch a puppet show, dance, or play.

Conclusion

In conclusion, autonomy is of significant value for all people who are capable of it, including children, and hope plays an important role in enabling autonomy. I have explored what I call engaged hope and discussed how it differs from optimism, wishful thinking, or hopes that do not involve motivation to act and exploration of pathways to achieving what one hopes for. I have written about the implications of my arguments for early childhood education with a focus on how early childhood educators can enable children to develop and sustain engaged hope. I have argued that intellectual, physical, and artistic tasks provide opportunities for achievement and hence, for hope, and that children can hope not only for outcomes that they work toward on their own, but also, and more often, for achievements that require collaborative effort. Early childhood educators have a tremendous opportunity to support children as they develop goals, explore pathways to realizing them, and take steps toward the outcomes they hope for.

References

Arthur, L. and W. Sawyer (2009), "Robust Hope, Democracy, and Early Childhood Education," *Early Years*, 29 (2): 163–175.

Benson, P. (2005), "Taking Ownership: Authority and Voice in Autonomous Agency," in J. Christman and J. Anderson (eds), *Autonomy and the Challenge to Liberalism*, 101–126, Cambridge: Cambridge University Press.

Bovens, L. (1999), "The Value of Hope," *International Phenomenological Society*, 59 (3): 667–681.

Christman, J. (2018), "Autonomy in Moral and Political Philosophy," in E. N. Zalta (ed.), *The Stanford Encyclopedia of Philosophy*. Available online: https://plato.stanford.edu/archives/spr2018/entries/autonomy-moral/.

Day, J. P. (1969), "Hope," *American Philosophical Quarterly*, 6 (2): 89–102.

Deci, E. L. and R. M. Ryan (2008), "Facilitating Optimal Motivation and Psychological Well-Being across Life's Domains," *Canadian Psychology/Psychologie Canadienne*, 49 (1): 14–23.

Dillon, R. S. (1992), "Respect and Care: Towards Moral Integration," *Canadian Journal of Philosophy*, 22 (1): 105–132.

Mackenzie, C. (2000), "Imagining Oneself Otherwise," in C. Mackenzie and N. Stoljar (eds), *Relational Autonomy: Feminist Perspectives on Autonomy, Agency and the Social Self*, 124–150, New York: Oxford University Press.

Macleod, C. (2003), "Shaping Children's Convictions," *Theory and Research in Education*, 1 (3): 315–330.

Maddux, J. E. (2009), "Self-Efficacy: The Power of Believing You Can," in S. J. Lopez and C. R. Snyder (eds), *The Oxford Handbook of Positive Psychology*, 2nd edn, 323–333, Oxford: Oxford University Press.

McGeer, V. (2008), "Trust, Hope and Empowerment," *Australasian Journal of Philosophy*, 86 (2): 237–254.

McNulty, J. K. and F. D. Fincham (2012), "Beyond Positive Psychology: Toward a Contextual View of Psychological Processes and Well-Being," *American Psychologist*, 67 (2): 101–110.

Meirav, A. (2009), "The Nature of Hope," *Ratio*, 32 (2): 216–233.

Mullin, A. (2007), "Children, Autonomy and Care," *Journal of Social Philosophy*, 38 (4): 536–553.

Mullin, A. (2011), "Gratitude and Caring Labour," *Ethics and Social Welfare*, special issue on Ethics of Care, C. Koggell and J. Orme (eds), 5 (2): 110–122.

Mullin, A. (2014), "Children, Paternalism, and the Development of Autonomy," *Ethical Theory and Moral Practice*, 17: 413–426.

Pettit, P. (2004), "Hope and Its Place in Mind," *The Annals of the American Academy*, 592: 152–165.

Rand, K. L. and J. S. Cheavens (2009), "Hope Theory," in S. J. Lopez and C. R. Snyder (eds), *The Oxford Handbook of Positive Psychology*, 2nd edn, 323–333, Oxford: Oxford University Press.

Shade, P. (2006), "Educating Hopes," *Studies in Philosophy and Education*, 25: 191–225.

Smith, N. (2008), "Analysing Hope," *Critical Horizons: A Journal of Philosophy and Social Theory*, 9 (1): 5–23.

Snyder, C. R. (2002), "Hope Theory: Rainbows in the Mind," *Psychological Inquiry*, 13: 249–275.

Warwick, P., A. Warwick, and K. Nash (2018), "Towards a Pedagogy of Hope: Sustainability Education in the Early Years," in V. Huggins and D. Evans (eds), *Early Childhood Education and Care for Sustainability: International Perspectives*, 28–39, New York: Routledge.

White, K. Meyer (2013), "Associations between Teacher Child Relationships and Children's Writing in Kindergarten and First Grade," *Early Childhood Research Quarterly*, 28: 166–176.

Yeung, D. Y., S. M. Y. Ho, and C. W. Y. Mak (2015), "Brief Report: Attention to Positive Information Mediates the Relationship between Hope and Psychosocial Well-Being of Adolescents," *Journal of Adolescence*, 42: 98–102.

10

Enacting Twenty-First-Century Early Childhood Education: Curriculum as Caring

B. Denise Hodgins, Sherri-Lynn Yazbeck, and Kelsey Wapenaar

Worlds seen through care accentuate a sense of interdependency and involvement. What challenges are posed to critical thinking by increased acute awareness of its material consequences? What happens when thinking about and with others is understood as living with them? When the effects of caring, or not, are brought closer? Here, knowledge that fosters caring for neglected things enters in tension between a critical stance against neglect and the fostering of speculative commitment to think how things could be different.
María Puig de la Bellacasa, *Matters of Care*

The pedagogical inquires that we (Denise, Sherri-Lynn, and Kelsey) draw on in this chapter took place on the unceded traditional territory of the Lekwungen-speaking peoples, and we acknowledge that the Songhees, Esquimalt, and WSÁNEĆ peoples have continued relationships with the land today. We offer our acknowledgment with gratitude that as uninvited settlers we have the opportunity to research, teach, and live on these lands. We also offer this acknowledgment and gratitude knowing that it is not the culmination of our responsibility, but rather it is only the beginning. In our work as educators, we are committed to the labor of becoming accountable to the complexities, demands, and active ethical and political answerabilities of living in settler colonial spaces.

Centuries in the making, this ongoing collective work is a twenty-first-century necessity, one that is deeply entangled with other twenty-first-century challenges. Children today are inheriting the legacies of colonization, human-caused climate change, mass species extinction, rapid technological advancements, and mass migration and displacement. Innovative pedagogies within the field of early childhood education (ECE) are urgently needed to address, respond to, and engage with the realities of twenty-first-century children, families, and communities (Common World Childhoods Research Collective 2015; Pacini-Ketchabaw and Taylor 2015; Skott-Myhre et al. 2016; White et al. 2017). Just as previous movements such as industrialization and urban change gave birth to new approaches and practices to early learning and care, the twenty-first century requires novel questions and pedagogies that extend how and what ECE requires and responds to. The inquiry moments and reflections that we share with you in this chapter take this call seriously, focusing on the potential that a feminist materialism reconceptualization of care holds in efforts to unsettle Euro-Western developmental and anthropocentric hegemony and reimagine pedagogies for and with twenty-first-century children.

The moments and reflections recounted here have emerged through an ongoing action research study with early childhood educators and young children that began in 2011 at a university-based child care center in British Columbia (Canada) with five different programs: one for infants, two for toddlers, and two for children aged three to five. The purpose of this research is to implement, disseminate, and extend pedagogical approaches outlined in the *BC Early Learning Framework* (Government of British Columbia 2008a, b). As an action research project, we investigate and experiment with pedagogical approaches and understandings through inquiry work and make these (partially) visible through the process and products of pedagogical narrations (Government of British Columbia 2008b; Hodgins 2012). The information generated through the inquiries is integral to the daily planning and development of the curriculum and pedagogical approaches in the participating programs.

We come to this work in different roles: Denise Hodgins as a pedagogist and researcher; Sherri-Lynn Yazbeck and Kelsey Wapenaar as early childhood educators and co-researchers in our collective inquiries. This chapter draws on three inquiries from our work; one that took place in 2012–13 within one of the toddler programs, and two that are, as we write, still taking place within the programs for three to five year olds. Our (re)presentation is a trace of our collective thinking, offered as a provocation to consider how complex conceptualizations of more-than-human relationality might help educators to enact a care(ing) curriculum that responds to the material, colonial, and environmental legacies that we all live with and bequeath to children. The chapter begins with an introduction to the feminist materialism conceptualization of care that is engaged with in this chapter, followed by three stories from our work, and concludes with considerations about crafting conditions for enacting curriculum as care(ing).

Conceptualizing care through feminist materialism

Feminist theorizing has played a significant role in challenging taken-for-granted assumptions about gender hierarchies used to regulate behavior and opportunities, including in relation to care practices (de Beauvoir 2011/1949; Friedan 2013/1963). Importantly, a feminist ethics of care (Held 2006; Noddings 2003/1984, 2005; Tronto 1993, 1995) has helped to illuminate the under-valuation of care as both a value and a practice.

This feminist ethic challenged care as understood through a public–private binary and thus opened up envisioning care outside of personal (individual) abilities and affects, beyond the reaches of home life, and as an ethic of interdependence that is always already politicized. This vision influenced pedagogical theorizing to challenge understandings and practices of care as simplified and uncontextualized (in ECE, see Dahlberg and Moss 2005; Dahlberg et al. 1999; in children's services and care work, see Jones and Osgood 2007; Moss and Petrie 2002; in elementary schooling, see Noddings 2003/1984, 2005). These challenges have mattered greatly in our work with young children, educators, and families, where care has predominantly been understood through Euro-Western traditions and seen as an un-problematic, apolitical, universal principle that educators (caregivers) simply know how to execute (Thompson 2015).

Added to this theorizing have been our engagements with recent conceptualizations of care within material feminism theories (Barad 2007; Haraway 1994, 2008, 2016). Of particular importance to this chapter is María Puig de la Bellacasa's careful (re)reading of critical feminism and an early feminist ethics of care that emerged from Joan Tronto's work. With a feminist materialist, more-than-human relational ontology, Puig de la Bellacasa (2017) thickens this ethics of care to include both human and nonhuman relationality and interdependence, where care operates with/in nature–culture assemblages. In other words, care emerges and exists through already entangled networks of human and nonhuman, material and discursive, perceptible and unexpected actants (Latour 2005). With Bruno Latour, actants are understood as any thing that acts upon another actor (both human and more-than-human), and assemblages are that which is gathered/entangled. For Latour, assemblages are not only that which is "there" but also why/how that which comes together *and* their generative potential. Attending to these assemblages is how, for Latour (2004), matters of fact (indisputable and simply there) become matters of concern.

Puig de la Bellacasa is theorizing within this Latourian landscape, reading it through a lens of feminism that "engages persistent forms of exclusion, power and domination" (2011: 91). She extends Latour's matters of concern with her proposal of matters of care—not to replace "concern at the heart of the politics of things" (89) but to thicken the vision and consequent action. For Puig de la Bellacasa, the use of the word *concern* instead of *fact* brings "connotations of trouble, worry and care" (2011: 87). But the word *care*, she explains, pushes more toward "a notion of material doing" (2011: 90). In her words:

> As is the case with most feminist attempts to re-affect the objectified world, this way of knowing/caring in our staging of things relates to a politics of knowledge, in that it generates possibilities for other ways of relating and living, it connects things that are not supposed to reach across the bifurcation of consciousness, and transforms the ethico-political and affective perception of things by the way we represent them. (99)

In Puig de la Bellacasa's early publications theorizing care, she defines care as "an affective state, a material vital doing, and an ethico-political obligation" (2011: 90). That triplet (an affective state, a material vital doing, and an ethico-political obligation)—entangled, inseparable, essential—is what we have been increasingly working to attend to in our pedagogical research and practice. This is not an idealized or simplified vision of care where all would be well if only we tried hard enough, if only we just learned how to really care. A feminist ethics of care has been instrumental in making visible that "these three dimensions of care—labor/work, affect/affections, ethics/politics—are not necessarily equally distributed in all relational situations, nor do they sit together without tensions and contradictions" (Puig de la Bellacasa 2017: 5). As educators, we are curious (and hopeful) about the possibilities for pedagogies that "carr[y] the triptych of care as 'ethics-work-affect' into the terrain of the politics of knowledge, into the implications of thinking with care" (Puig de la Bellacasa 2017: 13). What might living such pedagogies create for twenty-first-century childhoods? What is required?

In the sections that follow, we mobilize these perspectives in our exploration of the ethico-political and more-than-human relations that are always already situated with/in the ordinary routine encounters of children, teachers, materials, and places with/in early childhood curriculum in order to disrupt child- and future-centered developmental interpretations of pedagogical encounters and to rethink "caring for young children" amid the colonialist, social, and environmental challenges that exist today. As noted, we do so through the sharing of three stories that have grown within our action research inquiries. In the first story, I (Denise) review how thinking with Puig de la Bellacasa's conceptualization of care came into our work, initially through an inquiry that explored gender, care, dolls, and cars to become a methodological and concerted approach to our current research inquiries. In the second story we (Sherri-Lynn and Denise) share narratives and reflections of an ongoing inquiry that explores the complex entanglements of children, forest, other species, and bike jumps. The third story is another ongoing inquiry that we (Kelsey and Denise) are in the middle of, one that focuses on investigations and experimentations through gardening. We share these three stories *not* as a means to recount what we "found" in those particular inquires, but rather to illuminate our grapplings and engagements with an extended, feminist materialism, ethics of care. Our stories do not conclude with tidy declarations about dolls, cars, forest, or garden and child relations, though we have written about this research more extensively elsewhere (Haro Woods et al. 2018; Hodgins 2014, 2016; Waapenar and DeSchutter 2018). Consistent with our understanding of care as a doing that refuses taken-for-granted or "easy" notions of care, our caring is an ongoing practice that resists the certainty allowed by bounded or romanticized conceptions of care as a straightforward, universalized, intact act. For us, caring requires that we actively refuse to rest with conclusions, instead doing care as a constant attention to complexity, uncertainty, and situatedness. The three stories we share argue for living "caring in all its senses as a core needed practice" (Haraway 2008: 332) but not simply or only because we work with young children. As Moss (2017) has cautioned, there is a danger that the use of the word *care* in relation to early childhood reifies a view that "'care' is of exclusive or even particular relevance to young children" (13). Like Moss, our thinking is that an ethic of care is a core needed practice that reaches well beyond early childhood, one that "should inform all aspects of life and includes attentiveness, responsibility, competence and responsiveness" (Moss 2017: 13, drawing on Tronto 1993). While we do not definitively sum up our little stories, we do conclude each section by offering our momentary, tentative understanding of caring—this, for us, often involves asking questions and sharing our discomforts, rather than articulating a solution-oriented or "perfect" care that has resolved our uncertainties. We then conclude our chapter with a few considerations about how to create conditions for enacting such a care(ing) curriculum.

Baby dolls and toy cars—Coming to care

In my (Denise's) doctoral research, an inquiry that explored how conceptualizations and practices of gender and care are intra-actively related

(Barad 2007), the participating educators and I came to recognize that emerging gender and caring subjectivities touch many material-discursive practices in, near, and far from the classroom (Hodgins 2014, 2016). While care was a subject of research in that particular study, I have come to recognize that care was also a doing. This began to fuel my curiosity about the potentiality of putting care to work as a conceptual framework and method in ECE research and practices intended to, as Donna Haraway says, "get at how worlds are made and unmade, in order to participate in the processes, in order to foster some forms of life and not others" (Haraway 1994: 65).

When the educators and I began that research, we observed and documented moments of practice for the purposes of further dialogue and pedagogical experimentation, in relation to considering gender and care. At the beginning I asked the educators not to change their routine or setup; we would document what the *BC Early Learning Framework* calls "ordinary moments" (Government of British Columbia 2008a) and look for jumping off points related to gender and care that we found intriguing/interesting. When we (re)viewed the early documentation, the educators and I were drawn to particular moments involving baby dolls and toy cars. We did not set out to explore dolls and cars, but we were pulled to these moments and, like the children, drawn to these materials. The educators and I became deeply curious about what the dolls and cars might teach us about gender and care. Haraway describes curiosity as "the beginning of fulfillment of the obligation to know more as a consequence of being called into response" (Gane and Haraway 2006: 143). As I re-reflect on those early moments of our research through the lens of Puig de la Bellacasa's triptych of care as ethics–work–affect, being called into response was a mode of care that we lived in/through our inquiry (see Hodgins 2019).

As researchers and as educators in practice, we are not outside of what we research or teach. Kim TallBear refers to this understanding as "feminist objectivity—that is, inquiring not at a distance, but based on the lives and knowledge priorities of subjects" (2014: 7). We followed the dolls and cars because they mattered to most of the children and to some of the educators, because dolls and cars are deeply connected to their worlds. We became obliged to know more. We were not only studying care, we were doing care. By tracing some of the webs of relatedness in relation to the classroom doll–child and car–child moments, we explored the developmental logics for having baby dolls and toy cars. We traced the production, marketing, and curricular histories and presents of the objects, as well as our own experiences (memories) with/of dolls and toy cars. We were troubled by their abundance (Are so many necessary?), their plasticity (Are they safe?), their production (Are they ethically made?), their genderedness (Who are they *really* for?), and their pedagogical foundations (Do baby dolls really teach nurturance, acceptance, self-worth, innocence? Are toy cars really only about active indoor play, or useful only as an accompaniment to other, better, materials?). And, yet, at the same time, we were drawn to, moved by the care these materials evoked. As we came to care for these materials—their histories, their presents (and presence)—we came to recognize that it is not only that these materials matter to some children and adults, but also that the mattering of these materials matters (see Hodgins 2014, 2016, 2019).

Puig de la Bellacasa asks, "What does it mean to think of agencies of care in more than human terms?" (2017: 21). In our dolls and cars research, it meant tracing webs of relatedness beyond the developmentalist framings that position children's relations with the world within exclusively human contexts, where the world and materials exist for use in children's development. It continues to mean researching our (the educators and researchers whom I continue to work with) ongoing efforts to reimagine and live pedagogy as emerging through less-than-seamless, often unequal, always imperfect human and more-than-human relations. It also complicates dominant assumptions that we (educators, childhood studies researchers) are simply/only accountable to the children and families we work with. One of the anxieties that emerged in our research was the realization that we cannot care for everything or everyone all of the time and that caring for one could be (often is) at the expense of another (Puig de la Bellacasa 2017). Who and what will we choose to be accountable to and for in our everyday actions of care as ethics–work–affect?

While I first began thinking about Puig de la Bellacasa's conceptualization of care as a material vital doing, an affective state, and an ethico-political obligation during my doctoral dissertation research, this conceptualization has continued within the other research projects the educators, children, and I have engaged with. Over the years, pedagogical inquiries have included charcoal, paint, clay, textiles, tape, sound, movement, dance, Haro Woods, composting, gardening, and multispecies relations with deer, birds, and worms. These inquiries have emerged through the curiosities of the children, educators, and researchers. As with the dolls and cars, something calls us into response, and our curiosities move us to know more. They are what Puig de la Bellacasa might call our "webs of care obligations" (2017: 220). But, as she notes, "These obligations are not all equivalent; they are contingent on situated ecological terrains. This journey doesn't add up to a smooth theory of care with no loose ends" (220).

The questions we wrestled with through our dolls-and-cars inquiry were not easy, romanticized visions and enactments of care. No simple and agreed upon conclusions about whether we should or should not have dolls or cars in the classroom emerged, but rather the complexity of these taken-for-granted materials as entangled with children and educator onto-epistemological subjectivities became visible through that research (Hodgins 2014, 2016). And we have grappled with this kind of complexity—who and what will we choose to be accountable to and for in our everyday actions?—in varying ways, attending to various concerns (cares), during all of our inquiries since then. Carrying the triptych of care into our curriculum and pedagogy has been about living the difficult, uneven, and layered labor of persevering with care in complex contemporary worlds.

Bike-jump Pedagogies—Persevering with care

The university where we work is located on the edge of what is now collectively referred to as Haro Woods, a 21-acre urban, second-growth forest that is made up of mostly designated parkland. The 3.6-acre portion owned by the university is located in the northeast corner of campus, with the remaining portions that are owned by the Capital Regional District (two parcels that total 3.9 acres) and the District of Saanich (14.2 acres) lining it on two sides. Before colonization severed the Songhees, Esquimalt, and WSÁNEĆ peoples' occupation and management of the land that the university sits on today, the area "contained a mosaic of Douglas fir and grand fir (*Abies grandis*) forests, Garry oak meadows, forested creek ravines, and wetland habitats" (Harrop-Archibald 2008: 20). Eight distinct First Nations families "lived, fished, hunted and harvested these lands" (Saanich Parks and Recreation Department 2017: 4). Today the most dominant plant communities in Haro Woods include the red-listed Douglas fir, dull Oregon grape, and arbutus trees. In British Columbia, "red-listed communities are those at greatest risk of being lost, largely due to clearing land and harvesting resources for agriculture and development" (12).

The educators and children have a deep, care-filled, and complex relationship with Haro Woods. Their everyday curriculum touches this place through activities such as walks in the forest and listening and watching for the multiple species that move along and over the fence line, and we have conducted several inquiries in and with this place. Over the last two years some of the program's educators, families, and pedagogist researchers have been participating in the consultations with the District of Saanich about the current and future use of this place. There are many (sometimes contentious) voices and perspectives that have been part of that process (Saanich Parks and Recreation Department 2017). In the middle of that work, I (Sherri-Lynn) wrote a narration, a narrative and visual story (see Figure 10.1), about some of the complex encounters that have shaped our participation and shared it in a digital collective of educators and researchers called the Early Childhood Pedagogies Collaboratory (https://www.earlychildhoodcollaboratory.net; see also Haro Woods et al. 2018). The following narrative is called Bike-jump Pedagogies.

> Pacini-Ketchabaw, Kind, and Kocher (2017) write of encounter as "a moment of meeting, where things and forces and human and non-human beings come together in spaces of difference." In this meeting, they say, "we decide how to respond—whether to follow, join with, intervene, provoke, perhaps work against. Something is set in motion in this encounter" (34). We live in a juxtaposition, a contradiction, when it comes to our encounters with the bike jumps of Haro Woods. The large mounds of compacted soil draw us in with our desire to climb, slide, and challenge our bodies. But they push us away too. We discover they are created from dug up soil resulting in exposed and cut tree roots, erosion, disrupted worms and suffocating moss, lichen and wood bugs found on sticks and logs buried to support the form. One day we enter the forest ready to climb and "play," the next we are armed with shovels and a wheelbarrow to deconstruct, rebury roots, "rescue" the more-than-human-others. This continuous, non-linear tug-o-war leaves us both overjoyed and saddened by the jumps. These encounters are messy and disruptive—for bikers, for more-than-human-forest-others, and for ourselves. Cohabitating in these contact zones—these juxtapositions, these contradictions—require us to "grapple" with the "sticky knots" (Haraway, 2008) that thrown-together differences often produce. Bike-jump pedagogies ask us, can we begin to understand what it means to care, how to care, and be care(full), with(in) not only bike jump encounters but all encounters, by continuing to look for those interdependent, interconnected, messy moments that bind us together?

Since writing Bike-jump Pedagogies, the question asked at the end of the narration continues with much complexity. While the Saanich Parks and Recreation Department acknowledges that "unapproved bike-jump building can damage the understory, tree roots and soil … [and that] it also causes conflict between those that build and use the jumps, and those that resent the damage it causes" (2017: 17), the "unapproved bike-jump building" has not only continued but increased in scope.

Figure 10.1 Bike-jump Pedagogies (Author photograph).

Concerns about whether, and how, the bike-jump building impacts the ecosystem of Haro Woods have led us to thinking about the impact that *our* footsteps through Haro Woods and Finnerty Ravine have on this ecological terrain. For example, how are *we* contributing to the ongoing erosion to what some call Finnerty Creek, but the children years ago named Worm River? Should we be limiting where the children go in their forest explorations, perhaps by not walking through/in the creek bed? In November 2017, we noticed how wide the creek bed was compared to previous years and the ongoing erosion, and we have begun raising these questions with the children. What do the children think about this boundary—not going into the creek? Or the possible boundary of not being able to reach Grandma Tree (another beloved place marker) if the proposed bike park gets built, as Grandma Tree will be fenced within it (Saanich Parks and

Recreation Department 2017)? Grandma Tree is a large tree in the forest that the children have named. We think she's a Bigleaf Maple, *Acer macrophyllum*, but we're not totally sure. While we often research to "know more," usually in response to children's prompts and questions, we like the ambiguity of not knowing for sure, almost like we know her in a different way, a less "scientific" way (Kimmerer 2003, 2013; Narda Nelson personal communication, April 10, 2018). It is actually the way we know a lot of inhabitants and places in Haro Woods.

The tensions and questions exist alongside being drawn to the bike jumps. The same children who care for the inhabitants of the forest, the trees, and soil that is used to build the jumps also enjoy the jumps. This is no smooth, straightforward theory of care, where one is either simply for or simply against the bike jumps (or the trees, or Haro Woods, or the bike jumpers, or the humans who want the bike park built elsewhere). The following narrative draws on a very recent encounter that took place nearly two years after the moments retold in Bike-jump Pedagogies above.

> Some move quickly down the trail, their bodies effortlessly glide over tree roots and rocks; others meander slowly behind, examining moss, picking up sticks, looking for banana slugs. All of a sudden, without warning, the group stops, someone calls out "deer," and we watch silently as two deer move cautiously across the trail, seemingly aware of our presence. Once the deer are on the other side, we pick up momentum again; this time we all move quickly—we are on our way to the Roundabout. Just as we turn the corner, the group stops again, and some children crash into each other, falling to the ground; the reason: bike jumps—"new jumps!" a child excitedly proclaims. There are several jumps made of soil from the forest floor and supported by large cut branches, small boulders, and what looks like old carpet. Simultaneously, excitement and outrage over the new jumps erupts, but we continue to move down the trail. Some propel their bodies up and over, while others move to the edge, squeezing between jumps and holes (left from where the soil was removed) as they attempt to stay on the path. The three-feet-tall jumps stop at the heart of the Roundabout and end with a low-banked mound leading down another trail and supported by sections of a tree trunk. Once we all arrive, I notice a group of children looking closely at a newly cut tree. As I approach one child exclaims, "They cut the tree with the woodpecker holes!" Another calls out, "Look at all these wood bugs!" Several children come over to examine the stump. What stands before us is a roughly cut tree trunk where a rotting tree once stood. We have been watching this tree for a while now. It lacked branches and did not stand very tall, but it proudly displayed the work of a woodpecker and many tiny bugs and was also home to many fungi during our wet and rainy season. The children are saddened by

the loss of the "woodpecker tree" (see Figure 10.2). What will happen to the birds that visited it? Where will the wood bugs live now? One child angrily asks, "Why do they [the bike jumpers] cut the trees? Somebody lives there and eats there, too!" As we stand in mourning for the tree and its inhabitants, a voice by the low-banked mound calls out, "I found the woodpecker holes." The speaker is standing over the supports of the mound looking down at the work of its former visitors. Taking a closer look, we realize the trunk of the tree has been cut into several sections to support the banked mound.

Our engagements with the bike jumps continue, as do our emerging multispecies, ethico-political forest relations (see, for example, on Twitter #bikejumpvoices, #HaroWoods, #facetimingcommonworlds). The children and educators do not always agree about which actions to take with/in these relations, but we work to make space for the multiple perspectives and possibilities, and

Figure 10.2 Woodpecker tree taken for bike jumps (Author photograph).

to talk (take) seriously the consequences of our engagements—we have come to learn that maintaining this focus on uncertainty and accountability is an act of caring. Thinking-with care is relational work. We are in it: in relationship learning and living *with*. Necessarily, as Kim TallBear's feminist-Indigenous approach illuminates, "putting ethics and standpoint first" (2014: 6). And, as Puig de la Bellacasa (2017) makes clear, not once, but again and again. "Thinking with care also strengthens the notion that there is no one-fits-all path for the good. What *as well as possible* care might mean will remain a fraught and contested terrain where different arrangements of humans-non-humans will have different and conflictive significances" [italics in original] (Puig de la Bellacasa 2017: 220).

Garden Pedagogies—Persevering with care

Kelsey:	What's happening in the garden?
O:	Where is the garden?
Kelsey:	Everywhere, our community garden? The yard garden?
O:	Oh yah. I like the community garden.
Kelsey:	What do you like about it?
O:	The raspberries.
Kelsey:	What makes a garden a garden anyways?
S1:	SEEDS!
S2:	Soilllllll.
D:	I think seeds growing and growing and growing and growing SO big that they're big stuff.
Kelsey:	What if the seeds don't grow so big though?
D:	Then there would be no plants.
Kelsey:	Is it still a garden then?
D:	Well if it grows a little. They just have to keep trying.

Kelsey, thinking as she listens to the children: What assemblages of bodies make a garden, a "garden"? When do they move from being isolated bodies? What motions need to be in movement? How do we understand "gardens"?

We are in the middle of our second year of a garden inquiry that began one early spring in our classroom by starting basil and pea seeds inside and preparing the various garden beds outside in our yard. While we have planted and tended our little gardening areas before, this was the first time that we decided to focus on gardening itself as a collective project. Since we began thinking–doing gardening, our project has traveled well beyond the fence line of our childcare center. Shortly after our decision to focus on gardening, we were granted one of the plots in the university's community garden and we—the children, families, and educators—began to work in this new-to-us place. These early gardening experiences led to curiosities about weeds (vs. plants), pests (vs. helpers), wild (vs. cultivated), borders, and time. Thinking with our yard garden and community garden further led to wondering about possibilities of *what else can be a garden* (Wapenaar and DeSchutter 2018). Where does the garden begin and where does it end? What *is* a garden? Our collective grapplings with/in the (bordered) yard and community gardens, particularly our struggling with (and problematizing of) the colonial inheritances that have shaped our understandings and practices of gardening, were carried into this year's inquiry work and our efforts to think differently about gardens/gardening.

Kelsey: Let's go looking for surprise gardens.
Child: Mystery gardens!!

On our walks through and beyond campus we have begun to take (a different kind of) notice. Robin Wall Kimmerer (2013) suggests that paying attention acknowledges that we have something to learn from intelligences other than our own. "Paying attention is a form of reciprocity with the living world, receiving the gifts with open eyes and open heart" (222).

The community garden was too wet to go to, so we decided to go to the forest as an extension of thinking about boundaries. We walked with the intention to consider whether the forest is a garden too. We gathered at the waiting log where I [Kelsey] asked the children their thoughts on the question. Some say yes, some say no, and a few ideas are shared as to how it might become a garden, if it isn't already. We asked ourselves: If it IS a garden, whose garden is it? Narda reminded us about Earl Claxton Jr.'s perspective as a Tsawout Elder, Knowledge-Keeper, Story Teller, and ethnobotanist when he shared with us his thoughts on similar questions about Haro Woods a few years ago. Earl basically told us that we "look like you really enjoy being here, but it is more than a place to look at and have fun to my people. This was a gathering place. Walking in the forest is like walking through the grocery store … "

Along the walk we saw mushrooms that looked like they were growing up through layers of lasagna leaves on the forest floor and thought about whether the creek could be a garden for fish (who once swam in Finnerty Creek). As we walk through Haro Woods, photographing the mushrooms, talking about the water running through Worm River (see Figure 10.3), Earl's reminder echoes in my [Denise's] ears. A reminder that the land we walk over and through has a history far longer than the children's and our (the educators') relationship with this place. A land "owned" by districts and a university, a land seen and experienced through lenses

Figure 10.3 Can the creek (Worm River) be a fish-garden? (Author photograph).

of recreation and enjoyment. What does it mean for me to know, to remember, to share with the children that there are histories here other than our own? Is it enough? Am I as a settler and an uninvited guest on this territory (as we continue along our walk through "Haro Woods" and beside "Finnerty Creek") now just that little bit less complicit in ongoing settler-colonial violences, less culpable, because I remember, because we mentioned it to the children? Is it enough? And if it isn't, what else do we (must we) do?

In the first year of our garden inquiry we (the five educators in the program and both pedagogist researchers) read chapters of Kimmerer's book *Braiding Sweetgrass* together. Kimmerer's stories did something to our ability to listen and to take seriously the children's imaginative theories about the gardens. These stories of colonial histories and presents that touch garden(ing) do more than complicate our inquiry conversations; they rupture romanticized, apolitical understanding of "young children and gardening."

After hearing Kimmerer present a lecture at our university, we were prompted to think more about the children's history of naming special places within the forest. Worm River. Grandma Tree. Moss House. Big Rock. The Roundabout. Waiting Log. Is it problematic that we were not correcting the children's naming? Should we be sharing the scientific names? What about the Indigenous language names? We are conscious of the powerful colonial tool of linguistic imperialism, overriding Indigenous names with Euro-Western ones (Kimmerer 2015). Is the children's desire to name plants, places, and landscape forms a reflection of the process of building relationships with the more-than-human place inhabitants? "The names we use for rocks and other beings depends on our perspective, whether we are speaking from inside or outside the circle" (Kimmerer 2003: 3). In the absence of knowing Lekwungen names for these plants and places, maybe the children's naming is indicative of their feeling inside a circle. Thinking with Kimmerer, perhaps this naming does not solely originate from the child, but from the *relationship* between the plant and the child. The names are partly how plants and species make themselves known to us. If we listen. As noted before, "we know her [Grandma Tree] in a different way, a less 'scientific' kind of way," that perhaps matters more than we have previously attended to. Kimmerer reminds that "science can be a language of distance which reduces a being into its working parts; it is a language of objects" (2013: 49). She also reminds us of how language that objectifies matters:

> Our toddlers speak of plants and animals as if they were people, extending to them self and intention and compassion—until we teach them not to. We quickly retrain them and make them forget. When we tell that the tree is not a *who*, but an *it*, we make that maple an object; we put a barrier between us, absolving ourselves of moral responsibility and opening the door to exploitation. Saying *it* makes a living land into "natural resources." If a maple is an *it*, we can take up the chain saw. If a maple is a *her*, we think twice. [italics in original] (Kimmerer 2013: 57)

Kimmerer refers to this as the grammar of animacy, and with it argues that "we don't need a worldview of earth beings as objects anymore. That thinking has led us to the precipice of climate chaos" (Kimmerer 2015: 21: 02). With Kimmerer, we have begun to shift our language, begun to reconsider what gets the "it," and the children continue to be important guides in this work. Watching and listening to the children sing and tell stories to the growing seeds, finding little papers of notes the children had left for the seeds, noticing that the children notice and attend as much to the "unwanted" plants (weeds) as to the growing "wanted" ones. Garden pedagogies have provoked our thinking about what it means not only to care for, but to care with. This work and our growing questions continue with/in our various gardens, questions, and actions that now intersect with another inquiry project that explores climate change and trees (see Twitter #climateactionchildhood, #trees). For us, caring is a practice of complexifying our everyday encounters with gardening–place relations: How do we listen? Who and what do we listen to/for? Whose voices (get to) count? What is required (of us)?

Figure 10.4 Caring for marigolds in our yard garden (Author photograph).

In our yard garden plot, I noticed S and C were squatting near the marigold flowers carefully wrapping tissues around them (see Figure 10.4). Pondering curiously as I watched, I wondered what this meant. S explained that she was "covering them in blankets to keep them warm."

Crafting conditions of/for/with care

With the children, educators, and families we work with, we have been thinking carefully about engagement with the places we touch: what we take out, what we move, what we leave, who and what is here beyond us, and what our (in) actions mean for these places, our world. There are no tidy or finished answers. Ultimately, our inquiries have led us to think about what kind of citizens we, as educators, are producing. What kind of citizens are we *hoping* to produce? In the dolls and cars research, this really showed up to us in terms of consumerism and ecological footprint, as well as gendered subjectivities (Hodgins 2014, 2016). Putting care to work in the forest and in our gardens has particularly illuminated that as citizens, we are here with many others—and that our human needs (desires) may not (perhaps should not) be the driving force in our pedagogical decision-making (Haro Woods et al. 2018; Wapenaar and DeSchutter 2018).

Puig de la Bellacasa notes that "an ethical reorganization of human-nonhuman relations is vital, but what this means in terms of caring obligations cannot be imagined once and for all" (2017: 24). She proposes that "caring is more about a transformative ethos than an ethical application. We need to ask 'how to care' in each situation" (Puig de la Bellacasa 2011: 100). So, in this not-so-smooth journey with lots of loose ends, innumerable questions, and no finished answers, our aim is to, as Haraway says, "stay with the trouble" (Haraway 2016).

Part of my (Denise's) work as a pedagogist is to support educators in practice to persevere within the complexities of their work and grapplings along the journey, not for the purpose of reaching or producing an end product but, rather, to live the questions (Hodgins et al. 2017). This requires trust—of each other as colleagues, of the children as knowledge keepers and generators, of the process to "stay with the trouble." It requires trust because it also requires risk: risk to try otherwise, risk to not know, risk to dedicate labor toward creating novel pedagogies, and risk to be in relationship (learn) within a collective. This journey is about supporting each other as we craft pedagogies that then keep carrying a shape-shifting triptych of care, pedagogies that keep demanding things of this care. This is a vision of early childhood education akin to what Peter Moss (2014) sees as built on a "story of democracy, experimentation and potentiality" rather than the neoliberal story of markets, quality, and high returns. Here, care as ethics–work–affect favors process over instrumentality, taking seriously the relational work of caring within uncertain, precarious, and inequitable times.

As educators, we are asking ourselves how we make space for practice as an ethical journey. How do we grapple with and invent collective possibilities here, in environmentally compromised, settler-colonial, capitalist, more-than-human spaces? Who and what will *we* choose to be accountable to and for in our everyday actions of care as ethics–work–affect? Our questions and troublings have emerged through purposeful inquiry work, wherein we have made time to document, discuss, think, and experiment together. Sometimes that discussion time is two minutes passing each other on the floor or talking during naptime while we simultaneously keep one ear to the nap room and the other in our inquiry conversation. We have also, since 2011, reimagined and played with how we use our time, what we dedicate our time to, letting go of some time-taking activities in order to make space for other (new) ones. Importantly, the doings and dialogues that emerge through our inquiries together ripple into living the day-to-day curriculum in the centers. Questions raised and knowledges generated do not stay contained within the garden plot or forest trail. For example, shredding newspaper for the compost bin turns to reading headlines about pipelines and Idle No More; biking along the concrete path in our yard turns to path-sharing with a snail. Without our longtime inquiry questioning, we likely would have bypassed (dismissed) the children's request to know what those newspaper words said, likely thought, "Oh, we probably shouldn't read *these* headlines." Without the children being an integral part of these questions and conversations, they may not have thought to divert their biking activity in order to share the path with a snail. And these everyday curricular moments travel home and back again through our (both the children and the educators) conversations with families, friends, and community members. When care is understood as always extending beyond pre-articulated practices, living curriculum as care(ing) requires taking accountability, action, and relationship—ethics, work, and affect—as pedagogical touchstones.

Conclusion

Moss (2017) recently heralded that "it is time for the [ECE] resistance movement to envision alternative futures, to discuss and design conditions that might enable these futures to come into being" (12). We agree. As government begins to significantly invest in the creation of systems for delivering and supporting early learning and care (Alberta Government 2018; CBC News 2018; Government of British Columbia 2018; Government of Canada 2017), the time is now to advocate for early childhood education beyond neoliberal, market-based rationalizations (Moss 2014). The time is now to recognize that early learning and care pedagogies developed solely on nineteenth- and twentieth-century principles and practices do not have the capacity to address the legacies faced by children in the twenty-first century.

With the teachings from Kimmerer (2003, 2013, 2015), we are compelled to recognize that the time is now to support pedagogical approaches that recognize development as a complex entanglement of human and more-than-human relations and to understand that the actions we take in our practices with children, families, and communities are already ethical and political.

In a 2015 keynote address at the Geography of Hope conference in California, one of the stories that Kimmerer shared was from the teachings known as the

"Prophecies of the Seven Fires." "In this era of accelerating climate change, in the era of the sixth extinction" (10:04), Kimmerer poses the question "How do we care for the many other beings [plants, land, non-human species] who have cared for us [humans] since the beginning of time?" (10:25). She noted that at "this time we are living in, this time of great change and of great choices" (10:39), "we stand altogether at a fork in the road" (11:38) and offered that "the prophecy tells us that we have to make a choice between the path of materialism and the path of spirituality and care and compassion" (11:58).

Through the stories that we have shared in this chapter, we hope it is evident to the reader that this choice Kimmerer speaks of is not smooth, tidy, or easy and that "the path of spirituality and care and compassion" will not look the same for all.

"So, while we do not know how to care in advance or once and for all, aspiring speculatively for situated ethicalities is vital because no 'as well as possible' on Earth is conceivable without these agencies" (Puig de la Bellacasa 2017: 221). "With a triptych notion of care involving maintenance doings, affective relations, and ethicality as well as political commitment" (218), our suggestion is that *caring* may well provide avenues for educators to enact and foster curriculum as generative, experimental, and democratic for all. We offer these stories of twenty-first-century politicized curriculum as not simply a call for what might be possible or a call for what is necessary, but as examples of curriculum as care(ing) that are already being lived.

References

Alberta Government (2018), *Supporting Affordable Child Care*, https://www.alberta.ca/release.cfm?xID=5575245BFEB77-AD12-8A53-492760435BC4DF10.

Barad, K. (2007), *Meeting the Universe Halfway: Quantum Physics and the Entanglement of Matter and Meaning*, Durham, NC: Duke University Press.

CBC News, (2018), *Western Education to Lead the Provincial Early Learning and Child Care Centres*, http://www.cbc.ca/news/canada/london/western-centre-early-learning-child-care-1.4590392.

Common World Childhoods Research Collective (2015), *Home Page*, http://commonworlds.net/.

Dahlberg, G. and P. Moss (2005), *Ethics and Politics in Early Childhood Education*, London: RoutledgeFalmer.

Dahlberg, G., P. Moss, and A. Pence (1999), *Beyond Quality in Early Childhood Education and Care: Languages of Evaluation*, London: Routledge.

de Beauvoir, S. (1949/2011), *The Second Sex*, trans. Constance Borde and Sheila Malovany-Chevballier, New York: Random House.

Friedan, B. (1963/2013), *The Feminine Mystique (50th Anniversary Edition)*, New York: W.W. Norton & Company.

Gane, N. and D. Haraway (2006), "When We Have Never Been Human, What Is to Be Done? Interview with Donna Haraway," *Theory, Culture, Society*, 23 (7–8): 135–158.

Government of British Columbia (2008a), *British Columbia Early Learning Framework*, Victoria: Crown Publications, Queen's Printer for British Columbia, http://www.bced.gov.bc.ca/early_learning/pdfs/early_learning_framework.pdf.

Government of British Columbia (2008b), *Understanding the British Columbia Early Learning Framework: From Theory to Practice*, Victoria: Crown Publications, Queen's Printer for British Columbia, http://www.bced.gov.bc.ca/early_learning/pdfs/from_theory_to_practice.pdf.

Government of British Columbia (2018), *Child Care B.C.: Caring for Kids, Lifting up Families*, http://bcbudget.gov.bc.ca/2018/childcare/2018_Child_Care_BC.pdf.

Government of Canada (2017), *Federal-Provincial/Territorial Early Learning and Child Care Agreements*, https://www.canada.ca/en/early-learning-child-care-agreement.html.

Haraway, D. (1994), "A Game of Cat's Cradle: Science Studies, Feminist Theory, Cultural Studies," *Configurations*, 2 (1): 59–71.

Haraway, D. (2008), *When Species Meet*, Minneapolis: University of Minnesota Press.

Haraway, D. (2016), *Staying with the Trouble: Making Kin in the Chthulucene*, Durham, NC: Duke University Press.

Haro Woods, N. Nelson, S. L. Yazbeck, I. Danis, D. Elliott, J. Wilson, J. Payjack, and A. Pickup (2018), "With(in) the Forest: (Re)conceptualizing Pedagogies of Care," *Journal of Childhood Studies*, 43 (1): 44–59.

Harrop-Archibald, H. (2008), *University of Victoria Natural Features Study Phase Two: University Cedar Hill Corner Property, Garry Oak Meadow and Camus Meadow Area, Finnerty Ravine, Haro Woods, South Woods, Lower Hobbs Creek/Mystic Vale*, https://www.uvic.ca/campusplanning/assets/docs/Natural%20Features%20Study%20Phase%202_PART1.%20Jan.3-08.pdf.

Held, V. (2006), *The Ethics of Care: Personal, Political and Global*, New York: Oxford University Press.

Hodgins, B. D. (2012), "Pedagogical Narrations' Potentiality as a Methodology for Child Studies Research," *Canadian Children*, 37 (1): 4–11.

Hodgins, B. D. (2014), "Playing with Dolls: (Re)storying Gendered Caring Pedagogies," *International Journal of Child Youth and Family Studies*, 5 (4.2): 782–807.

Hodgins, B. D. (2016), "Hope and Possibilities with/in Car(e) Pedagogies," in H. Skott-Myhre, V. Pacini-Ketchabaw, and K. Skott-Myhre (eds), *Youth Work, Early Education, and Psychology: Liminal Encounters*, 113–130, New York: Palgrave Macmillan.

Hodgins, B. D. (2019), "Caring: Method as Affect, Obligation and Action," in B. Denise Hodgins (ed.), *Feminist Postqualitative Research for 21st-century Childhoods*, London: Bloomsbury Publishing.

Hodgins, B. D., L. Wanamaker, and K. Atkinson (2017), "(Re)imagining and (Re) engaging in Relational Encounters: Communities of Practice for (Re)vitalizing Pedagogies," *Association of Early Childhood Educators of Ontario eceLink*, 1 (1): 23–34.

Jones, L., and J. Osgood (2007), "Mapping the Fabricated Identity of Childminders: Pride and Prejudice," *Contemporary Issues in Early Childhood*, 8 (4): 289–300, http:// dx.doi.org/10.2304/ciec.2007.8.4.289.

Kimmerer, R. W. (2003), *Gathering Moss: A Natural and Cultural History of Mosses*, Corvallis: Oregon State University Press.

Kimmerer, R. W. (2013), *Braiding Sweetgrass: Indigenous Wisdom, Scientific Knowledge, and the Teaching of Plants*, Minneapolis, MN: Milkwood Editions.

Kimmerer, R. W. (2015), "Mapping a New Geography of Hope," [Video file], https:// www.youtube.com/watch?v=QhQKdJHLDcw.

Latour, B. (2004), "Why Has Critique Run out of Steam? From Matters of Fact to Matters of Concern," *Critical Inquiry*, 30: 25–48.

Latour, B. (2005), *Reassembling the Social*, New York: Oxford University Press.

Moss, P. (2014), *Transformative Change and Real Utopias in Early Childhood Education: A Story of Democracy, Experimentation and Potentiality*, New York: Routledge.

Moss, P. (2017), "Power and Resistance in Early Childhood Education: From Dominant Discourse to Democratic Experimentalism," *Journal of Pedagogy*, 8 (1): 11–32.

Moss, P. and P. Petrie (2002), *From Children's Services to Children's Spaces: Public Policy, Children and Childhood*, New York: RoutledgeFalmer.

Noddings, N. (1984/2003), *Caring: A Feminine Approach to Ethics and Moral Education*, 2nd edn, Berkeley: University of California Press.

Noddings, N. (2005), *Caring in Education*, http://infed.org/mobi/caring-in-education/.

Pacini-Ketchabaw, V. and A. Taylor (eds) (2015), *Unsettling the Colonial Places and Spaces of Early Childhood Education*, New York: Routledge.

Pacini-Ketchabaw, V., S. Kind, and L. Kocher (2017), *Encounters with Materials in Early Education*, New York: Routledge.

Puig de la Bellacasa, M. (2011), "Matters of Care in Technoscience: Assembling Neglected Things," *Social Studies of Science*, 41 (1): 90.

Puig de la Bellacasa, M.. (2017), *Matters of Care in Technoscience: Speculative Ethics in More Than Human Worlds*, Minneapolis: University of Minnesota Press.

Saanich Parks and Recreation Department (2017), *Haro Woods Park Management Plan: Draft*, http://www.saanich.ca/assets/Parks~Recreation~and~Culture/Documents/ Haro-Woods-Management-Plan-DRAFT.pdf.

Skott-Myhre, H., V. Pacini-Ketchabaw, and K. Skott-Myhre (2016), "Introduction," in H. Skott-Myhre, V. Pacini-Ketchabaw, and K. Skott-Myhre (eds), *Youth Work, Early Education, and Psychology: Liminal Encounters*, 1–13, New York: Palgrave Macmillan.

TallBear, K. (2014), "Standing with and Speaking as Faith: A Feminist-Indigenous Approach to Inquiry," *Journal of Research Practice*, 10 (2): N17. http://jrp.icaap.org/ index.php/jrp/article/view/405/371.

Thompson, D. (2015), "*Stories of Multiage Child Care*," PhD diss., University of Victoria.

Tronto, J. (1993), *Moral Boundaries: A Political Argument for an Ethic of Care*, New York: Routledge.

Tronto, J. (1995), "Care as a Basis for Radical Political Judgments," *Hypatia*, 10 (2): 141–149.

Wapenaar, K. and A. DeSchutter (2018), "Becoming Garden," *Journal of Childhood Studies*, 43 (1): 81–86.

White, J., S. Kouri, and V. Pacini-Ketchabaw (2017), "Risking Attachments in Teaching Child and Youth Care Twenty-First-Century Settler Colonial, Environmental and Biotechnological Worlds," *International Journal of Social Pedagogy*, 6 (1): 43–63, https://doi.org/10.14324/111.444.ijsp.2017.v6.1.004.

Index